# THE WEALTHY INVESTOR

# THE WEALTHY INVESTOR

*A Total Approach to Investing for Wealth*

## BERNICE COHEN

Cartoons by

ORION
BUSINESS
BOOKS

First published in Great Britain in 2000 by
Orion Business
an imprint of The Orion Publishing Group Ltd
Orion House, 5 Upper St Martin's Lane, London WC2H 9EA

A CIP catalogue record for this book is available
from the British Library

ISBN 1 84203 021 3

Cartoons by
McLACHLAN

Set in ITC Stone Serif
Designed by Staziker Jones, Cardiff
Typeset at The Spartan Press Ltd,
Lymington, Hants
Printed and bound in Great Britain by
The Bath Press, Bath

To Julian, Steven and Anthony,
dividends of immeasurable value

Previous books by the author:

*The Cultural Science of Man* (3 volumes)
*The Edge of Chaos*
*The Armchair Investor*
*The Money Maze*
*Financial Freedom*
*Treasury of Investment Wisdom*

# Contents

# ACKNOWLEDGEMENTS

The idea for this book came from two sources: Bill Williams' book, *Trading Chaos*, (Wiley), and the 'No-Brainer' portfolio featured in the *Investors Chronicle* of 21 August 1998. I have used these two notions as the jumping off point for the 5-Level Learning Progression to plan your way to wealth and portfolio-building, instead of relying solely on good stock-picking routines. Although *The Wealthy Investor* has greatly modified these two themes, I am grateful to both sources for the initial ideas I found there.

The other important thankyou I want to make here is to the hard-working team at Orion Business Books who have provided help, encouragement and great support throughout the lengthy process of turning my manuscripts into finished books. This is the fifth volume we have produced together, so a hearty thankyou to everyone concerned is definitely long overdue.

# INCORPORATE THE
# **FASTER GAINS PAYS** SYSTEM
# INTO YOUR 5-LEVEL LEARNING
# PROGRESSION TO CREATE
# LONG-TERM WEALTH

**F**undamental facts: get a general overview of the company and what it is doing.

**A**nnual earnings per share: the company's latest annual results should show growth of 20 per cent or more.

**S**upply–demand: check what supply and demand factors govern the share price.

**T**echnical analysis: use the share price chart to determine short and long-term prospects for the company's share price.

**E**fficient management: check out the management of the company and its ability and motivation to increase shareholder value.

**R**ich in cash: ensure that the company is healthy in cash terms and has minimal debts.

**G**rowth in earnings per share: ensure that the company's EPS growth shows at least a doubling of figures over five years.

**A**ctive monitoring: ensure performance stays on track by monitoring the company and its share price regularly.

**I**nstitutional support: keep an eye on what the main institutional investors are doing in the market.

**N**ew: watch out for new products, new management and a new high in the share price.

**S**tock market direction: make sure you know where you are in the economic cycle and how this will affect the market.

**P**ortfolio-building: is an integral part of the 5-Level Learning Progression. Portfolio-builders invest for the long term and are psychologically more willing to ride out the dips.

**A**sset allocation: distribute your funds between different asset classes; cash, property, pension funds, foreign and UK equities to diversify the risks.

**Y**ields: a buy-and-hold investment philosophy enables the portfolio to achieve a high and rising return over the long term.

**S**ector analysis: to distribute cash among companies in different market sectors, to avoid holding a portfolio that is focused on too few sectors.

# INTRODUCTION – GO THE FULL DISTANCE

*'He that lives upon hope will die fasting.'*

*Benjamin Franklin (1706–90), American scientist and statesman*

This book is a sequel to *The Armchair Investor*, which sets out my favourite stock-picking system, FASTER GAINS. Many investment books focus on a stock-picking system; it is the investors' search for the Holy Grail. For the long-term, I now think stock-picking alone is incomplete. To become wealthy, you need a total package. Of course, a successful stock-picking system is essential, but to create real wealth during your lifetime, you have to build a planned programme around it. Too few private investors adopt this total approach.

*The Wealthy Investor* addresses this gap. It sets out the entire planned programme you need on how to proceed. While FASTER GAINS remains the key stock-picking system throughout the book, at its heart is a 5-Level Learning Progression to move the passive novice to active expert while setting out the time and money targets to follow to become a wealthy investor over the long term.

This approach mirrors the route used by over 60 per cent of the UK adult population when buying a home. Taking a mortgage for 25 years in order to own a home, has created long-term wealth for millions of people over the past 60 years. Homeowners happily plan a long repayment timetable to own their property and, perhaps, pass it down to their heirs; but few apply this admirable approach to building a balanced portfolio of company shares in order to create family wealth.

Throughout the twentieth century, apart from short-term setbacks, property has not only held its value, it has far exceeded the overall costs involved over a lifetime's purchase. Applying the same planned approach used for buying a home to portfolio-building over a period of 10, 15 or 20 years can build great tangible wealth, but few have availed themselves of this outstanding opportunity.

Why this difference? For two reasons, I believe: first, most homeowners buy a property as a place to live, not as an investment; and while it is fairly straightforward to buy a home on a mortgage, very few people know how to invest profitably on the stock market. Second, even if more people were to understand the basics of investing, few know how to plan an effective campaign to become really wealthy.

The central theme in *The Wealthy Investor* lies squarely on learning the skills for successful portfolio-building. This approach is far broader yet at the same time more focused than relying solely on one stock-picking system, however good. The book tackles all the issues facing beginners with no investment experience and no starting **capital** (terms in bold are explained in the Glossary at the end of the book). It also caters for informed investors who have some experience and some capital but have not considered adopting a total programme with realistic time and money targets to become wealthy long-term investors, rather than occasional successful stock-pickers. It helps these investors take the targeted-laser approach rather than the scattergun stock-picking route.

## INVESTMENT MATTERS

Being wealthy has never been more important than today. In most Western democracies, welfare provision is declining: more people will have to fend for themselves or grow relatively poorer. This problem is compounded by rising numbers of people reaching retirement. In Britain, one-third of the population will be over 50 years of age by 2006. In that year, in America the 'baby boomer' generation, born after the end of the Second World War, begin retiring.

With no regular income to rely on, pensioners depend on savings and assets they have accumulated during their working lives to supplement pensions and secure a comfortable lifestyle. With insufficient funds, retirement becomes a constant struggle rather than the long, happy holiday that aspiring retirees dream about. There is now a vast body of evidence to show that owning company shares is the best long-term route for achieving wealth. Yet the financial prospects for millions of pensioners and those approaching retirement look bleak. In Britain, despite building society flotations and the growth in numbers of personal **pensions**, over 60 per cent of the adult population do not own shares, that is, **equities (ordinary shares** in **publicly quoted companies)**. Moreover, 25 per cent of the population owns 73 per cent of the nation's wealth, leaving meagre pickings for the majority to survive on.

Are you among that privileged 25 per cent, or is being wealthy just an idle fantasy tied to winning the National Lottery? *The Wealthy Investor* sets out a complete planned programme on how to turn your dream of owning wealth into an achievable reality.

## THE ROAD TO RICHES

Building a successful business is the fairy-tale route to riches. The personal stories of Bill Gates of Microsoft and Michael Dell of Dell Computers illustrate what can be done. But accounts of these legends rarely dwell on their early difficulties: the endless 20-hour working days or the haunting threat of failure during the start-up periods before success arrives. For those of us who are not bright entrepreneurs, the doors to wealth can still be prised open. History shows that over the long term, as a way of generating wealth, equities outperform all other investments, including cash, UK-government bonds (called **gilts**) or property. Figures from Barclays Capital show that over the 80 years of 1918–1998 the **real** (after accounting for **inflation**) annual returns on equities averaged 8 per cent compared with 2 per cent on gilts. This difference (6 percentage points) is known as the **equity premium**. It is the difference between returns on equities and cash and represents the extra returns that investors expect for holding risky equities in preference to **capital-secure** cash or **fixed-interest** investments. Although they began as small businesses, Microsoft and Dell Computers are now public companies, quoted on the American Nasdaq **stock market**, the US market for young, growing companies, dominated by high-technology firms in their early development stages.

*'There are few ways in which a man can be more innocently employed than in getting money.'*

*Samuel Johnson (1709–84), Lexicographer*

Sadly, for most Britons, investing is often a hit-and-miss affair. Few are active investors but millions have haphazardly acquired a rag-bag of **privatisation** or windfall shares. Becoming a knowledgeable private investor is a much-neglected skill. Throughout their working lives, most adults are financial magpies, collecting assorted investments piecemeal. Typically, they might own a PEP, TESSA or ISA account, units in one or two **collective funds**, plus some privatisation shares. There may be one or two holdings of windfall shares from **demutualised** building societies or insurance companies that abandoned **mutual** status in the late 1990s to become publicly quoted limited companies listed on the London Stock Exchange.

An erratic approach to accumulating financial assets seems discouraging, but over more than 60 years it has not applied to buying a home on a 25-year mortgage. Clearly, most homeowners have failed to realise that there is a recipe for long-term financial success by applying the same planned route used for buying a home to portfolio-building over a period of 10, 15 or more years. I believe learning how to accumulate a balanced **portfolio** of company shares can build more tangible wealth for you and your family than you ever dreamed could possibly be acquired.

Yet, once you have the right attitude and make a long-term commitment to creating this wealth for yourself, you will have taken the second most important step necessary. Reading *The Wealthy Investor* is clearly the first step as it sets out the entire programme on how to proceed. As you start to master the 5-Level Progression covered in the following pages, you can begin to make an amazing transformation to your current personal wealth, even if at present it is totally non-existent.

## CREATE REAL WEALTH

Essentially, all you lack is an active investment approach and a planned programme. Active investing does not mean trading frequently to make quick gains. Very few people have either the time or the inclination to do this. On the contrary, it means learning the skills needed to find some investment treasures – companies that can grow your initial investment three, five, even ten times over while you are holding them. Being an active investor means learning how to choose for yourself the company shares you want to own that will enable you subsequently to reach your target wealth. You then buy and hold these shares in a managed portfolio until the story that initially prompted you to buy them no longer applies.

Many investment books focus on stock-picking systems. They can provide excellent results, as I am well aware, since I have used my own stock-picking system, FASTER GAINS, as described in *The Armchair Investor*, to multiply my capital six times over in nine years, from mid-1990 to mid-1999, although I spent plentifully from my growing funds and also tried to recoup some of that spending periodically, by saving whenever possible.

Becoming a successful private investor took me up a steep learning curve. I made countless mistakes, which I now see would have been fewer and less costly if I had developed my version of the 5-Level Progression, described in later pages, much earlier. My stock-picking system evolved as I read about systems practised by successful investors, most of them operating in America. I did not start consistently applying FASTER GAINS until 1992, but by 1997 I began thinking there could be a better route to acquiring wealth than relying solely on a choice of hopeful prospects.

For thousands of investors, stock-picking is the key to success. They buy shares in promising companies and make useful gains. However, I suspect few of them build balanced portfolios for long-term results or set themselves realistic time and money targets that would better focus their efforts. Of course, stock-picking systems run by dedicated operators produce wealth, and most investors have limited funds; so stock-picking will always play an important role. However, I think it should be a central feature within an overall plan, as indeed it is in the 5-Level Learning Programme described in *The Wealthy Investor*.

## THE INTENTION TO BE RICH

To reach your targets you need a focused approach: once you set your targets and make the right commitment, your whole attitude to saving and investing will dramatically change. Your goal is to build a portfolio of a few choice company shares, even if you start with nothing. Being wealthy is your long-term target.

## 'A wise man will make more opportunities than he finds.'

*Francis Bacon (1561–1626), Philosopher and Lord Chancellor of England*

During the 1990s, as I learned the skills for successful investing, the personal stories that most impressed me were about superb entrepreneurs and prodigiously successful investors. Many businessmen made fortunes exploiting their personal ingenuity; Bill Gates and Michael Dell, among others come instantly to mind.

In Britain in the 1970s and 80s, members of both the Sainsbury and Tesco families amassed huge wealth by converting small shops into vast super-market chains. As regular shoppers, we were suddenly intent on locating shopping-list items while pushing trolleys around the endless isles. If we had given more thought to assessing this grocery transformation, we might have seen the enormous future potential of this new shopping concept. I recall visiting a Tesco store still under construction with half the shop veiled behind massive tarpaulins. Yet the sound of cash tills ringing was clearly audible above the bustle at work behind that veil.

In recent years, figures show supermarket chains impose the highest price mark-ups, according to suppliers. From 1993 to 1998, shelf prices increased by nearly 16 per cent at Tesco and 15 per cent at Sainsbury, much higher than the rate of inflation. Perhaps shareholders get a better deal than shoppers. When the supermarket chains floated on the stock market over 20 years ago, we could have joined this epic growth story, if we had taken the time and trouble to appreciate what was happening right under our noses. The moral of the tale is not that we must be related to successful entrepreneurs to share their wealth: if they float their family firm on the stock market, we can become part-owners in the enterprise early in its development.

This latter idea, then, was the second strand to my thinking that stock-picking may be only half the story. It grew when I read about two truly great investors: Peter Lynch, fabled one-time manager of Fidelity's flagship American **mutual fund**, Magellan; and Warren Buffett, the billionaire American investor. I was increasingly aware that these masters of their art spend time and effort researching which shares to buy because they are looking for the next Microsoft or Tesco shares to own for decades. When they find these gems, they hold them long term, expecting to make huge profits by being part-owners in just a few select success stories. There are not many companies as successful as Microsoft, Gillette or Coca-Cola, even in America, that great nursery for budding entrepreneurs. And, sadly, in Britain they are even rarer. So when we find them, we must invest for the long ride if we want to enjoy all the wealth benefits that part-ownership brings.

I firmly believe we can all copy the examples of great investors, even if our efforts are more modest. They are undoubtedly brilliant stock-pickers, but long-term portfolio-building is the cornerstone of their success. The key is to take the long perspective and use a total investment plan such as the planned programme advocated in *The Wealthy Investor*. This programme has an international dimension: it can be applied to any major stock market, using the **FTSE 100** in Britain, the Dow Jones or **S&P indices** in America, the **Nikkei 300** in Japan or the **Dax** in Germany. These are all benchmark indices covering the performance of their respective stock markets.

## A STAGED APPROACH

If stock-picking is not the whole answer, how should private investors proceed? A better way is to choose a stock-picking system that works for you and use it as a key theme within a complete planned programme. In *The Wealthy Investor*, the stock-picking system is FASTER GAINS, with PAYS added, to emphasise the role of portfolio-building, plus the planned programme that incorporates a universal 5-step learning progression. The latter is a well-proven learning technique, applicable to many skills; it takes the trainee from novice to expert, working at his or her own pace and moving steadily from one level to the next as skill and confidence increase. I first read about 5-Level learning in Bill Williams' book, *Trading Chaos*, which helps losing market traders improve their performance. My use of this technique is diametrically opposite to his. He helps short-term speculators enhance their returns: I want to help long-term investors achieve lasting wealth.

A staged approach to acquiring a new skill covers a wide range of topics: learning how to become a top-ranking golfer or pianist are examples, while running the marathon is another. It may take 12–15 months of regular training to be able to run over 26 miles in less than three hours. Unfit runners may never achieve this target, while less enthusiastic starters might not complete the training course. Discouraged, many abandon the attempt before the race begins. Learning any skill demands dedication, perhaps in equal measure to talent. Or consider a physical-fitness exercise schedule.

City dwellers with sedentary jobs can improve their fitness by undertaking a progressively graded exercise regime. These might build up from a 10-minute daily session of easy exercises to longer work-outs involving more strenuous routines. The 5-Level Progression detailed in this book is ideal for learning essential investment skills. Coupled with portfolio-building, it is a powerful combination.

How much money then, do we need to be wealthy?

*'Not only strike while the iron is hot, but make it hot by striking.'*

Oliver Cromwell (1599–1658), Lord Protector of England

## TARGET YOUR FUTURE WEALTH

A target of £1 million seems right, and certainly is possible in the long term once the planned programme is successfully underway; but in Britain, to join the ranks of the top 4 per cent of wealthiest people in 1998 you would have needed financial assets (excluding your home) worth over £50,000. This includes saving for a pension, but at retirement your pension fund buys an **annuity** and becomes your replacement income. With that conversion, it disappears from your accumulated capital or financial assets. Of course, owning assets of about £50,000 is not a prescription for wealth. In 1998, only 147,000 high net worth Britons owned assets of more than £500,000; their numbers are estimated to rise to 166,000 by 2005. So to join the élite core of wealthy individuals in Britain, you should target a figure of around £500,000. Yet it might take 15–20 years to build a sum of this size starting with no capital at all. But if inflation continues, even at an average modest rate of around 3.5 per cent a year for 20 years when you have finally amassed £500,000 it's **purchasing power**, or what you can buy with it, will have halved to about £250,000 by 2020. You might be running faster just to stay in the same place because, however low the rate of future inflation, after 20 years you may need well over £1 million to be among the richest 1 per cent of Britons.

Another way to view wealth targets is to judge what income you receive from capital of £1 million. In a bank account earning 5 per cent interest every year, £1 million provides £50,000 to spend. As long as it stays on deposit, that £1 million can earn £50,000 in interest every year. This level of unearned income sounds attractive, but there are snags. First, interest rates fluctuate, and so in some years, when you may only earn 3 or 4 per cent interest, your income is smaller; second, the interest is subject to tax, which at a top rate of 40 per cent reduces your £50,000 free cash to £30,000. And, finally, if inflation continues to average 3.5 per cent each year, your £1 million nest egg will steadily lose its purchasing power. History shows that throughout the twentieth century, money saved in deposit accounts rarely kept pace with inflation.

*'Investors want only one thing: a reliable way to identify the companies most likely to experience strong, sustained growth.'*

*Hugh Addersey-Williams*

By contrast, investing £1 million in a well-chosen group of growing companies gives your funds a better chance of outpacing inflation. Over the years, your capital rises in real terms. This sounds more promising, but yet again there are snags. First, inflation may switch into **deflation**, when the general level of prices falls across the whole economy. At such times, equities tend to perform poorly. Second, although successful companies pay shareholders twice-yearly **dividends**, these usually amount to between 1.5 per cent and 4 per cent annually, depending on the purchase price when you bought your shares. With a balanced portfolio of around a dozen to fifteen shares worth £1 million, your dividends might amount to 3 per cent or £30,000 each year, subject to tax. This is by no means a vast sum, so you may need a pension or part-time income as a supplement.

As dividends, like deposit-account interest, fluctuate in value, your available income will vary year by year. However, companies that grow consistently increase their dividend payments over time. With a carefully selected range, you will own what I call the 'Have your cake and eat it' portfolio. Your capital regularly rises in value while your income grows steadily, every year. This is an ideal wealth-creating formula.

## TIME AND MONEY TARGETS

Surprisingly, it seems, even owning £1 million is not the great prize we expected. But put this disappointment into perspective: how much capital do you own now? If the answer is around £50,000, the interest it will earn in a bank deposit account paying 3.5 per cent after tax is a modest £1,750, far below the £30,000 income with a £1 million fund. Targets of £500,000 to £1 million seem impossibly high for people who do not own a small business capable of expansion. Yet I believe they are achievable with a staged approach: you set your first goal, act to reach it, and then set targets for a higher goal, simply by continuing to follow the successful route of the planned programme that enabled you to achieve your first goal.

Reader: *'Do you realise how old I'll be when I become wealthy using your plan?'*

Answer: *'The same age as you'll be if you don't use this plan!'*

Growing rich with the planned programme is like learning to ride a bicycle; the hardest part is gaining the confidence to know you can balance yourself on two narrow tyres without falling off. Once you have mastered the art of balancing, you can ride your bicycle for longer distances than you thought possible when you were wobbling along the road in your early attempts. Similarly, as we will soon see, a target of £500,000 can be reached by moving steadily towards it, following the 5-Level Progression with its main ancillary themes. And, once the project is operating well, moving on to higher goals is similar to riding further distances on your bike.

The goals you set are attainable by owning a balanced, well-managed share portfolio; this is your wealth-creating project. To reach your goals, you need to follow all the aspects of the total planned programme. The learning process involved is similar to learning to balance yourself on a two-wheeler bicycle. Once you have mastered the skill, you can balance your growing portfolio over the long term as expertly as you can ride your bicycle over longer distances.

## THREE INVESTOR GROUPS

At the outset, there will be three groups of investors, labelled for our purposes, Streams A, B and C, as follows:

- *Stream A investors* are novices with no previous experience of the markets and no initial capital. Following the 5-level route, they may need 20–25 years of steady progress to build a fund worth £500,000: this is the time required to buy a home on a mortgage. Although house purchase is an entirely passive exercise, to grow wealthy you must develop your investment skills to ensure you can acquire a portfolio of this magnitude and implement a **saving** schedule simultaneously to ensure your funds reach the target size. This investment regime is ideal for those aged 30–40 who want to build sizeable retirement nest eggs.

- *Stream B investors* with some market experience plus a modest capital sum of £15,000 at the start (of which £10,000 will be invested) may also need 15–20 years to accumulate £500,000. They can move rapidly through the early Levels, I and II, to fit their learned experience into the 5-Level Progression, although they may still want to spend three or four years moving through Levels III and IV to reach Level V. Those aged 40–50 might fit this category.

- *Stream C investors* could achieve this goal within a much shorter time frame, as they begin with over £20,000 of capital. If they have some market experience, they too might work quickly through Levels I, II and perhaps even III, taking advantage of their current investment skills to move on to Level IV. There they begin to modify an existing portfolio to match the type of long-term portfolio recommended in Level V. People in middle-life, building funds for retirement, might be in this stream.

## INVESTOR STREAMS USING THE PLANNED PROGRAMME

There will be three streams of investors, A, B and C.

*Stream A* – have no capital and no investment experience at the outset.

*Stream B* – have capital of at least £10,000 plus some experience at the outset.

*Stream C* – have capital in excess of £20,000 and some investment experience.

*'Each entry of debts paid brings us closer to freedom.'*

*Mark Bryan and Julia Cameron,* The Money Drunk

However long it takes to reach the first target of £500,000, there is a proven historical record during the twentieth century of increasing long-term growth the longer assets are left in the stock market. Although the past is only a rough guide to the future, a fund of around £1 million or more, therefore, could be achievable after about 25 years by simply continuing with Level V investing – the highest level – once your funds have reached £500,000.

*'When money breaks down, morality breaks down too.'*

*Kevin Jackson,* Ten Money Note

## PACE YOURSELF

With this long time-scale, the task looks daunting, especially if you have no starting capital. Fortunately, this is not the case. In fact, I think a successful result is attainable once you accept that you can achieve the targets you set yourself over the time you require to reach them. Two factors determine how quickly a novice progresses through the five levels. First, how the markets behave and, second, how rapidly your investment skills improve. The two are closely linked: improve your investment skills and you benefit faster from changing markets, thereby increasing your wealth. Clearly, investors in both Streams B and C can make more rapid strides.

*The Wealthy Investor* takes an entirely new look, with investing by portfolio-building for the long term as its central theme, working to time and money targets. As few private investors tackle their investments in this way, I believe the book will help them focus their energies on a key ambition that unites them all: the intention to become wealthier in the future than they are today. For all three investor streams, moving from one level to the next depends on when you are consistently making profits on your paper or real portfolios and when you personally feel confident about moving on.

While there are no shortcuts, using the planned programme you can pace yourself to arrive at the successful result you initially set – say £500,000 within 12–15 years. The beauty of this programme is that you can stop being active at any level along the route and settle with the amount of capital you then have. You can resort again to being passive, as outlined in Levels I and II, by making two adjustments: you should hold an equivalent sum in a **FTSE All-Share tracker fund** equal to the final size of your portfolio, to reduce your risk level; and, second, you must do a regular yearly review. Both modifications are explained in Level I.

The planned programme can be compared with a visit to Singapore's Night Safari Park. This unique tourist attraction is a zoo safari of nocturnal animals in an open forest setting. Your ticket comes with a map so you know in advance where all the different animal attractions are when you take the monorail train around the park. You might travel round the whole circuit without stepping once off the train, but there are three different stations where refreshments are available and from where trails are laid out so you can visit various animal exhibits. You can alight at any station to do one, two or all of the different walks, or stop for a snack. You decide.

There are similar choices with the planned programme. You set your targets at the outset. *The Wealthy Investor* is like the monorail train; it conducts you on your journey from beginning to end. This introduction is your map of how your future route will unfold. The 5-levels in the planned programme are similar to the three stations along the route. Even a tourist on holiday needs energy to walk around the three safari trails at 10 o'clock at night in a temperature of 30 degrees centigrade with humidity around 100 per cent. Similarly, it is equally true that some effort is needed to work through the 5-Level Progression but, as on the safari, you can pace yourself, take as long as you need, and enjoy the unique experience of creating tangible wealth to acquire a better lifestyle than you currently have.

So let us look now at the elements that comprise the 5-Level Progression.

## THE PLANNED PROGRAMME ROUTE TO WEALTH

To create wealth within a reasonable time of around 15–20 years, you need to learn how to become an active investor, and this is a central purpose of the 5-Level Progression. It moves you from novice to expert at the pace you set yourself. At the outset, you begin with a regular savings regime, holding either a paper or passive portfolio for some years, depending on which investor stream you are in. The savings regime and passive portfolio allow you to make an early start in building your funds over the first 5–8 years.

The essential elements within the 5-Level Progression are as follows:

- adopt a consistent savings regime;
- start as a passive investor;
- follow the market cycles;
- create your own Top Ten Portfolio;
- progress to the higher levels: III, IV and V.

*'The point of investment is to insure yourself against risks.'*

*Investors Chronicle*

## The Essential Elements in the 5-Level Progression

When you adopt the 5-Level Progression from novice to expert investor, you learn to become an active investor within about 8 years. This progression helps you obtain the best possible result: you grow your savings and portfolio faster than if you remain totally passive. The five factors listed above that allow the persistent trainee to accumulate wealth according to his own set targets can be expanded upon as set out below.

## Adopt a Consistent Savings Regime

Past evidence shows that 60 per cent of returns from a share portfolio are achieved by reinvesting the **gross** dividends, that is, without deduction of tax. Government action has now made it impossible to reinvest gross dividends, and so a regular savings regime replaces the role that reinvesting gross dividends played, to increase your potential returns.

## Start as a Passive Investor

Start as a passive investor yet learn to be an active investor: the move from initially being passive to being active may take about 6–8 years. This timetable moves a Stream A novice from paper investing and relying on a share portfolio that is automatically chosen at the start, to acquiring the skills to choose a self-selected portfolio to generate long-term wealth. Both Stream B and C investors with some market experience can move more rapidly from passive to active, applying the topics covered in *The Wealthy Investor* to improve their existing portfolios.

Passive investing begins with a portfolio consisting of the top ten largest UK FTSE 100 shares by **market capitalisation**. This is the Top Ten Portfolio. These ten companies are, by definition, the most valuable, as market capitalisation is the price of the share multiplied by the number of shares in issue. These 10 companies will be the most successful in the year you buy your portfolio as viewed by the whole investing community, but changing fortunes of these and others in the FTSE 100 list mean they may not necessarily remain the most successful over ten years. This explains why holding this passive portfolio over 15–20 years may prevent a passive investor building substantial wealth. Some of these top companies may even perform poorly over that period. We will see this shortly in a Top Ten Portfolio held from mid-1988 to mid-1998. Follow the complete programme to avoid the disappointment of underperformance.

Market Capitalisation = Share price × Number of shares in issue

## Follow the Market Cycles

Follow the market cycles to gain the maximum benefit from every major upward trend. Historically, the market makes a big upsurge on average once every 3–4 years. Over a period of 10–12 years, there may perhaps be three market corrections when prices fall and three major upswings when prices rise. Investing early in a rising market makes a huge impact on the speed at which a portfolio grows. Following market cycles can therefore increase your wealth.

## Create Your Own Top Ten Portfolio

Create a Top Ten Portfolio by learning how to run a paper portfolio of the top ten companies in the FTSE 100 index. Within 6–9 months of starting the planned programme, you should buy your own Top Ten Portfolio as a passive, automatically chosen portfolio. If you have a minimum of £10,000 in capital (with, in addition, a reserve fund of at least £5,000) you should start investing early, while acquiring the skills to become active. As you monitor this portfolio continually it becomes semi-passive. While this portfolio is running, you begin learning to run a paper portfolio based on FASTER GAINS and consisting of small, growth companies. Later, when you have converted this to a real portfolio, you set up another paper portfolio for big or medium-sized companies, different perhaps from the ten you already own.

## Progress to the Higher Levels: III, IV and V

As your knowledge and experience grow, you gradually convert the two paper portfolios one after the other, into actively managed portfolios. The first paper portfolio to convert, in Level III, is the one for small, growth companies with big profit potentials. Once that is running successfully, you set up the paper portfolio for larger capitalised companies in Level IV. In Level V, that too becomes active by converting the passive Top Ten Portfolio into an actively managed New Millennium Portfolio, holding self-selected shares that can grow seven or ten times over 15–20 years. The selection may include FTSE 100 shares or companies in the **FTSE 250 index**, plus some small fast-growing companies.

## TARGET COMPANIES TO OWN

There are fewer genuine growth companies in Britain than in America and many that show great promise subsequently disappoint. Examples include the retailers Body Shop, Next, JJB Sports and Laura Ashley; but there are others, such as Ferguson International, the mini-conglomerate label-maker, and the drugs firm, Medeva. If a company you hold shares in suffers a severe setback, stay alert and ready to sell to reinvest in another company. Without this active approach, it is harder to grow your funds as rapidly as is possible if you own steadily growing companies. Many such companies exist, but you must run a system for finding and following them. Several major UK companies have produced remarkable returns: Airtours, British Aerospace, Glaxo Wellcome, SmithKline Beecham, Railtrack, Sage, Vodafone AirTouch and AstraZeneca. Search out young companies with similar growth attributes for your self-selected portfolio.

So let us look more closely at the essential elements in the whole planned programme, starting with the savings regime.

*'Turn every negative into a positive.'*

*Mark Goldberg, multi-millionaire owner of Crystal Palace football club*

## THE SAVINGS REGIME

A consistent savings regime is vital to success to replace the role previously taken by reinvesting gross dividends. Save consistently by building up capital in a tracker fund within a tax-free ISA. (The details are covered in Level I.) While this should achieve a higher growth rate than a cash fund, it carries more risk. Cautious investors begin by saving the cash element in an ISA, until they have confidence in their newly acquired skills.

Stream A investors, with no starting capital or experience, should aim to save £2,000 a year. If the tracker savings achieve a 10 per cent growth rate, they can buy their Top Ten Portfolio within six years from savings of approximately £12,200. After 15 years, savings of £2,000 a year could produce about £56,000 (schedule (1) in the box on page 17). Your savings will grow faster if the stock market grows as well in future as during the 1980s and 1990s, but we cannot rely on this. A 10 per cent growth rate may be too optimistic; saving £2,000 a year at 7 per cent a year growth would produce £45,000 over 15 years (schedule (2) in the box). Whether the savings grow at 10 or 7 per cent a year, the results can be greatly improved with a rising savings scale: £2,000 a year for 5 years, followed by £3,000 a year during years 6 to 10, and £4,000 a year during years 11 to 15. With this staged regime, total savings of £43,000 can reach £78,000 at 10 per cent (schedule (3)) or £64,600 at 7 per cent (schedule (4)) after 15 years.

---

**STREAM A INVESTORS WHO BEGIN WITH NO EXPERIENCE AND NO CAPITAL**

(1) **Aim to save £2,000 a year with 10% growth.** Estimates of the progress of this saving are as follows:
a) After 5 years, £2,000 grows to £9,280
b) After 10 years, £9,280 grows to £27,100
c) After 15 years, £27,100 grows to £56,000
**Turn £28,000 of saving into £56,000**

(2) **Save £2,000 a year with 7% growth** would produce:
a) After 5 years, £2,000 grows to £8,880
b) After 10 years, £8,880 grows to £24,000
c) After 15 years it will be around £45,100
**Turn £28,000 of saving into £45,100**

(3) **Save at a rising scale with 10% growth** a year, would produce:
a) After 5 years, £2,000 grows to £9,280: (total saved £8,000)
b) After 10 years, £9,280 grows to £33,250: (total saved £23,000)
c) After 15 years, £33,250 grows to £78,000: (total saved £43,000)
**Turn £43,000 of saving into £78,000**

(4) **Save at a rising scale with 7% growth** a year, would produce:
a) After 5 years, £2,000 grows to £8,880: (total saved £8,000)
b) After 10 years, £8,880 grows to £29,700: (total saved £23,000)
c) After 15 years, £29,700 grows to £64,600: (total saved £43,000)
**Turn £29,700 of saving into £64,600**

---

*'When I think of all the sorrow and barrenness that has been wrought in my life by want of a few more pounds per annum than I was able to earn, I stand aghast at money's significance.'*

*George Gissing (1857–1903), English novelist*

## PORTFOLIO-BUILDING

Building a portfolio is the backbone of your financial strength. The portfolio ultimately consists of a carefully chosen group of company shares with the potential for substantial growth. A motivating way to view this is with money-doubling targets, as used by professional investors. Apply it first to the passive Top Ten Portfolio. You progress faster using two strategies: invest your accumulating savings and become active and more knowledgeable by advancing to higher levels.

Investors in Streams B and C, with capital of £10,000 or more, begin passive portfolio-building within a few months of starting the programme. As a guide, money can double roughly every five years (see box below). From the start to year 5, £10,000 doubles to £20,000: between years 6 and 10, this doubles into £40,000: from year 11 to 15, another doubling turns £40,000 into £80,000. The total fund increases by adding the savings regime. The best result is achieved with schedule (3), where savings of £2,000 a year, rise to £4,000 in year 11. With a 10 per cent growth rate, this adds another £78,000 by year 15, lifting the total portfolio to £158,000 (shown below).

These figures ignore the potential to improve the portfolio's growth by being an active investor. You avoid the danger of 'reading history backwards' because an active investor will make portfolio adjustments to reduce the underperformance if markets do not perform as well in the future as they did between 1975 and 1999.

---

**MONEY DOUBLING FOR STREAM B INVESTORS BEGINNING WITH INITIAL CAPITAL OF £10,000:**

Year 1 to 5 double the initial capital £10,000 into £20,000
Year 6 to 10 double again: £20,000 into £40,000
Year 11 to 15 double again: £40,000 into £80,000
Add schedule (3) savings of £2,000 a year, rising to £4,000 in year 11: £78,000
**Total Capital £80,000 + £78,000 = £158,000**

---

*'Poverty is no disgrace to a man, but it is confoundedly inconvenient.'*

*Rev. Sydney Smith (1771–1845), Canon of St Paul's Cathedral*

## Plan to Build £500,000 Within 15 Years

Stream C investors might achieve wealth of around £500,000 within about 15 years (see box below) if their starting capital (say about £55,000) is invested in conjunction with savings schedule (3). Money doubling in the portfolio over the first five years lifts it to £110,000: another doubling from year 6 to 10, brings it to £220,000: one more doubling, from year 11 to 15, produces a fund of about £440,000 after fifteen years. When savings from schedule (3) of £78,000 are added, the total reached is £518,000.

---

**STREAM C INVESTORS BUILD £500,000 WITHIN 15 YEARS**

Years 1 to 5 double the initial capital of £55,000 to £110,000
Years 6 to 10 double again: £110,000 into £220,000
Years 11 to 15 double again: £220,000 into £440,000
This schedule assumes savings of £2,000 a year at 10%, rising to £4,000 in year 11 as part of the total, yielding a further £78,000
**Total capital £518,000**

---

## Money Targets for Portfolio-building

When you put the savings regime and portfolio-building together, you can match the money and time targets, to give an estimate for how your funds can grow once the key elements of the planned programme are operating. During the first 5–8 years, as you ascend the 5-Level Progression, your results will depend greatly on the underlying strength of the market. However, during the following years, the growth of your funds will be greatly influenced by your ability to manage your portfolio actively and to hit these targets at your own pace (see table on page 20). This breakdown of the long-term targets is purely a guide to help you focus on your eventual goal of creating wealth. That goal becomes more reachable when you attach real time and money targets to it. This is the key point of outlining the breakdown details.

**BREAKDOWN OF THE LONG-TERM TARGETS**

| Years | Stream A (£) | | Stream B (£) | | Stream C (£) | |
|---|---|---|---|---|---|---|
| 0 to 10 | savings | 20,000 | savings | 38,000 | savings | 38,000 |
| | portfolio | 50,000 | portfolio | 80,000 | portfolio | 220,000 |
| *Subtotals* | | *70,000* | | *118,000* | | *258,000* |
| | | | | | | |
| 11 to 15 | savings | 78,000 | savings | 78,000 | savings | 78,000 |
| | portfolio | 80,000 | portfolio | 250,000 | portfolio | 440,000 |
| *Subtotals* | | *158,000* | | *328,000* | | *518,000* |
| | | | | | | |
| 16 to 20 | savings | 100,000 | savings | 100,000 | savings | 100,000 |
| | portfolio | 150,000 | portfolio | 400,000 | portfolio | 750,000 |
| *Subtotals* | | *250,000* | | *500,000* | | *850,000* |
| | | | | | | |
| 21 to 25 | savings | 150,000 | savings | 150,000 | savings | 150,000 |
| | portfolio | 350,000 | portfolio | 650,000 | portfolio | 950,000 |
| **Totals** | | **500,000** | | **800,000** | | **1,100,000** |

*'Genius does what it must, and Talent does what it can.'*

Welsh proverb

In the breakdown analysis above, most investors would merge the savings regime and portfolio after following the programme for 8–10 years. Money saved over six months might be invested in shares as soon as a promising opportunity arises. In the table they are treated separately, to show the impact of savings on the totals achieved. Saving plays a vital role in reaching your targets.

It is hopeless to set a huge target of £500,000 and aim for it in one giant leap. Break the long-term targets down into smaller stages: first, years 0 to 5; next, years 6 to 10; years 11 to 15 then, years 16 to 20; and then years 21 to 25. Smaller time and money targets are more manageable. You focus on reaching one pair of targets before moving on to the next. The table is a guide, however, indicating key signposts along the route for setting time and money goals.

## DOUBLING ON THE DOW

The table highlights the pivotal role of the savings regime, especially for investors with no starting capital. The sooner you begin your Top Ten

Portfolio, the less time you may need to reach the targets, assuming you avoid buying at a market peak. The history of America's Dow Jones Industrial Average (DJIA, or Dow), the premier benchmark index, illustrates long-term money doubling in action. The Dow only includes thirty major **blue chip** companies, such as Walt Disney, McDonald's and IBM, and is unweighted. This means each of the thirty shares has an equal weighting in the index although some are clearly much larger by value, sales revenue or profits. Being unweighted is a serious defect but the Dow has dominated Wall Street thinking almost from its 1897 inception. When I began writing *The Wealthy Investor* in the autumn of 1998, the world was gripped by the aftershocks of the international global crisis. The Dow stood at 8000, having recovered slightly from the September lows of 7700.

Since the Dow has been an important forward indicator for more than a century, we can follow its long-term fortunes. After hitting 100 for the first time early in 1905, it drifted for the next 20 years. During the great bull market of 1928–9 it hit a high of 386, but after the October 1929 crash and the depression of the 1930s, it was back again at 100 in 1941. The story of money doubling on the Dow then comes alive. It took 61 years (to 1966) to increase ten times, from 100 to 1,000. The next tenfold rise, from 1,000 to 10,000 only took thirty-three years, when the Dow briefly went through 10,000 in March 1999. If the US economy manages to grow by an average 5 per cent a year, the Dow could reach 100,000 by 2046! In my view, this is not an impossible target.

There were several significant lengthy pauses along the route, mainly around these big round numbers. At the start of the twentieth century, the Dow struggled for over twenty years to leave the first hurdle of 100 behind. But having arrived at 1,000 in the mid-1960s, it then took another 16 years, to 1982, to decisively break through the 1,000 barrier. Finally, it made the next ten-times leap in just seventeen years, leaving 1,000 behind in 1982 to hit 10,000 in 1999. The lessons from studying the Dow underscore the importance of creating wealth while the markets are rising. Once you have achieved that wealth, long periods of inactivity on the markets will not be a cause of concern.

## IMPOSSIBLE TARGETS?

The American economy is far more dynamic than the economies of continental Europe or Britain, so you may think the targets suggested in the table on page 20 are totally beyond reach – simply too remote to be meaningful. However, I have a friend whose grandmother invested £3,000 in 1963 (roughly equivalent to £50,000 in 1999 money) in a pharmaceutical company now in the FTSE 100 index. That sum had grown to £1,100,000 by 5 November 1999, after 35 years in the market. During this time, the shares were split into smaller units and mergers increased the company's size. In 1998, the growing yearly dividends on this magnificent nest egg produced an additional £12,500. I personally am half way through the programme now, in Level V and moving towards my wealth target, hoping to achieve it within ten to twelve years of starting to invest in 1990. In 1998, Neil Train, newly arrived manager of three major funds at M&G, the investment funds group, had money-doubling targets for his funds. He planned to turn £800 million into £8,000 million (that is, £8 billion) in ten years. His target is to grow the funds he manages by adding one zero. An investor hoping to match his target wants to grow an initial capital of £10,000 into £100,000 in ten years. If you start in Stream C with £50,000, you might reach £500,000 in ten years.

*'You have to earn intuition. It comes from years of day-to-day experience with the markets and an understanding of your reactions to a host of market situations.'*

Tom Belsanti, trader on the Chicago Mercantile Exchange

## THE TWO PORTFOLIOS: TOP TEN AND NEW MILLENNIUM

Two portfolios form the anchor for the whole project. The idea for them evolved from an *Investors Chronicle* article suggesting what might have been achieved by holding a passive portfolio over the long term.

### The Top Ten Portfolio

The passive Top Ten Portfolio is based on this idea. The *Investors Chronicle* article showed the performance of a portfolio of the ten biggest UK companies by market capitalisation, held for ten years. Investing £1,000 in each of these ten companies in mid-1988 with dividends reinvested, and holding until mid-1998, the £10,000 grew to £48,000. An accurate return was not calculated as several of the ten demerged parts of their businesses into freely floated companies during the term. BAT (British American Tobacco) demerged Argos, the catalogue retailer, in 1991, which was subsequently taken over by Great Universal Stores in 1998. The chemicals giant, ICI, demerged Zeneca in 1993. On its first day as an independent pharmaceutical company Zeneca was 634p. By mid-1998 it was more than three times higher, at 2560p. The **conglomerate** Hanson, comprising a diverse group of companies, split into four separate businesses, while Centrica demerged from British Gas. When all this company activity is included, the portfolio probably grew to about £60,000.

Twice money doubling, would have produced £40,000 but the real portfolio growth, to around £60,000, or 500 per cent, gives a measure of what a passive portfolio can produce with favourable stock market conditions. Even using the figure of £48,000, the portfolio grew 380 per cent while the FTSE 100 index rose from around 1875 in mid-1988 to 6179 by July 1998. This rise of 4,304 points, or 230 per cent, is well below the returns on the chosen ten companies. As we shall see, consistent out-performance by the top ten companies is a long-term trend, perhaps not yet fully recognised by the majority of investors.

However, benchmark indices, like the FTSE 100 or FTSE All-Share index, are averages only. As an active investor, holding a portfolio selected with a proven system, you are well placed to beat the averages. Clearly, there are many ways to value companies, as we will see in Level II, but market capitalisation measures a vote of confidence by investors in a company. Their buying bids up the price and the market capitalisation: their selling sends the share price down along with the market capitalisation, as the company loses favour with investors. In time, as an active investor, you will choose promising companies regardless of their FTSE 100 ranking; but, initially, following the top ten has merits.

Despite the disappointing performance of some of the *Investors Chronicle* top ten, the broad principle of using a passive portfolio along similar lines is sound. The long-term history of the market suggests it is possible to repeat this 1988–98 performance over any 10–12 years, even though 1988–98 was an excellent investment period. A target to turn a minimum of £10,000 into around £50,000 should prove reachable, to double the starting capital more than twice over.

## The New Millennium Portfolio

The second portfolio in the project is more important. It is the actively managed New Millennium Portfolio. By converting the Top Ten Portfolio from passive to active by using the 5-Level Learning Progression, greater returns are possible, as suggested from analysis of the *Investors Chronicle* portfolio, described on page 24. During the 5-Level Progression, the passive investor slowly converts a Top Ten Portfolio into a self-chosen active New Millennium Portfolio. It will contain 10–15 FTSE 100 or FTSE 250 companies that have been followed in a paper portfolio which showed the potential to substantial future growth. The target is to turn £10,000 into £100,000 plus, within ten to twelve years, by combining the portfolio with the savings regime. Dividends and interest earned are reinvested at least once a year to boost the returns.

## THE ORIGINAL *INVESTORS CHRONICLE* PORTFOLIO

This portfolio produced a total return with gross dividends reinvested of just over £48,000 (see table below) but, as noted, it ignored the major impact made by companies that floated off subsidiaries that subsequently grew into successful independent companies. The average UK income unit trust produced only £33,800 over those ten years, while the average UK growth unit trust only managed £31,200. These comparisons illustrate the benefits that private investors may gain by making their own financial decisions.

*'Invest in stocks to make money, not to preserve capital.'*

*Peter Lynch,* One Up on Wall Street

### THE ORIGINAL INVESTORS CHRONICLE PORTFOLIO AS AT MID-1998

| Company | Value of Holding (£) |
|---|---|
| BAT | 5,600 |
| BG (British Gas) | 5,400 |
| BP | 5,700 |
| BT | 5,300 |
| BTR | 1,600 |
| Glaxo | 10,100 |
| Hanson | 2,100 |
| ICI | 2,700 |
| Marks & Spencer | 3,900 |
| Shell | 5,800 |
| **(Total Initial Capital £10,000)** | **48,200** |
| **Average UK growth unit trust** | **31,200** |
| **Average UK income unit trust** | **33,800** |

This portfolio, called the 'No-Brainer Portfolio', appeared in *Investors Chronicle*, 21 August 1998.

*Sources*: Autif, Datastream/ICV

*'There is virtually no kind of situation that can't be handled with a system.'*

Robert R. Godfrey, *author of* High Bond Yields

## FOLLOW RISING STARS

A closer look at how these 10 companies performed over 10 years is instructive. The table on page 24 shows 5 of the 10 grew to about £5,500, although the average growth was £4,820. Two poor performances were not offset by Glaxo's sparkling result. Hence, this portfolio is fairly typical: several average performers, a couple of poor results and two or three stars.

The portfolio was unchanged for ten years: in that time the FTSE 100 index rose 230 per cent (from 1875 to 6179) but the *Investors Chronicle* portfolio rose 382 per cent, although probably by 500 per cent when the many company demergers are taken into account. However, by ignoring the demergers, the BAT, BG, Hanson and ICI results are understated. BG and Hanson probably turned £1,000 into about £6,000. Adding Zeneca to ICI and Argos to BAT lifts those two outcomes to about £8,000. Including the demergers, three companies (BAT/Argos, ICI/Zeneca and Glaxo Wellcome, after the 1995 merger) produced above-average results.

Glaxo was the star performer, turning £1,000 into £10,100. Neil Train will be hunting for the next Glaxo, to add one zero to his investment. We want the New Millennium Portfolio to do this, turning £10,000 into £100,000 in ten years. Glaxo was a huge success right from the 1984 launch of the FTSE 100 index. As the seventh-largest company in that index at the time, it had a market value of £2.6 billion. By August 1998, in the top-ranking position, it was worth £65.5 billion. In 1995, Glaxo swallowed Wellcome, but the great growth surge was internally generated and derived from the success of Zantac, a blockbuster treatment for stomach disorders.

## AVOID FALLING STARS

The performance of Britain's premium retailer, Marks & Spencer illustrates the need to be active. Over this ten-year period, the company turned £1,000 into £3,900, below the group average of £5,500. By 1998, the growth story had faltered: the company had embarked on an ambitious expansion plan, to take its successful retailing formula abroad, but the downturn in the global economy blew the plans off course, hitting profits. In November 1998, Marks & Spencer reported lower **interim** (half-yearly) pre-tax profits for the first time since 1991. In January 1999, it issued a profits warning on prospects for the full year. The company's place in the élite 100 FTSE index fell: as the 5th ranked company in January 1984, it was 10th by January 1995, 12th in January 1996, 15th in January 1998 and by November of that year, when the 23 per cent profits decline was announced, it was down to 21st position.

BTR was the worst performer in the portfolio, gaining only £600 in ten years. BTR is a conglomerate, similar to Hanson. From 1995 to 1998, the shares fell 80 per cent behind the market. In January 1984, BTR was the 8th largest FTSE 100 company and was still ranked 10th in January 1996, but by January 1998 it was 35th and in 86th place by November 1998. Then, unexpectedly, an announced £9 billion merger with engineering company Siebe changed the story. As BTR and Marks & Spencer slid down the FTSE 100 table, their poor performance reduced the overall growth of the portfolio. They added £5,500 (£3,900 + £1,600), but if *each* had produced an average growth of £5,500, the portfolio would have been £5,500 higher by mid-1998. The 5-Level Progression has a disciplined routine to eliminate poor performers and improve a portfolio's growth prospects.

## THE TURBULENT FTSE 100

General Electric Company (GEC), the third most valuable FTSE 100 company in 1984, was 19th by November 1998. In January 1999 it split itself into two divisions, planning to merge the aerospace division with British Aerospace and rename the remaining business Marconi. Meanwhile, mobile phone operator Vodafone became an outstanding superstar whose history covers the lifetime of the FTSE 100. Launched in 1984 as a division of Racal Electronics, the security, defence and telecoms combine run at that time by Sir Ernest Harrison, it demerged from Racal in late 1988 with a market capitalisation of £1.7 billion. As Vodafone rose through the rankings, so did its value and share price. It was placed 24th in 1995 and at 8th position by October 1998. Demerged at 170p (before accounting for share splits), it reached 950p by mid-1998, a spectacular growth of 1,574 per cent, with a market value of £29.4 billion (note that the shares were split again in October 1999 as explained on page 93). The *Investors Chronicle* portfolio was passive, held unchanged for ten years, so it completely missed the opportunity to invest in this fantastic UK success story. In January 1999, Vodafone won a takeover battle for AirTouch, the largest American mobile phone operator, to double its size and create the largest mobile operator in the world with a market capitalisation of about £68 billion. On completing this takeover in 1999, Vodafone AirTouch became the third-largest FTSE 100 company.

Constant jostling of FTSE 100 companies with their changing fortunes is a total surprise, but offers alert investors an exciting glimpse of how to multiply wealth many times by exploiting such fluctuations. There is opportunity aplenty, from watching this erratic league table, to maximise profits by being active. Starting with a passive portfolio, the investor holds the UK's biggest, most successful companies. Some may fall, relative to the rest, but once a year he discards those that fall below the top ten, reinvesting the proceeds in new top-ten entrants to maintain the portfolio's performance. This creates the semi-passive Top Ten Portfolio. When he is ready to take active control, he will have gained the confidence to buy companies with potentials like the young Vodafone that he has followed in his paper portfolio. The Top Ten Portfolio converts into the active New Millennium Portfolio, with a higher chance of reaching the wealth targets than is possible by holding the passive portfolio long term.

*'By definition, the FTSE 100 is a winners' index. Like the Premier League, the worst teams keep getting rooted out, and you have to be good to stay in the top tier.'*

*Robert Buckland, UK equity strategist at NatWest Stockbrokers, 1994*

By Christmas week of 1998, I was running a paper Top Ten Portfolio to monitor its progress and report on company changes and news flows throughout the book. Since July 1998, BAT had demerged its insurance interests, and mergers between BP and American Amoco, UK Zeneca and Sweden's Astra plus BTR and Siebe were planned. Meanwhile, a pre-Christmas rally lifted some of the companies we shall be following to new all-time highs, so there was, as ever, plenty of action. During 1999 the pace of change accelerated yet again.

## THE 5-LEVEL PROGRESSION IN OUTLINE

The move from passive to active investor is a central theme in the planned programme, at the heart of the 5-Level Progression, to which we now turn. In the following chapters, we will cover each level in depth, but here is a broad introduction, to give a general outline of the five phased stages.

## LEVEL I – Preliminary Steps: The Early Stages

You learn to know your investor type and understand the market's rhythms. When you can recognise the phases of the cycle you can spot a market trough and improve your prospects for making larger gains in the next uptrend. You set up your savings regime, with a budget and wealth check.

You create a paper version of the Top Ten Portfolio at the outset, to follow the fortunes of the top companies for 6–9 months or a year. When market conditions look favourable, you set up the passive Top Ten Portfolio to hold for at least 10 years or until you are ready to progress to higher levels. Stream A novices with no capital run a Paper Top Ten Portfolio while progressing through the early levels, so they keep up with Stream B and C investors to gain hands-on experience even though they need larger savings or longer time to build their wealth. Investors with some market experience might move speedily through Levels I and II. They set their targets and find the appropriate level where they begin working on the detail.

Stream C novices, with capital of over £20,000, could increase the opening portfolio size so as to have more of their funds growing faster from an early date.

Tools for Level I: which newspapers and journals to use and choosing a stockbroker.

*'The luck of having talent is not enough; one must also have a talent for luck.'*

*Hector Berlioz (1803–69), French composer*

## LEVEL II – The Passive Investor: Settle in and Pace Yourself

You learn to evaluate growth and value shares, how to use FASTER GAINS and understand basic fundamental and technical analysis. You learn how to create a paper portfolio and check it regularly to stay on track. Aim to move to Level III when this paper portfolio shows consistent profits.

Stream B and C investors continue with the Passive Top Ten Portfolio, as for Level I, but it undergoes the first stage of conversion from passive to active by becoming semi-passive. It can potentially grow faster if investors discard those companies that have fallen below the top ten by market capitalisation and reinvest the proceeds in the new top ten entrants once a year. Stream A investors stay with the Paper Top Ten Portfolio but do the same exercises on paper as Stream B and C investors, while learning Level II and saving to open their own Top Ten Portfolio.

Extra Tools for Level II: Software for following the market and company shares.

## LEVEL III – The Active Investor: Begin Relying on Your Growing Expertise

Change your perspective and success becomes achievable. You learn to follow the market and know how it is affected by business cycles in the economy. You examine the signals that identify the onset of recession and understand the key issues in portfolio-building, using FASTER GAINS PAYS.

Stream B and C investors close the paper portfolio for small, growth companies and set up a real portfolio to hold small growth companies with big potentials that they found by running FASTER GAINS. At the same time they continue with the semi-passive portfolio, as described in Level II. Stream A investors close the Paper Top Ten Portfolio when they have accumulated £10,000 with the savings regime, preferably while in Level II or in Level III. They open a real portfolio, to join Streams B and C.

Investors follow the big capitalisation stocks to find the growth stories.

Additional Tools for Level III: obtain real-time prices or Teletext, to follow the companies being tracked.

## LEVEL IV – The Self-Confident Investor

Your first wealth targets look achievable. You learn to manage your portfolio as an active investor and follow companies with strong growth stories, whatever their size. Learn to recognise potentially profitable growth in recovery stories. The Top Ten Portfolio continues to be semi-passive as you discard any of your ten companies that fall below tenth ranking. You continue with the portfolio for small growth companies, adding new holdings as opportunities arise. Open a paper portfolio for FTSE 100 or FTSE 250 stocks with growth or recovery stories using FASTER GAINS if applicable. Compare these companies with the ten currently held in your Top Ten Portfolio. Move to Level V when this paper portfolio shows consistent profits or when you feel ready to progress. The target is to turn the initial £10,000 into £85,000 plus, including extra growth from the small company portfolio.

A new tool is the Internet but it can be used earlier.

## LEVEL V – The Wealthy Investor

Your initial wealth targets are within sight. Most investors will have reached years 6 or 8, depending on the rate of progress. You close the paper portfolio for big-capitalisation growth companies while continuing to follow these stocks to find growth stories. Buy the successful growth companies being followed in the paper portfolio to replace some of the companies held in the Top Ten Portfolio, which now becomes the actively managed New Millennium Portfolio. It has become a self-chosen portfolio where each company held shows the best possible chance of creating real wealth over a period of 10–20 years. You learn how to choose companies to hold in this portfolio and how to decide if or when to sell.

Run the portfolio of small growth companies with big potentials based on timing market cycles and FASTER GAINS. Merge it into the New Millennium Portfolio so you are now running only one portfolio. Allocate 5–8 per cent of the portfolio for special situations, where you look at new industries with exciting growth potentials. This portfolio section can enhance overall growth, but needs careful monitoring and is an optional addition.

Continue with the savings regime by directing all savings into the combined portfolio. Aim to achieve a target of around £500,000 within 12 to 15 years of embarking on the planned programme. The objective is to hold a balanced, wealth-creating portfolio to provide a rising income plus capital growth to maintain a comfortable standard of living.

The target is to turn the initial £10,000 in year 1 into £500,000 within 6–8 years of embarking on Level V (perhaps 15–20 years in total).

## GET STARTED

Here, in outline, is the essence of the complete planned programme. It is not a formula for instant wealth. Rather, it is a self-improvement system for private investors wanting to gain investment expertise. You can reach a higher living standard than you currently have by exercising investment skills learned through a phased progression. I believe everyone is born equipped with a menu of skills, like options on a personal computer. You can activate different computer options by a simple click on the mouse: the dormant skills we are all capable of learning, such as investment expertise, need a similar effort to that involved when you first learned to run your computer. I feel sure we can tackle far more of these new techniques than we give ourselves credit for.

Too few people use a planned approach to grow wealthy. Moving step by step, each target becomes achievable in turn. The sooner you start, the earlier you will move through your chosen series of time and money targets and the larger the wealth pot you can accumulate. You may not want this wealth for yourself, but once you have it, there are many ways to employ it productively.

*'As a means, I saw that money was almost absolute: it could realise every fantasy of creation or murder.'*

James Buchan, The Psychology of Money

## HOW TO USE THIS BOOK

You can approach your 5-Level Progression along several routes. You might read through the whole text once or twice, to get a general sense of the complete programme; but reading the book is not the same as using it constructively to achieve high-level results. Or you might prefer to focus first on this Introduction: it is your map to begin planning your target time and money goals. Or you might work first through Levels I and II before you focus on the level you think best fits the stage of investor expertise you have reached.

Reading is the core of your project. So where should you start? At first, I suggest you read right through *The Wealthy Investor*. Subsequently, concentrate on the Introduction and browse through Level I, which covers the reading materials you should use for the early steps. If you have starting capital or previous experience, you might decide to jump straight to a higher level. Set aside at least 7 hours a week for reading. This can be in two or three large blocks or as one hour a day. You decide. Use a special book to record your whole programme – a separate notebook, a workbook in your personal organiser, or a file on your personal computer. Your chosen system keeps all your working papers together to help revision, by looking back on your early efforts as you progress.

Begin by re-reading the Introduction and then read Level I to start your savings regime, do a wealth check, set your time and money targets, and start your Paper Top Ten Portfolio. The paper portfolio is useful for all investors, even if you already run your own portfolio using your favourite stock-picking routine.

Work to a schedule of 6–12 months for each level, whatever your experience or size of capital. The time commitment need not be very great once the paper portfolios are set up, but the best results come from setting your time and money targets and then working steadily towards them. Don't put yourself under pressure to become wealthy. There is no rush. It is better to act smart than fast.

In summary, here is the action plan to start your programme:

1. Allocate at least 7 hours for reading each week.
2. Start a workbook to monitor your results.
3. Re-read the Introduction and read Level I to start your savings regime.
4. Do your wealth checks.
5. Set your first time and money targets.
6. Set up your Paper Top Ten Portfolio.
7. Plan to spend 6–12 months on each level.

With the essential elements defined, we are ready to embark on the first level, the preliminary steps. Even if you have some stock market experience, I think you will find setting time and money targets is useful and the market cycle analysis helpful for fine-tuning investment decisions. Making money with the planned programme is the ultimate treasure hunt, first on paper and then for real. We can all enjoy this exciting search while generating the wealth we want to own.

---

**KEY POINTS TO REMEMBER**
........................................

1. Make a lifetime commitment to create your own wealth.
2. Aim to build a wealth-creating portfolio of company shares, not a random mix of individually picked shares.
3. Use the planned programme to pace yourself.
4. Set achievable time and money targets.
5. Be willing to stop at any level, but aim from the outset to go the full distance.

---

*'You cannot teach a man anything; you can only help him to find it within himself.'*

*Galileo Galilei (1564–1642), Italian Mathematician and Astronomer*

# LEVEL I – PRELIMINARY STEPS

## The Early Stages

*'Trust in yourself. Your perceptions are often far more accurate than you are willing to believe.'*

Claudia Black, American social psychologist

However experienced you are, the preliminary steps of Level I are useful. The early stages launch the programme for novices but most of them apply to everyone. A structured action plan is indispensable. The value and practical application of a savings regime is central to success. Setting time and money goals and preparing a yearly wealth check help you stay on target. Running a paper portfolio is productive for finding and tracking promising companies before you invest. Understanding the rhythms of market cycles is essential background material. Investment timing is a difficult skill to master, so any insights that improve your ability to time buy or sell decisions well are valuable. Together, these preliminary steps form your action plan for Level I.

Your Level I action plan covers the following steps:

1) Begin the savings regime. Examine the key issues for the savings regime:
    a) budget to find the money to save;
    b) do a wealth check, to establish your starting financial position;
    c) decide which type of investor you are, so you can then
    d) decide on the right place to put your savings.
2) Examine recent market cycles to recognise the rhythms of the market.
3) Obtain and use some essential tools to begin learning about investments.
4) Identify recognisable features during a market cycle.
5) At the outset, establish the paper portfolio for the current top ten companies.
6) Prepare to buy your own Top Ten Portfolio.
7) Complete the checklist to decide where the cycle is before you buy your portfolio.
8) Choose a stockbroker and open an account.

## COMPOUND THAT GROWTH

In 1998, an American study used two investors (we'll call them Max and Mary) to illustrate investment growth. The study showed that the largest gains come from starting early, rather than investing more, but later. Both saved $2,000 each year; Max invested in equities for 40 years, from age 26 until he retired at 65; but Mary only invested for 7 years, from age 19 to age 26. With a 10 per cent average annual growth rate each year, Mary had a larger fund at 65. Her $14,000 over 7 years of savings, ($2,000 × 7) became $930,641 after 40 years. Max saved $80,000 over 40 years ($2,000 × 40) and accumulated $893,704. However, the higher the rate of return, the greater the benefits from investing early. For Max and Mary, with the same investments but assuming a 5 per cent rather than 10 per cent rate of return, the results are very different. Max would have $173,680 and Mary only $106,371. Yet, as before, Mary invested only $14,000 compared with $80,000 by Max, so Mary's return was higher although her final sum was lower.

For readers too late to start at 20, do not fret. I began at 53 and have created a healthy nest egg for my family. Anne Scheiber's story is far more impressive. She began investing on Wall Street aged 50 with just $5,000 when she retired in 1947. When she died, she had turned that into a superb $20 million. She was a classic long-term, self-taught private investor, teaching herself the main investment skills. As she lived to be 101, her money was compounding over 50 years of active investing. On her death it all went to charity. When you become an active, knowledgeable investor, no matter at what age you begin, you can be wealthier than you ever dreamed was possible.

## BEGIN YOUR SAVINGS REGIME

In my book, *The Money Maze*, I borrowed a helpful idea from the Beardstown Ladies, who run a famous investment club from their home town of Beardstown, Illinois. Their 'pay-yourself-first' fund captures the essence of saving as a high priority; it puts the savings regime at the top of the budget – as important as cash for food, heat or light and paying the mortgage. A 'pay-yourself-first' fund is central to the programme as it makes your savings regime a vital rung on your ladder to success.

While you are working, your income is regular money from a reliable source. Working for a living is exactly that: earning the money to live on, day by day. You should juggle your current expenses so as to find cash for a savings fund. As you progress through to higher levels, you will learn to judge when to plough the money saved into your portfolios. Eventually, after working through the planned programme, you can live like a Lord on unearned income paid each year as dividends on the equities you own.

Your growing capital, including these savings, is the focus of all your efforts; it is your passport to wealth. Learning how to manage your money will help you protect this precious capital from loss. To reach your ultimate targets your financial assets must grow steadily. Their values will fluctuate at times, with market conditions, but the trend should be upwards. If you eat into your capital for whatever reason, you reduce your chance of hitting your targets. Vanishing capital means vanishing dividends, but evidence shows that reinvesting the dividends plays a proven role in a portfolio's growth.

For a decisive impact on your investment funds, aim to save £2,000 a year or 7 per cent of your **take-home pay** after tax and National Insurance deductions. Copy Mary's example and save 10 per cent in the early years. Later, you might reduce that amount, although this may affect your targets. The stock market rose strongly in the 1980s and 1990s. We will discuss its amazing performance shortly, and in Level III we examine the favourable background conditions that made it possible. It would, however, be unwise to rely on such an excellent future performance.

When you start investing, you may be lucky enough – or clever enough – to buy exciting companies that grow substantially within your portfolio. Yet, even with one or two such gems, it is certainly easier to grow wealthy when stock market conditions are favourable and prices rise. If the stock market dawdles, so may your funds, but by adding in a steady schedule of savings you can greatly enhance your results.

*'A budget can transform your prospects for becoming wealthy.'*

## Prepare Your Current Budget

The first step is to find some money to save. Launch your savings regime and then decide where to put this cash so that it grows while your investment skills improve. Some people will have spare cash to start a savings fund immediately, and if you live within your income, saving will pose no problem, although some spending cuts may be needed to save 7 per cent regularly each year.

However, you may not know exactly how much cash you can save. Or you may suspect that you spend more than you earn. A preliminary assessment of your current budget will quickly divulge how much cash, if any, is free. A prepared budget shows you exactly what is happening to your income now: how much money is being earned and how much is spent. Ideally, your income should cover all outgoings; but if it does not, a budget will reveal the overspend.

First, collect all your income slips, bank statements and bills covering the last twelve months. These provide rough guesses about your expected income and expenses over the coming twelve months, but estimates using last year's figures are good enough. List all your monthly incomes, bonuses, dividends and bank interest, plus all your expenses: rent or mortgage, food, travel, heating, household bills, pension contributions and car expenses. Additional expenses, such as entertainment, clothes, cigarettes or holidays, must also be included, plus an entry for one-off items, which I lump together as 'extras'. These might be birthday or wedding presents, buying a book or CD on impulse, new car tyres or other unplanned outlays. From this list of *monthly* figures, you can calculate the *annual* totals. By deducting the total annual expenses from your total annual income, you find the balance and can see whether you are spending less than you earn. It is then a small step to allocate some free money to your new savings fund.

However, if you rely on an overdraft, or spend every penny you earn, your annual expenses may equal or exceed your income. With the introduction of personal loans in the 1980s, and the expansion of available credit through store and credit cards, we have become a nation of seasoned debtors. Personal household debt doubled during the 1980s. This spending is counterproductive for wealth seekers. If it applies to you, adopt a budgeting routine as the natural follow-on step to find the money to save.

### The Budget Routine

Regular budgeting is essential when your expenses exceed your income. It puts you in control to pay off short-term debts and find your savings fund. Habitual high spenders should resort to belt-tightening when last year's budget reveals the size of the overspend. You found it from your budget, but that is now history; your income was either spent or saved and cannot be changed. But this does not apply to *next* year's income.

You now devise two more budgets: the first, your *target budget*, sets out new lower spending targets; and the second, your *working budget*, will keep your spending down to the limits you have set through the year ahead. Examining the details of expenses in last year's budget enables you to revise your spending downwards in order to create the new target budget, including your savings fund. You arrive at the sum you plan to save by shuffling the figures for your expenses around and deciding on the main areas where reductions can be made. You can track where the money is going every month by filling in the expenses rows on your new working budget, as shown in the table on page 39. This is one of the most methodical ways of keeping within your revised spending targets.

*'If we do not solve the problem of the budget, we will not solve any other problem.'*

*Yevgeny Yasin, former economics minister in Russia, 1998*

This routine is as boring as it sounds, and so one alternative is to focus just on the key issues. From last year's budget, you can see at a glance the size of your overspend. You now know how you allocated all your income, so you can immediately start pruning. Cut your spending to the amount you earn, and then go further to find your target savings fund of £2,000 a year or 7 per cent of take-home pay, whichever fits the overall budget. How rapidly your situation improves depends on the size of the excess spending and how many 'extras' are amenable to vigorous cutting. If your gross income is £25,000, your after-tax take-home pay will be about £20,000. Save 10 per cent and squirrel away £2,000 a year. If that looks impossible, aim for £1,400, to tuck away 7 per cent a year. Over time, add to your savings, perhaps when you have a pay rise.

With the savings figure decided, reorganise the expenses that can be reduced, so your budget will balance for the next twelve months. Set maximum spending limits for big items that vary. You obviously cannot economise on expenses such as the mortgage, council tax or insurance payments as these are effectively outside your control, but many others in the budget can be adjusted. The final revised figures create your target budget. Each budget has different amounts of reducible expenses, but suppose you spend £240 a month on clothes, magazines and extras: can you shrink it to £150 a month to save £90? Can you economise on travel or your mobile phone tariff? Find another £80 for a monthly total of £170 and your savings regime starts with £2,040 a year.

With your revised spending levels set, enter your monthly target budget. Use the empty columns alongside to complete the working budget expenses at the end of each month, shown in the table below. Use a cash book or a computer program to record income and expenses details, both daily and weekly. Enter the daily totals in a pocket notebook or on a prepared budget grid in a personal organiser. At the end of each week, the totals go to preparing the monthly figures. Using this routine, you are able to monitor and modify your spending almost as it happens, for the next twelve months. If your first guesses were wildly wrong, routine monitoring amends the errors. Major firms track their expenditure by running budgets. You quickly spot an overspend if it emerges and can correct it promptly. During the next month, focus on the area where an overspend arose, to correct it and get back on to your target budget.

## TARGET AND WORKING BUDGETS FOR ONE MONTH

| Item | Last Year's Budget | Target Budget | Working Budget |
|---|---|---|---|
| *Monthly Income:* | | | |
| Monthly income | £ | £ | £ |
| Spouse/partner's income | £ | £ | £ |
| Bank etc. interest | £ | £ | £ |
| Bonuses | £ | £ | £ |
| *Total Income (after tax)* | £ | £ | £ |
| | | | |
| *Monthly Expenses:* | | | |
| My savings fund | £ | £ | £ |
| Mortgage/rent | £ | £ | £ |
| Food | £ | £ | £ |
| Council tax | £ | £ | £ |
| Household bills | £ | £ | £ |
| Car insurance & tax | £ | £ | £ |
| Petrol & travel | £ | £ | £ |
| House insurance | £ | £ | £ |
| Clothing | £ | £ | £ |
| Car & other loans | £ | £ | £ |
| Entertainment | £ | £ | £ |
| Holidays/Christmas | £ | £ | £ |
| Pension & life assurance premiums | £ | £ | £ |
| Extras (credit cards) | £ | £ | £ |
| *Total monthly expenditure* | £ | £ | £ |
| **Balance:** | **£** | **£** | **£** |

## 'If you want to feel wealthy, you must make more each month than you spend.'

*Mark Bryan and Julia Cameron,* The Money Drunk

Budgeting works well on overspending by comparing each completed month's outlay with the target budget. If spending on extras is over budget in May, buy less in June. When June's allowance is spent, defer more spending until July. Routine budgeting will help you meet your wealth targets, but it may require a diligent effort for some years. If your spending habits are easily changed, you may master your savings regime without budgeting, even if you are overspending when you prepare your first budget.

### Budget Short Cuts

I discussed detailed budgeting in *The Money Maze*, but it is a tiresome chore.

Tackle it by spotting troublesome areas where your spending was high last year. Focus on one or two such areas, to short-circuit budgeting tedium. Locate what I call 'budget black holes'. Most people have pet spending habits to which they are addicted; if they are ignored, considerable sums simply disappear down these black holes.

You may know which items would respond to drastic revision. Major pruning there should correct any excesses. Could you cut next year's clothes budget in half, buy fewer books or visit the theatre less often? Persevere strictly with budgeting to reduce the size and number of the black holes, and your budget will soon respond. Acquire this habit, and you are close to your first goal: to find some cash for your savings regime.

## The Yearly Wealth Check

A wealth check is a snapshot of your financial health, to see how you are moving towards your targets. I discuss the value of a yearly wealth check in all my personal finance books. It is important because when you manage your own personal finances it is vital you know how your budget is faring and the approximate size of your **net worth**. This is the balance of your assets after deducting your debts. The wealth check consists of your annual budget plus your net worth statement. If you consult a financial adviser, his first task when you meet is to prepare a wealth check to discover what shape your finances are in. Now you are your own adviser, you can do this exercise for yourself.

Annual Budget + Net Worth Statement = Yearly Wealth Check

The wealth check is important to reveal at the outset – and, indeed, at least once every year – two vital financial statistics: first, whether you can increase the amount you save out of income; and, second, what the value of your accumulated capital is to date. If your salary rose by 6 per cent one year, could you raise your savings by 3 per cent, even before allocating extra money to spend? The net worth statement is the rapid route to discovering how many assets (possessions) you own and the size of your debts or liabilities. Knowing this information, you are well placed to chart your progress for the next year, to meet your targets and reach your goals. Having prepared your annual budget, therefore, you are but a small step away from completing your wealth check.

The initial check reveals whether you can save £2,000 a year or if you need smaller steps to get there. It will also disclose whether you are a Stream A investor (no starting capital), one from Stream B (£15,000 in starting capital), or someone in Stream C (more than £20,000 at the start). You can then plan future time and money targets, as set out in the Introduction to this book. Make rough estimates of your savings over 10 or 20 years and do money-doubling figures for growing your capital. Alternatively, just add a nought, to arrive at a reasonable 10-year target for the size of your future portfolio.

Keep all your personal details on your annual budget and net worth statements in one notebook, or together in your personal organiser or personal computer. With all the information in one place, it is easier to check your progress over several years. Prepare your opening asset position and compile your first set of time and money targets. Write down your initial money targets for the next 5 years.

## Prepare Your Net Worth Statement

The net worth statement contains two lists. The first shows all your assets: your house, car, jewellery, antiques, deposit accounts and items with a monetary value, using rough estimates. You may guess the value of your house, based on others in your area, but when you sell, the price is what the buyer will pay, and may not match your estimate. In relation to your investment portfolio, the FTSE 100 is updated every 15 seconds throughout the day and prices change continuously, so you only know its approximate worth. Without accurate values for your assets, you can never exactly determine your wealth; but when you have a substantial portfolio of financial assets, this vagueness no longer matters.

The second list contains all your outstanding debts: your mortgage, loans on a car or furniture, university loans, credit-card or store-card debts which will not be repaid within the interest-free period, plus any other debts. Add up the items on each list and deduct the figure of your total debts from your total assets to produce the balance of your current wealth. This is your net worth, as shown on the worked example in the table below.

In the net worth example, a deposit account holds £10,500. If your initial position is similar, you may think you are ready to open your Top Ten Portfolio. However, there is a credit card debt of £4,500. Even without that, it would be unwise to invest £10,000, leaving only £500 on deposit. This sum is far too small for an emergency fund to cope with any unexpected expenditure. So if your net worth statement looks similar to this example, how should you proceed?

The top priority is to start budgeting and repay the whole credit-card debt. Set target instalments to pay it off within 12–18 months. Until you rebalance your budget and start a savings regime, further progress is impossible. You can be running your Paper Top Ten Portfolio all the while

**YEARLY NET WORTH STATEMENT AS AT . . . (You enter the date here)**

| Assets | Current Value (£) |
|---|---|
| House | 95,000 |
| Car | 8,000 |
| Building society deposits | 10,500 |
| Pension Fund | 12,000 |
| **Totals** | **125,500** |

| Outstanding debts | Current Value (£) |
|---|---|
| Mortgage | − 75,000 |
| 3-year loan | − 7,250 |
| Credit card debts | − 4,500 |
| Hi-fi system | − 1,200 |
| **Totals** | **− 87,950** |

**Net Worth £37,550**

you are eliminating the debt and building your savings. With the debt repaid, on an average income of £475 a week, aim to save between £1,750 and £2,000 a year in monthly instalments of £146–£167. Alternatively, savings of £150 a month as a good round number, produces an extra £1,800 saved each year. Repaying debt while saving every month is difficult. You might decide, like some marathon runner hopefuls, that the effort is not worth the prize – we are not all destined to be wealthy. But if budgeting and saving are burdens while you are working, the prospects when your income ceases at retirement might be worse. Rather than abandon the whole exercise, take longer to repay the debts while building your capital. Throughout, if you run a paper portfolio, when you have about £15,000 saved you can open your real Top Ten Portfolio, with £5,000 set aside as an emergency fund. If your ultimate goal is to be wealthy, the time you take to start is flexible, especially if you learn to master the skills to put your finances in better order.

## 'Anyone who says that money doesn't matter has never had to live without it.'

*Mark Bryan and Julia Cameron,* The Money Drunk

If you have £10,500 on deposit at the outset, but no debt, two years of saving plus interest could produce between £3,760 and £4,600. With interest added, your deposit account might reach about £11,250, giving you total capital of between £15,010 and £15,850 (see workings below). It would then be safe to close the paper portfolio and invest £10,000 in your Top Ten Portfolio, with around £5,000 as a reserve fund.

### SAVING OVER 2 YEARS, WITH BUILDING SOCIETY CASH ADDED

| Date | Savings Fund (£) @ £1,750 a year | Savings Fund (£) @ £2,000 a year | Building Society Cash (£) |
|---|---|---|---|
| At Outset | Nil | Nil | 10,500 |
| After 2 years with interest | 3,760 | 4,600 | 11,250 |
| *Add* b/society cash | 11,250 | 11,250 | |
| **Total** | **15,010** | **15,850** | |

If you have debts and little or no cash on deposit, you may be alarmed to discover your net worth is negative, with total debts greater than your assets. This is not a cause for panic. The point of a yearly budget and net worth statement is to reveal your annual wealth check and expose its defects as well as its strengths. It is far better to know the extent of your negative savings than to continue blindly until financial disaster looms. When you know your financial position, you can monitor your progress as you move through the 5-Level Progression. If you have large debts, more budgeting may be needed and a larger savings regime might improve the situation. Examining your first financial situation, even if it is poor, triggers the motivation to move up through the five levels and reach your wealth targets. This works for determined characters. In 1990, I began with huge debts. I ran a strict budget for 4 years to shrink the debts, and I still managed to create a sizeable portfolio within 8 years by staying with my targets. However, as my wealth grew the targets moved so that I could use the growing funds productively.

*'Taking a new step, uttering a new word is what people most fear.'*

*Fyodor Dostoyevski (1821–81), Russian novelist*

## What Type of Investor Are You?

Having compiled your budget and net worth statements, you can see at a glance where you put your money in the past. How much have you saved in deposit accounts? Do you have other financial assets – a pension fund, PEPs or unit trusts, perhaps? If all your money is in National Savings products or deposit accounts, it is clear you are either a cautious saver or you do not know how to use equity-based investments to your advantage. Are most of your assets tied up in your home and deposit accounts? Your wealth check gives you an instant picture of the type of investor you are. Evidence shows that most British people avoid equity-based investments, even if they own a few shares in a privatised company or demutualised building society. If your assets fit this description, you are a cautious investor. But this may be through lack of knowledge about equities. Adopting the 5-Level Progression can change that to your financial benefit.

Before you put your savings to work, decide what type of investor you are: nervous, taking a balanced view, ready for some risk, or a mixture of these. Complete novices should be ultra-cautious while learning core investment skills. Begin slowly, while overcoming early fears. As you progress, the fears should recede. The paper portfolios play a dominant role in the early stages of the 5-Level Progression, so you gain plenty of paper experience to help you master your initial anxieties. Using an equity-based fund to try and grow your savings fast would not be sensible if you are constantly worried. Decide early whether this description fits you. Even if you realise the helpful role that equities play in building wealth, avoid them until your confidence grows. Beginners should feel comfortable with their level of involvement while they learn basic essentials. The aggressive route will suit people with some experience of markets or novices keen to move rapidly up all five levels; they will need, however, to devote more time and effort to improving their expertise and knowledge of the markets.

*'Over the years, Engels gave generously to Marx – almost two thousand pounds between 1866 and 1869 alone. Sometimes he posted five pounds cut in half to deter thieves, sometimes much larger sums.'*

Edna Healey, Wives of Fame *(on Jenny Marx)*

Knowing your investor type is powerful information: slot it into your database of facts about yourself as a successful investor to judge how you will react to unexpected market events. Your investment personality is closely linked to your commitment level. Despite the great attraction of creating wealth, that ultimate goal may not persuade everyone to complete the 5-Level Progression. Many people cannot devote enough energy to achieving great prosperity, but if you treat the planned programme as a lifelong hobby you will ultimately reap huge rewards. Managing your money is probably the best hobby you can cultivate because if you are successful, it will pay for all your other hobbies.

## Put Your Savings to Work

Having found the cash to save, help it grow while you run your Top Ten Portfolio. Where you save depends on your attitude to **risk**, that is, the risk of losing money. Moving from novice to expert along the 5-Level planned route reduces risk as your expertise improves. When knowledge rises, risks diminish. Investors should listen to their inner voice if it cautions against risk; it is warning you to act slowly. This is sound advice for everyone at times. A slow, cautious start is eminently sensible.

Where, then, should you put your monthly savings? They should grow faster in tax-free schemes, but try to match your investor type with where you save. Do you prefer cash or equities? Cautious savers should choose cash funds; tracker funds will suit passive investors who want equity-based savings.

*'All money, properly so called, is an acknowledgement of debt.'*

*John Ruskin (1819–1900), author and artist, social reformer*

### Saving Cash

Two major government-approved tax-free plans, Personal Equity Plans (PEPs) and Tax-Exempt Special Savings Accounts (TESSAs) were superseded by Individual Savings Accounts (ISAs) in April 1999. No new annual PEPs and TESSAs could be opened after that date, but ISAs are less generous, with lower tax advantages than the plans they replaced. The cash element earns gross interest, but rates were falling from mid-1998. The amount you can save is smaller than in TESSAs. Existing PEPs can continue, with no **capital gains tax** payable on equities sold within them, but the dividend tax credit fell from a rate of 20 per cent (prior to April 1999) to 10 per cent thereafter, equal to the level of tax credits in the equity part of ISAs. Tax credits will end in 2004, although capital gains within both PEPs and ISAs will remain tax-free.

Other products offer tax advantages. As limits on the cash saved each year in an ISA are low, these may be needed. If you want to build a cash fund above the ISA limit, the extra can go into tax-free **National Savings** or a high-interest deposit account, although this latter would be subject to tax. If you can ignore short-term stock market gyrations, consider an equity-based tracker ISA. We will look at these options in turn, and a summary of the most important features is given in the table below.

---

### SUMMARY OF CHOICES FOR YOUR SAVINGS REGIME

| | | |
|---|---|---|
| i) | **Cash** in a Tax-free Fund | National Savings or cash in an ISA |
| ii) | **Cash** in a higher interest account | Savings are not tax-free |
| iii) | **Units** in a Tracker fund | Savings in an ISA are only tax-aided |

---

### GUIDE TO THE MAIN TAX-FREE SCHEMES

| Feature | Tessa | Pep | Isa | National Savings |
|---|---|---|---|---|
| 1 Tax exemption on interest | Yes | Yes | Yes | Yes[a] |
| 2 Capital gains tax exemption? | Not applicable | Yes | Yes | Not applicable |
| 3 Maximum annual investment | Nil after April 1999 | Nil after April 1999 | £7,000[b] £5,000[c] | £20,000 per person £40,000 per couple |
| 4 Easily withdrawn? | No | Yes | Yes | Yes |
| 5 Level of risk? | Low[d] | High | Low – cash[d] High – equity | Low[d] |

*Notes:* [a] on some products only; [b] 1999 only; [c] 2000 and each following year until 2008; [d] but there is a risk inflation will reduce the purchasing power of the capital.

### *Tax-Free Saving in an ISA*

Individual savings accounts, ISAs, were launched in April 1999. The cash-only 'mini' version allows £3,000 to be invested in the tax year 1999/2000 and £1,000 each year thereafter for at least ten years. The 'maxi-ISA' consists of a £3,000 cash element in the first year (6 April 1999 to 5 April 2000) and £1,000 a year thereafter, until 2008 on current legislation. A maxi-ISA may also contain an equity element comprising the total £7,000 investment permitted in the first year and £5,000 a year thereafter, with no money allocated to cash. The insurance element of £1,000 a year seemed unpopular with both savers and ISA providers. Originally planned to be simple, easy-to-use schemes, ISAs became complicated, with great confusion among providers and the public. Articles on ISAs appear regularly in the financial press. Here, we focus only on how ISAs aid your plan to be wealthy. We will look, therefore, at cash ISAs and the equity element for building savings.

Cash ISAs work like tax-free savings accounts: rates vary for each account. Phone and postal accounts pay more than branch-based ones. Ideally, they should have no notice periods for withdrawals. With the ISA cash limit set at £1,000 from 6 April 2000, for savings of £2,000 a year you must put the balance elsewhere. You can buy £1,000 of National Savings products that are either tax-free or paid gross but subject to tax. You could open a high-interest or instant-access account, without early withdrawal penalties, but taxpayers will be liable for tax. Money-market unit trusts are another alternative, but capital values are not guaranteed and again they are liable for tax. You could buy £1,000 of tracker fund units each year, using an equity-based ISA for the tax benefits. The annual limit is £5,000 a year, ignoring the cash element, and so if you increase your savings, your contributions can reach that level in this or later tax years.

*'You never answer my letters, so I have written you a short one. I send you half a ten pound note and you must write by return of post to say if you got it. Then I will send the other half.'* [Equivalent to about £1,200 in 1998 money]

*Letter written by Anna Maria Bowker to her son, Holden, 28 November 1858*

### National Savings Inside and Outside an ISA

Cautious savers rely on safe, ever-popular government-backed National Savings. They can now enjoy this safety within the National Savings ISA. It offers tax-free benefits plus the government guarantee, with the same flexibility on withdrawals as other ISAs, an advantage over those National Savings products with fixed periods and early withdrawal penalties. It is suitable for higher-rate taxpayers, despite the low savings limit that covers all ISAs. This ISA meets the government's Cat standard (see below) and the government backing is a bonus over other cash ISAs, because the Cat standard does not guarantee against loss but only guards against hidden costs, charges or unfair conditions. The National Savings ISA is more accessible than other National Savings products that are available through post offices or by post.

With the maximum allowed in a National Savings cash ISA, you can buy other National Savings products with higher limits. Tax-free savings certificates, either index-linked or ordinary (and children's bonds), offer

---

**FACTS ON ISAS**
........................

1. ISAs are tax-free individual savings accounts that replaced PEPs and TESSAs in April 1999.
2. ISAs have three elements: an equity component, which can be invested in shares, unit trusts, investment trusts, gilts or bonds; a cash element, which can be saved in a bank or building society account, or in the National Savings ISA; a life assurance element, which can be allocated to certain insurance products.
3. In the first year, 6 April 1999 to 5 April 2000, the total tax-free allowance is £7,000, but it falls to £5,000 in subsequent years. In the first year, the full £7,000 can go into equities, or £3,000 can be diverted into the cash element and £1,000 into insurance. From April 2000, the allocation can be either the full £5,000 in equities or £1,000 each in cash and insurance and the balance in equities.
4. There are two types of ISA: minis and maxis.
5. A maxi ISA can contain all three elements, shares, cash and insurance although the whole sum, either £7,000 (year 1) or £5,000 (each following year) can be invested solely in shares. The alternative is to take out three mini-ISAs: one for shares, a second for cash and the third for insurance. You can invest only £3,000 in the equities mini-ISA.
6. A 'Cat-marked' ISA has government approval. Cat covers 'Cost, Accessibility and Terms'. A Cat-marked ISA must not charge more than 1 per cent a year as a management fee and cash ISAs must pay interest that is not more than two percentage points below the current base rate as set by the Bank of England.

---

Note: This is not a comprehensive guide to ISAs, it is intended to clarify the main points.

good returns, notably for higher-rate taxpayers. The rates are guaranteed for 5 years but as there are penalties on early withdrawal, do not buy if you might invest this cash in your portfolio before the term ends. Index-linked savings certificates guarantee to beat inflation, but when inflation is low, so are the returns. As with all savings accounts, base-rate cuts reduce the interest paid. Follow rate movements to catch current issues before they are closed and replaced by a new issue with a lower rate.

Other National Savings products, namely the investment account, income bonds and First Option bonds, pay interest gross but that interest is liable for tax.

### High-Interest Accounts

In the late 1990s, falling interest rates posed problems of low interest for cash savers, but competition for their money increased as new entrants expanded the existing choice. Some retailing chains and supermarkets offered financial services, including instant-access accounts with attractive interest rates. Organisations such as Saga, for the over-50s, and some major insurance companies entered the market. The Prudential's Egg account, launched in a blaze of publicity in autumn 1998, met a huge response, offering as it did 8 per cent interest when competitors were offering 7 per cent. Building societies, banks and financial institutions set different rates, and eventually all rates fall into line with base rates, but the speed at which they move is highly variable. This throws up a wide range of interest rates, so the best-buy tables constantly change.

Choose a safe haven for your savings, focusing not on rates but on the reputations of the companies offering the accounts – if you have money in an institution that fails, compensation is limited to £18,000 per person (although this limit excludes National Savings, whose products are fully backed by the UK government). Use large, well-established companies or spread your cash among different savings products. Look for those with consistently competitive rates over a prolonged period.

## 'Man can learn nothing except by going from the known to the unknown.'

*Claude Bernard (1813–78), French psychologist*

### A Tracker in an ISA

With the maximum in a cash ISA, you could open an ISA tracker fund. Trackers rely on a simple idea that is effective for savings by Level I, II and III investors: they track one particular stock market index, which acts as a benchmark for investment performance. It may be the FTSE 100 index, or the more broadly based FTSE All-Share index, covering over 800 companies. There are numerous types of trackers, but these two main UK indices are the most popular and have attracted a large group of tracker unit-trust funds, run by some of the largest, most influential UK fund management groups and insurance companies, many of which also offer ISA trackers.

Trackers are 'passive', aiming to closely match the performance of the particular index being tracked. Although they employ managers, the share selection is automatically achieved by following only companies listed in the index. This makes trackers different from actively managed funds, which instead aim to beat the market through share selections based on a particular investment or stock-picking system. Tracker managers monitor their funds to replicate the return obtainable by owning shares in *all* the companies in that index. This is difficult for small FTSE All-Share trackers: because they lack the funds to hold shares in 800 companies, they buy only a representative selection, a weighted sample, to match the complete index. Even large trackers may not achieve an exact match as they pay commissions on buying or selling, and prices change while the proper weighting for a new holding is built. They receive dividends on the shares held, however, although dividend payments are not calculated in the index. Very large funds, like Virgin or Legal & General, running FTSE All-Share index trackers valued at over £1 billion, are less volatile, with fewer swings, than small trackers. Managers have their own selection methods, and so performances differ: and some funds have a better record of matching the index than others.

The tracker fund manager must change his shareholdings with the quarterly revision for the index. Every three months the changes reflect alterations in the ratings of the listed companies, as their fortunes fluctuate. For the FTSE 100, almost every review brings changes: two or three new entrants replace a corresponding number of expelled companies whose value has fallen below the required level. Some companies get suspended – this occurred to Maxwell Communications, Robert Maxwell's flagship company, in December 1991. The government's privatisation programme created several huge publicly quoted companies: British Gas, British Telecommunications, BP among many. At their flotation, other companies left the index to accommodate these new higher-worth issues. Similar changes followed when some of the largest mutual building societies and insurance companies floated as public companies. Halifax and Norwich Union were large enough to enter the FTSE 100 index at the next review date after launch, ousting less valuable companies. If businesses hit management or trading problems, a falling share price may reduce the market value so far that the company loses its index slot. This fate struck Polly Peck in 1991, when it dramatically collapsed. In 1998, Next, the fashion retailing group, issued a profits warning after a season of poor sales. The company slid down the FTSE 100, causing its expulsion.

The quarterly review of index components makes continuous monitoring necessary for funds to match the index. So trackers are more active than is realised, even though they are limited in their choice of company: they must add index newcomers and sell the leavers. **Active fund managers** avoid this constraint, searching for companies with profit potentials, regardless of size or index listing. Yet this freedom of choice does not improve their performance. Statistics show that about 20 per cent of active managers match the market and fewer still – perhaps 10 per cent outperform it. In February 1999, the five-year record showed the average FTSE 100 tracker had grown by 84.6 per cent compared with 66.3 per cent for the average-growth unit trust. The five-year record to September 1998 showed a 94.4 per cent rise in the FTSE All-Share index compared with 75.2 per cent (capital plus income) for the average actively managed growth unit trust. For one-year periods within those five years, the index beat the active funds four times. Staying in step with the market seems a modest goal, but since the majority of active managers cannot do it, the tracker serves investors well. We will look below at reasons why I believe you have better prospects of outsmarting the index than the majority of professional fund managers.

## LONG-TERM TRACKING OF MARKET CYCLES

Tracker fund popularity grew as more investors realised that many active managers fail to beat the market. Investors worry that they will inadvertently choose poorly performing funds; automatic share selection for trackers eliminates that risk. Through more than 60 years, the stock market has risen over every decade. It rises for longer periods than it falls. With your money in a tracker, you benefit with every rise. This removes some of the uncertainty linked to actively managed funds. You also avoid the need to choose a fund manager who performs well, because you know that, whatever the index does, your fund will closely match it, reducing the greatest uncertainty of stock market investing. Markets always fluctuate, but timing sales or purchases is a tricky skill. Avoid the misery of poor timing and remain invested through the dips, knowing your funds will grow with each upswing. Evidence repeatedly shows buying and holding good blue-chip shares pays rich rewards for patient investors. The Top Ten Portfolio is based on this historical fact.

The longer you keep your money in the market, the lower the risk. Resolve to keep your cash in a tracker for around ten years or until your investment skills can handle the decision on when to move it. Stay with the tracker even longer if you remain at Levels I or II. By moving through to Level V, you will actively manage both your funds and the risks. You will gain enough experience on market movements to time the transfer of your tracker funds into your own portfolio.

Cheaper costs for running trackers is another reason for their growing popularity compared with active funds. Trackers need not employ expensive professional analysts because they know which shares to buy or sell. Lower costs improve fund performance as smaller charges mean more money is invested in shares. With cheaper costs, many management groups run ISA trackers in addition to higher-cost, self-select equity ISAs.

*'What lies behind us and what lies before us are tiny matters, compared to what lies within us.'*

*Ralph Waldo Emerson (1803–82), American poet and philosopher*

## Spread the Risk

While you are learning, therefore, a tracker is a core savings vehicle. Buying tracker fund units, you immediately own a tiny share in many companies; 100 for the FTSE 100 tracker, or around 806 companies for the FTSE All-Share, depending on which index your fund tracks. On your own, you need several thousand pounds to buy a few companies. It is less risky to hold 100 companies than a few, and even less risky to own several hundred as you **diversify risk** by spreading your funds widely.

Trackers are invaluable for investors with limited funds. When you buy your Top Ten Portfolio, you only own ten shares, but they are the biggest UK companies and you monitor their progress while learning to be an active investor. However, by November 1999, a spate of mergers and acquisitions among these massive companies meant FTSE 100 trackers had more than half their money invested in just ten firms. More than 50 per cent of the value of the FTSE 100 consisted of BP Amoco, Glaxo Wellcome, BT, SmithKline Beecham, Lloyds TSB, Vodafone AirTouch, Shell, AstraZeneca and Barclays. Together, these ten firms accounted for most of the FTSE 100's rise from 1997. When you buy a Top Ten Portfolio, avoid duplicating those holdings with FTSE 100 tracker units as this increases your risk.

Invest in the FTSE All-Share index, where 70 per cent of the funds are in FTSE 100 companies. You will then hold shares in some smaller companies with greater growth potential. The larger the number of shares held, the lower the investment risks because a large loss in one company out of the current 806 makes a smaller dent in fund performance than a large loss in a portfolio of only 100. This logic also operates in reverse, for making big gains. We saw in the *Investors Chronicle* portfolio how the presence of one or two exceptional gains boosted overall performance. The impact would be much smaller if the portfolio held 100 shares.

Reducing risk is a top priority and is achieved in many ways; becoming more knowledgeable is the best route. Use trackers as they are less risky than actively managed funds, which assume greater risks by holding small, riskier shares mainly to make higher returns. A savings regime is ideal to reduce the risk of poor timing. Monthly saving prevents you buying your entire holding at a peak. Drip-feed your money into your tracker with a monthly plan – which is exactly what you do when saving through your monthly budget. Finally, reduce risk substantially by becoming active. Monitor your progress regularly to eliminate the poorest performers.

*'Measure the risk of doing nothing against the risk of acting and being right.'*

Avoid tracker funds that charge for monthly savings as this impairs the rate at which your funds grow. The fee is disproportionately large compared with the amount saved. A collection fee of £2 per month is 4 per cent if you save £50, but 8 per cent if you save £25 a month. However, monthly additions balance this out as you avoid the risk of investing a lump sum at a market high when prices are expensive. With a monthly plan, some units are bought at lower prices, reducing the average cost of the growing funds. Over a long period, these gains offset the monthly collection fee.

Tracker funds, however, are far from perfect investments. Because they slavishly follow the market, they will rarely outperform it. If the market falls substantially – perhaps by 20 per cent – the tracker will follow it. This could be doubly serious if the market suffered a prolonged downturn, as occurred in Japan from 1990 to 1998, where private investors lost a lot of their savings. Finally, there is a serious risk of market distortion now that institutional investors increasingly track the index. With their buying activity focused on the major stocks, they increasingly ignore smaller companies. Forcing up prices of shares in FTSE 100 companies created a damaging self-feeding spiral during 1998 and early 1999. This process could dramatically unwind, producing significant falls in these major stocks if the market entered a severe downturn.

---

**ADVANTAGES OF SAVING WITH A TRACKER FUND**

1. As the market spends more time rising than falling, you enjoy every rise.
2. The long-term market trend is up, and so your funds should grow over a 10-year period.
3. Knowing that the tracker will match the market reduces investment uncertainty.
4. You know the tracker will fall with the market, but will rarely fall further.
5. In a severe downturn, most actively managed funds fall further than the market.
6. You avoid the problem of choosing an active fund that underperforms the market.
7. Investing in trackers is cheaper than in actively managed funds as trackers do not have large budgets to cover company research and analysis.
8. If you invest with a monthly plan, you need not time buying your units.
9. Saving with a monthly plan averages down the cost of the units you buy.

**DISADVANTAGES OF SAVING WITH A TRACKER FUND**

1. Tracker funds slavishly follow the market, and therefore rarely outperform it.
2. When the market falls 20 per cent, so does the tracker.
3. In a prolonged market downturn, investors would lose a lot of their savings.
4. Institutional investors increasingly track the index and distort the weightings of companies both inside and outside the indices. This buying spiral could dramatically unwind, causing large drops in major stocks if the market fell.

## Which Tracker?

All trackers aim to match the index they follow, but differing share-selection methods and charging structures create differences in their matching skills. Many trackers have fees below 1 per cent a year, but some impose extras, like initial fees or regular savings charges. Small trackers also have problems matching index performance because their dealing costs are high relative to the fund size. Cautious savers and those who buy a Top Ten Portfolio should chose a FTSE All-Share tracker for exposure to a large number of FTSE 250 companies. If you run a paper portfolio or are less nervous, choose a FTSE 100 tracker, or compromise by splitting your savings between the two. Save for several years and build a fund of units in your tracker before selling to reinvest the proceeds in your growing portfolios.

In summary, there are four rules for how to choose a tracker:

1. Choose the right index to track:
   - FTSE All-Share index – if you want maximum UK diversification;
   - FTSE 100 index – to focus on the top 100 UK companies, which is riskier because the main FTSE 100 companies are concentrated in very few sectors.
2. Avoid extra fees, initial and/or regular savings fees.
3. Pick a big tracker to avoid underperformance.
4. Choose a fund with a low tracking error.

By holding a portfolio of the top ten UK companies by market capitalisation, you have bought your own tracker fund to follow the ever-changing fortunes of companies worth almost half of the total blue-chip list. Add in your savings, growing in a professionally run tracker fund. In Level I, therefore, you begin passively, but as you advance to Level V, you move from being passive to become your own active fund manager, in charge of growing your portfolio of company shares. This progression gives you a powerful head start for building wealth, but you may wonder why you should be more successful at beating the market than the majority of professional investors. This is an important issue, to which we now turn.

## Why You Can Beat Professional Investors

I see it as a salutary lesson for private investors that Bank of England officials could not anticipate that Britain's expulsion from the European Exchange Rate Mechanism in September 1992 would reignite the economy. They are paid to steer a stable course through the unpredictable waves of economic turbulence. We should be cheered to know that even smart, well-informed professionals occasionally lose control of events and cannot produce the results they want. Reading is the key to becoming smart and well-informed. We can then be managing our funds successfully.

Professional investors dominate market activity, but although they are the majority, evidence shows they rarely outsmart the markets. It is a known fact that most investors are consistently wrong. If this were not so, the majority would make moderate gains while a small minority made losses. Statistics show there are a few consistent institutional winners but the overwhelming majority perform poorly. Private investors can take a contrary view to try and make exceptional gains. Institutional investors rarely do this as they have two conflicting goals: they want to keep their jobs and make their funds grow. To keep their jobs, it is prudent to follow the majority. They rarely make sudden decisions or act swiftly, as private investors might. There may be layers of management to consult, or a house investment philosophy to follow, which limits a manager's freedom.

*'If you buy the same securities as other people, you will have the same results as other people. It is impossible to produce a superior performance unless you do something different from the majority.'*

Sir John Templeton, Investment fund founder

As the top priorities of professional fund managers differ greatly to yours, because they must hold down a highly paid job, they avoid extreme or controversial moves and stay with the herd. Your priority is to be wealthy: to achieve it you must remain highly focused, but this attitude might cost a professional his job. Institutional investors manage huge funds, often of several hundred millions of pounds. Making large percentage gains in enormous funds is far more difficult than doubling a small amount of capital: it is easier to turn £3,000 into £6,000 than £3 million into £6 million.

Finally, and linked to the problem of making large percentage gains, a proven way to maximise gains is to concentrate on a few choice companies where impressive growth will lead to large price rises. This is precisely what small investors usually do. With limited resources, they invariably adopt this winning strategy while perhaps not fully realising it. Holding only a few companies is technically impossible for fund managers, as in an emergency, massive holdings could not easily be sold; for this reason, most avoid holding just a few large stakes. A fund worth £500 million might hold 50–100 different company shares. If it held only 12, an average holding of around £40 million would represent about 5 per cent of the market capitalisation of some medium-sized companies. This would not be an effective investment strategy. Small investors, however, can hold a dozen shares, hoping seven or eight will produce superb returns to boost the performance of their funds way beyond the benchmark averages. It is easier to find 12 super-stocks than it is to find 100. This is the main reason why active private investors can realistically hope to both outsmart the market and 90 per cent of the professionals.

In summary, private investors enjoy several advantages:

- By the laws of averages, the majority of investors are consistently wrong. This is confirmed statistically, as the majority consists of institutional investors of whom about 90 per cent are poor performers. Active private investors are a minority and can reap high returns.
- Private investors can act in a contrary way, hoping to make exceptional gains. Institutional investors rarely do this because it is more prudent to follow the majority view.
- Private investors can move more rapidly on investment decisions than professionals and have more freedom of action.
- The top priority of private investors is to build capital and increase their income; professionals worry about retaining their highly paid jobs.
- Private investors manage small funds, where it is easier to make large percentage gains. This is far more difficult for professional investors to achieve as they manage huge funds.
- With limited cash resources, private investors must focus on a few companies only. This is a proven method of achieving superior returns and is more difficult for professional investors as they manage much larger funds and hold many dozens of different company shares at any time.

*'Time is the great teacher, but unfortunately, it kills all of its students.'*

*Hector Berlioz*

## Time to Back Britain?

A 1997 report by the Geneva-based World Economic Forum endorses the use of UK tracker unit trusts. Although it was issued before the 1998 global financial crisis erupted, adversely affecting emerging economies in South-East Asia and Russia, its message for British investors was positive. The report assessed 53 countries by their medium-term growth potential, based on such factors as government, finance, technology, management and labour force. In ranking nations according to their contribution to the forecast for total world economy growth, Britain was placed sixth.

This high ranking is excellent news, but most British adults have failed to enjoy the benefits of living in the nation boasting the second-largest stock market in the world and vastly larger than any in Europe. While the UK market expanded during the 1990s, the Tokyo market contracted, lifting Britain to second place. However, in 1999, when the European single currency (the euro) was launched, a merger of the German and UK stock markets was proposed, which could promote European markets. A thriving stock market brings wealth-creating possibilities for firms that tap it for funds to expand when good opportunities arise. Millions more of us should exploit this domestic source of wealth creation. Many large UK companies trade globally, operating in profitable markets around the world. Evidence shows that many of Britain's biggest companies outperformed European rivals, are consistently more profitable than their French or German counterparts, and have a better survival track record.

With so many benefits from holding shares, why isn't share ownership more widespread? While nearly half of all Americans own shares or collective funds, evidence shows that over 60 per cent of adults in Britain ignore equities for a variety of reasons. People misjudge risk, confusing short-term price volatility with the proven long-term potential. Equities are seen as an unreliable home for money that may be needed in a hurry, perhaps if incomes fall during recession when people may want to cash in some savings. Few people know they do not need a large starting capital to begin investing: a modest £25 a month will open a monthly unit trust account. Even fewer people know that passively tracking the market has produced excellent long-term results. When millions avoid investing in equities, they create rich rewards for those who do invest.

*'Money will come when you are doing the right things.'*

*Mike Phillips*

## ESSENTIAL STARTING TOOLS

Reading is a top priority to launch your planned programme, but stay with the basic essentials because financial information is expensive to buy. If you have too much data, the detail becomes overwhelming; indeed, reading it then becomes a chore. To plan your way to wealth, start with the financial press, but be selective. If the budget is tight, use your local library as it will take copies of all the daily broadsheet newspapers plus weekly investment journals. The *Financial Times* is a must; buy your own Saturday edition, as it contains good summaries of the previous week's news and events, but read the daily paper once or twice a week in the library if you are watching your expenses. You can there read the daily *Financial Times* plus the business sections of *The Times* or the *Daily Telegraph* without cost. To check on back copies, the Newspaper Library at Colindale, North London, is indispensable.

Begin with the Companies and Markets section of the *Financial Times*. It includes important news items on companies you are watching, with details and comments on half yearly (interim) and full-year (**annual**) **results** plus details on the amount and payment date of the next dividend. In weekday editions, the back four pages of the business section are a goldmine of information. Almost every quoted company, with yesterday's closing price and share volumes traded, is listed. The back page has a London Market Report, highlighting yesterday's key news items, where you can follow what analysts and brokers are saying about companies in your portfolio. Are they optimistic about prospects, or pessimistic? The report may quote a broker's target price forecast for a particular share. Also recorded here are the previous day's movements of the top 100 companies, with volumes of shares traded.

Periodically, the *Financial Times* changes the layout of pages providing financial data, but one of these back pages provides technical information on market activity. There are lists to record the numbers of shares that were rising, falling or the same at the previous day's stock market close. There are notable trends in such figures; when there are regularly more risers than fallers, it signifies a rising trend, or **bull market**. Another set of technical figures appears on this page as a list recording the number of share prices that the previous day made new highs and new lows over the past 52-week period. When these figures are heavily weighted on new highs, it may imply an approaching market peak. The London Market Report also includes a summary of yesterday's activity across the whole market, so you know how the market responded to expected or unexpected news items, international events, or big moves in foreign markets (perhaps Wall Street or Japan). All these details provide valuable clues about the main thrust of the previous day's market activity and the progression of long-running trends.

The back page of the *Financial Times* Companies and Markets Section shows a short-term FTSE 100 chart. There is a four-year FTSE 100 and Dow Jones Industrial Averages Index chart on an inside page of Saturday's Money Section. For a longer sequence, use a software chart package or consult *Investors Chronicle*. This latter carries vital weekly information across the whole global investment scene, with major sections and articles on the UK and details on every company result over the past week. *Investors Chronicle* is costly on subscription, but it is carried in all major libraries. A monthly magazine that earns its keep at a modest price (£30 a year in 1999) is *Money Observer*. It includes important articles each month on different aspects of saving and investing. Each edition lists the monthly, 6-monthly and yearly performance of every share, unit trust and investment trust.

There is a weekly listing of the top 200 companies in the Business section of *The Sunday Times* and *The Sunday Telegraph*. The ranking, market capitalisation and price for each company is given based on the previous Friday's closing price. With this you can quickly update prices and rankings of the top 10, plus the next 5 hopefuls lying just below them. The Business and Money sections of *The Sunday Times* carry major articles on key events, markets, companies and other major news items of interest. Another source of valuable information is to read each company's own annual report for those in your portfolio. Even if the accounting figures are unmanageable, there are sections of the report you will find informative. The *Financial Times* offers a free report service on most companies it lists.

PC buffs can browse the Web for additional information. The Internet brings an international electronic library on to your desk – new sites crop up daily. Use carefully chosen keywords to search for information, as specific keywords save time finding useful data. Visit me on <www.mrscohen.com> for investment and savings updates and the latest extracts from my diary. Finally, check the television coverage of business issues. The BBC runs *Business Breakfast* at 6.15 a.m. Every day, at 12.30 p.m. on weekdays there is *Working Lunch*, and BBC Radio 4 has extensive financial coverage.

Later, with improving skills, you might add other tools, but these few (summarised in the table below) comprise an essential toolkit for Level I.

**ESSENTIAL TOOLKIT FOR LEVEL I: WHAT TO READ AND WHERE TO FIND IT**

| What to read/use | Where to find it |
|---|---|
| 1. Closing daily prices for your top 10 or 15 companies | 1. On the back page of the Markets and Companies Section of the *Financial Times* |
| 2. News and company announcements on these top 10–15 | 2. The Markets and Companies Section of the *Financial Times* |
| 3. Major articles on companies investment and global economic events | 3. *Financial Times* and other newspapers (daily) <br> 4. *Investors Chronicle* (weekly) <br> 5. *Money Observer* (monthly) |
| 4. Top 10–15 company rankings | 6. *The Sunday Times* (Business section) |
| 5. Chart of the FTSE 100 and your top 10 companies | 7. In the financial press; or <br> 8. Buy a charting software package or search financial web sites, e.g. Updata |
| 6. Additional information for companies, markets and events | 9. Look on the Internet, where most financial institutions and newspapers have web sites. Visit my web site at www.mrscohen.com. I am running my own portfolio there. |
| 7. Company Annual Reports | 10. Direct from the company or with the *Financial Times* Report Service |
| 8. Television and radio coverage | 11. BBC's *Business Breakfast* and *Working Lunch*. BBC Radio 4. |

'*A lot of people criticise Formula One as an unnecessary risk. But what would life be like if we only did what's necessary?*'

*Niki Lauda, ex-Formula 1 racing driver and owner of Lauda Air*

## AVOID BUYING AT A PEAK

Some experts suggest you focus on stock-picking and ignore the market as you cannot guess what it will do. This argument implies that your investments can succeed even if you disregard events in the wider global economy. This may apply to brilliant stock-pickers but is poor advice for lesser mortals; I know from personal experience, as I did precisely this through outright ignorance when I began investing in the spring of 1990. Early in August of that year, when Saddam Hussein invaded Kuwait, global stock markets fell, nervous about low world growth and high oil prices should a Gulf War break out, which it duly did in January 1991. If I had paid attention to these global events, I would have realised that background conditions were adverse and prices would fall. By watching instead of ploughing straight into the market, I would not have promptly lost 7 per cent of my capital within six months. There are many helpful signals about timing investments if you know them. We discuss them throughout the book. Investing money is not an easy skill to master, and so private investors need all the helpful signs they can find. They are excellent to reduce the risks of being wrong.

For beginners, it is even more sensible to become familiar with the markets and try to assess the main trends. Follow the market and avoid investing a large sum as it peaks. You will not know you have inadvertently done this if, as I found in 1990, you do not understand how markets work. Sadly, you will soon discover your poor timing, because as the markets begin a rapid decline, your investment quickly shows a loss. Better to watch and decide what the markets are doing during your first 6–9 months before acting.

When the market nears a peak, statistically it is closer to a fall than a further rise. On some occasions, prices stay high for weeks, perhaps months. It is important not to get sucked into buying highly priced shares at this stage. Avoid this temptation and watch the action. By following the market's moves, you have a better idea of when it has risen strongly and for how long, and then you can make a more reasoned decision on investment timing. Wait patiently for prices to hit your 'buy price figure', as described in Level II. When markets seem to continue rising regardless of adverse background conditions, even when these look glaringly obvious, the chances of a sudden decline increase. Indeed, if an expected fall is long-delayed, when it arrives it may be steeper and faster-moving than usual.

Major advantages spring from assessing where the market is before you act. First, obviously, your money buys more units or shares when prices are low. Second, you make larger gains because *your money goes further as you bought more shares, and they were at a lower price when you bought them.* When prices rise again, you get this double benefit: the value of your holding increases as prices rise, and you are holding more shares than if you had bought them at a higher price. Third, as you own more shares, your dividends are larger because every share is entitled to the same dividend payment. Reinvesting dividends plays a big part in improving the growth of your portfolio, so any move that increases your dividends helps your funds to grow.

---

**BENEFITS FROM BUYING AT LOW PRICES**

.........................................................................

1. You buy more shares than when prices are high.
2. You therefore make larger gains when prices next rise.
3. You receive dividend payments on a larger number of shares.
4. If you choose well, you may not have long to wait before your investment is in profit.

---

*'The way to build long-term returns is through preservation of capital and home runs.'*

*George Soros, President of Quantum Funds*

## Follow the Market Cycles

Although this reasoning sounds eminently logical, evidence shows many investors ignore it. They buy as the market peaks, when newspapers and the media report on market rises. With few bargains around, this is entirely the wrong time to buy. You lose the big advantages we outlined that can be exploited when you can better judge how markets behave. At the peak, well-informed investors who follow events will be sitting on fat profits they have held, perhaps for months. They intend to sell, hoping naïve novices will eagerly buy their highly priced shares. Make sure these well-informed investors are not waiting for *you* by learning about market trends.

Of course, observers are right to say the market is unpredictable, but this does not mean it is a waste of time to follow it. On the contrary, rather than ignore the whole issue, knowing that markets are unpredictable is part of our toolkit to help us improve our investment timing. I like to compare learning about market moods with learning to live with a new partner. The problems of learning to know someone so you can live harmoniously together can be complex. How many friends or relatives do you have who have bad relations with brothers or sisters? This seems to happen more often to pairs of brothers or sisters; but in a marriage partnership, learning the other's moods can be equally fraught. There are occasions when you have no idea how your partner will react to an important event that affects your relationship. Conflicting attitudes to money or outside friendships are classic examples. But if you try to understand this behaviour, the longer the relationship lasts the more chance there is that you can anticipate unexpected reactions until, eventually, they cease to be so unexpected.

*'Friendships most often come under strain when money is involved.'*

This also happens with the market. Study its tantrums and surges and gradually you begin to follow the moods. It looks highly temperamental, but most investors, as a group, try to make sensible decisions. They have two principal aims: to grow rich and to avoid serious losses. This is exactly what you hope to do; all the manic behaviour revolves around these goals. Herd behaviour is powerful; investors are reassured by staying in the mainstream. Understand this insight and benefit financially from your knowledge by acting ahead of the crowd. Watch the market action and avoid the hugely expensive folly of buying near a peak. With routine watching, you gain the maximum benefit from every major uptrend even if you cannot precisely time the start. For these sound reasons, following the market's moods by reading is, in my opinion, time well spent for investors keen to learn new skills.

Of course, shares rarely rise or fall in unison. A company with splendid growth prospects might fall less far than others when a major global or national crisis erupts. Conversely, even with brilliant investment conditions and a booming market, some companies lag the main advance due to problems that affect their profits or generate losses. In the Introduction, we saw how this worked over 10 years for 10 UK companies: while the FTSE 100 index rose strongly and some companies made good progress, Marks & Spencer and BTR lagged the market between 1988 and 1998. By contrast, with its globally selling blockbuster drug, Glaxo Wellcome's share price rose by 901%.

## Collective Market Action

The market is a **leading indicator** because it responds rapidly to changes in the underlying economy. But the market consists of millions of investors: professional fund managers, company finance directors, insurance company fund managers, foreign bankers and private investors of many nationalities. Collectively, they often foretell changes in the economy. Travelling *en masse*, like a shoal of fish or a flock of birds in flight, their actions reflect the behaviour of the whole market. But you can rise above the institutional investor herd by acting ahead of the crowd, because your priority is not to keep your job as a fund manager but to plan your way to wealth.

In a recession, investors grow increasingly pessimistic that recovery will never come. Conversely, in a booming market, they become complacent or ignore underlying realities. Shares become overpriced and higher than fundamental values imply. Prices may hit a barrier at a peak, as we saw with the history of the Dow at 100 and 1000. Similarly, 2400 on the FTSE 100 became a barrier for a while in the late 1980s. Having overshot fair value, prices may pause while commercial events catch up. Market mood swings can be abrupt because, collectively, investors want to exploit good opportunities while avoiding large losses in a worsening outlook.

In Level III, we will examine the fluctuating relationships between the stock market and the real economy where we all live and work. But, here, we will look at how the market behaves as an entity composed of millions of individuals. Being a leading indicator, the market falls months before a recession arrives and rises ahead of the recovery, as investors anticipate both events, sometimes by several months. The reason is obvious when the moves are seen as mass investor reactions. They take fright about an impending recession and sell shares without waiting until the recession arrives: it might take months before adverse conditions affect the companies themselves. Many investors will have sold before the bad news announcements. Months later, major job losses are reported, profit warnings increase, factories close, fewer companies report profits rises, try to raise money in the market or engage in take-overs or mergers. News items are pessimistic on future prospects. If the recession is worse than forecast, sellers continue to sell, and prices fall further. But long before, the onset of the sentiment change will have coincided with the first falls in prices when the recession was still a distant threat. The market makes a big upsurge about once every three or four years. Over a span of 10–12 years, there may be three market corrections, when prices fall and three or four major upswings with rising prices. Investing early in a rising market can greatly enhance your portfolio's growth. So following market cycles is highly productive.

## 'You have to want what the market wants.'

Bill Williams, author of Trading Chaos

When we say 'the market', we lump together the actions of millions of people; but the FTSE 100 or All-Share indices reflect these group effects. Through the index, we monitor total investor activity by observing movements on a chart of an index. Stock market indices are benchmarks for fund manager performance because they reflect collective investor behaviour.

Volatility may rise dramatically, with wild price swings, seen especially at a market peak. Investors then are unsure about the market's future trend. Volatility also rises with unexpectedly high demands for shares that **market makers** did not foresee. When they are short of stock in a rising market, they face losses as they try to square their books. To cover their positions cheaply, they force prices higher. This can explain sudden surges that do not fit underlying fundamentals. The 8-week 26 per cent uptrend rally in October and November 1998 followed this pattern.

When the market rises strongly, optimism tempts in more buyers than sellers. Conversely, when prices fall – as seen on the falling index – the dominant activity comes from sellers and pessimism is widespread. However, most of the time, the market idles, dominated by neither buyers nor sellers. During long periods of indecisive movements, it is unclear which way the market will move until the uncertainty ends. These periods can be spotted on a chart as they produce trading ranges.

## The FTSE 100 Experience

Charts of the FTSE 100 or All-Share indices track investors' collective acts. During the 1980s and 1990s, as the market performed more strongly than the long-term average, there were longer periods of share buying than selling. When the market fell, for profit-taking or on bad news, selling outweighed buying. In periods when buyers and sellers were roughly matched, the charts of index movements have shown a narrow range. These consolidation or trading ranges can last for several months: they indicate investor indecision. It is difficult to guess which way the index will ultimately move; millions of investors, as a group, are dithering over the next direction for prices. This may all sound incredibly logical, but unless you know the way the market thinks, you cannot benefit from its many mood swings.

The chart (shown below) of the FTSE 100 shows the closing daily prices from its launch in January 1984 to 30 December 1999. It reveals 16 years of irregular market cycles. You glimpse the main market moods by checking the index level against horizontal lines across the chart, which indicate key levels. Checking the index against those lines, you can spot a trading range and see how long it lasted. The index is measured to one decimal place but we will use round figures for simplicity to work through these broad movements.

**FTSE 100 Index**

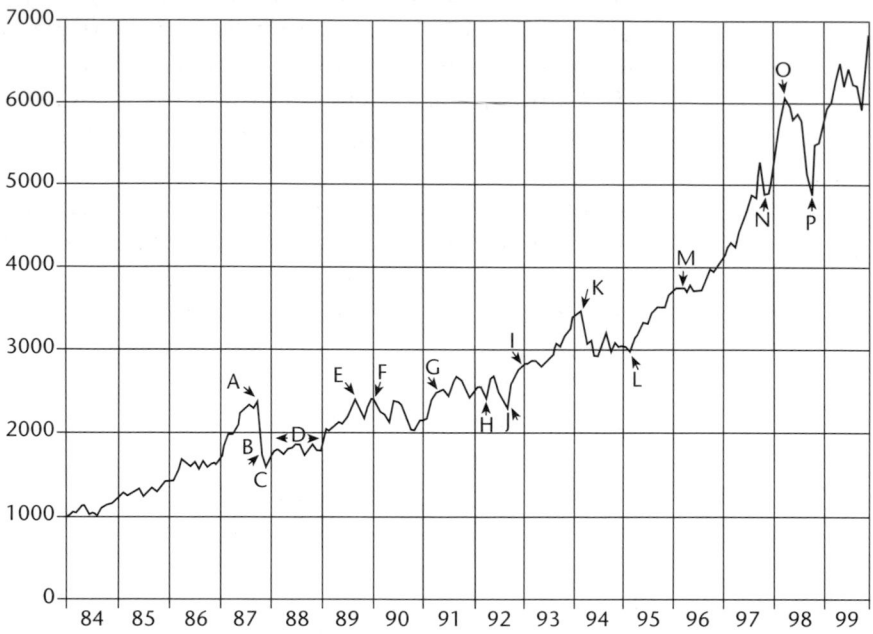

*'Am I thinking the way the market is thinking?'*

*Bill Williams*

The index rose in 1984 and 1985, but it was range-bound for several months during 1986. It rose and fell steeply in 1987 but was range-bound during 1988. As is widely known, there was a tremendous crash in 1987. Yet the FTSE 100 rose strongly and was up 785 points, or 47.6 per cent, from January to mid-July of that year (point A on the chart). In two working days in late October 1987 the index fell 500 points (from 2302 to 1802 – point B), an exceptional 22 per cent fall. The low point of the crash, a month later on 19 November, saw the FTSE 100 at a 12-month low of 1565 (point C). It ended 1987 4 per cent lower than it began. Following these huge gyrations, it is not surprising that 1988 was another undecided year, moving in a 200-point range (from 1700 to 1900 – see point D).

After a short upward leap in 1989, another range began and peaked at around 2400 (point E). The index had peaked in 1987 at around 2400 in July (A) and again in September. During 1989 and 1990, the index hit this same level three times (F) and stalled. Clearly, for many months 2400 was a barrier. Whenever the index hit 2400, sellers arrived in strength. However, in 1989 and 1990, the trading range lasted over a year and was 400 points (from 2000 to 2400), deeper than earlier ranges. This pattern recurred in 1991 and 1992, but the index finally shot above the 2400 barrier during the spring of 1991 (G) and then ranged between 2300 and 2700 until late in 1992. Once the 2400 level was breached, the market stayed above it. If there were a truly major collapse at some future date, this level of 2400 could be revisited.

More indecision occurred in 1992, with the trading range depth the largest yet, at 560 points, from a mid-summer low of 2290 (H) to a year-end close at 2850 (I). This represented a 24.5 per cent rise in just over three months. The market rose from September 1992 (J) right through 1993, to February 1994 (K), gaining 1,270 points, or 53.3 per cent over 16 months. This was investors' rapturous collective response to Britain's expulsion from Europe's Exchange Rate Mechanism.

The first decisive fall since the major 1987 crash occurred in 1994. The market fell 17.4 per cent, or 610 points, in five months. Yet more indecision followed in 1995, with a narrow trading range of only 200 points (3000 to 3200). However, March 1995 (point L) saw a dramatic change: the index climbed 12.3 per cent over 13 months from then until March 1996 (M). The next trading range, from March to July 1996, was followed by another major rise of 1,700 points (3600 to 5300), or 47 per cent in 13 months. In October 1997, the market took a sudden dive and in two months fell 550 points (N), equivalent to 10.4 per cent of its value. A strong recovery from November 1997 helped the market surge into 1998 rising by 1,429 points from January to mid-July (O) of that year. This rise was 30 per cent (from 4750 to 6179) in 7 months. From mid-July to early October of 1998, the market fell almost 25 per cent (6179 to 4649) in two and a half months (P). It then underwent one of the swiftest rallies ever, rising 1,200 points (almost 26 per cent) to 5850 in just 8 weeks. The rise continued into January 1999, and by March the FTSE 100 had shot past its earlier peak of 6179 to above 6360. In the summer of 1999 the FTSE hit 6600 before dipping back to 6200 in May and then scaling 6600 again in July. It then began a slow descent to 5950 by October before rallying up again during November. The FTSE 100 index ended 1999 at a high of 6930.

The foregoing description is summarised in the table below.

### MAIN MARKET MOVEMENTS ON THE FTSE 100 CHART, 1984 TO 1999

| Year | Action | Trading Range |
|------|--------|---------------|
| 1984 | Rising | |
| 1985 | Rising | |
| 1986 | Trading range | 1540–1700 |
| 1987 | Rise and fall | |
| 1988 | Trading range | 1700–1900 |
| 1989 | Rise and fall | |
| 1990 | Trading range | 2000–2400 |
| 1991 | Rise and fall | |
| 1992 | Trading range | 2300–2700 |
| 1993 | Trading range | 2800–2950 (February to July 1993) |
| 1994 | Fall and rise | |
| 1995 | Trading range | 2900–3200 (July 94 to March 1995) |
| 1996 | Trading range | 3600–3800 (March 1996 to July 1996) |
| 1997 | Rising | |
| 1998 | Rise, trading range, fall and rise | |
| 1999 | Rise and fall and rise | |

*'London will continue to be a great money centre. As a wealth creator it is without equal. It is even more exciting than New York.'*

*Tim Taylor, executive director of Merrill Lynch, November 1998*

In October 1987, global stock markets suffered some of their greatest and most rapid falls since the crash of October 1929. Investors suffered a truly harrowing experience. Yet over the next ten years most markets not only recovered but also moved to higher levels – except in Japan, which had specific domestic problems. On the 16-year chart, the 1987 crash, a momentous disaster at the time, seems little more than a temporary dip on the market's long-term progress. Through the twentieth century, charts show that the long-term trend has been upwards.

In Level III we will marry the market's movements with the underlying business cycle. Between 1984 and December 1999, the market rose by 593 per cent, ignoring dividends. There were four major declines, each lasting less than 9 months. Steep falls in 1987, 1990, 1994 and 1998 were followed by recoveries and trading ranges. There were several upsurges of 30–40 per cent, and some were larger. There were several trading ranges or consolidation periods, when investors were unsure about the next direction for prices. In Level II we will discuss clues offered by technical analysis to help you follow market movements.

Yet even if investors watched a trading range unfold, not knowing what the market would do next, it is clear that investing over 16 years was highly profitable. You must look back to 1973 for the last major **bear market** when prices fell consistently for months, taking the **FT 30** index down 74 per cent from its May 1972 peak. We cannot know whether this uptrend will continue, but this is the reason why becoming an active investor enables you to take the maximum advantage of market moves, whatever happens. When you can do this effectively, you can grow wealthier, even when the market is weak.

*'It is not because things are difficult that we do not dare; it is because we do not dare that things are difficult.'*

*Seneca (c 54BC–39AD), Roman writer of rhetoric*

## Identifiable Features During a Market Cycle

Charts consistently show that markets move in irregular cycles. If the cycles were regular, timing the market would be so easy that no one could make super profits. However, in the box below are listed some of the many identifiable signals for timing investment decisions. They indicate how the market generally behaves. Throughout *The Wealthy Investor* we discuss them all. Use the checklist to locate yourself in the cycle before buying your Top Ten Portfolio. You need an updated FTSE 100 chart to see the current cycle. Refer back to the Tools section in Level I for suggested ways to find a chart. Do not buy your own Top Ten Portfolio until you are comfortable with how your paper version is running.

---

**IDENTIFIABLE FEATURES DURING A MARKET CYCLE**

1. The market moves in trends, as seen on charts of FTSE 100 and All-Share indices.
2. Up trends are often longer than down trends, which may be shorter but steeper.
3. There are intermittent bouts of indecisive trading ranges, clearly seen on charts.
4. The long-term progress of the market is up, on a 20, 30, 50, or 80-year view.
5. Since 1984 and up to November 1999, there have been 7 uptrends, 4 major falls (1987, 1990, 1994 and 1998) and 8 trading ranges.
6. A price 'barrier' can emerge and block further rises. During 1987 and 1989, the 2400 level was a barrier for the FTSE 100 index.
7. If the index moves decisively through a price barrier, it may be years, if ever, until it falls below that barrier again.

---

## START YOUR TOP TEN PAPER PORTFOLIO

At the outset, and while you are learning about the major investment concepts, it makes sense to set up your first paper portfolio so that you can begin following the fortunes of the top ten UK companies. Follow the stages outlined below.

1. On a clean sheet in your personal organiser or personal computer, record all the details of your paper portfolio.
2. Start with an opening capital of £10,000, allocating £1,000 to 'buy' a holding in the top 10 companies by market capitalisation.
3. On paper, 'buy' each of the 10 holdings with £975, allowing £25 for costs. Example: £975/786p = 124 shares in SmithKline Beecham. Add £25 costs, total cost = £1,000. (Ignore the pence here.)
4. Watch the performance of these 10 plus the next 5 companies in the list in case one or two of your chosen companies fall below tenth position.
5. Keep a separate full record of every purchase and sale made.
6. Record the dividends as they are announced, the amount to be paid, and the payment dates so you can reinvest these dividends at least once a year.
7. Add the dividend payments to any cash left over from the initial investments, to keep your cash balances up to date.
8. Once a month, calculate the portfolio's value, adding in the dividends plus cash.
9. Follow the progress of your 10 companies plus the 5 on your stock watch-list by compiling a file of newspaper and journal cuttings.
10. Monitor the portfolio's progress regularly, at least once a month.

## PREPARE TO BUY YOUR TOP TEN PORTFOLIO

After following the fortunes of your paper portfolio for 6–9 months, you should have gained the confidence to buy your own Top Ten Portfolio, when market conditions look right. Time the current market cycle by completing the checklist (see next section), and examine ancillary signs to assess where the market is. These signs include the exuberance or pessimism of analysts or brokers, plus bonus levels in the City, as these reach stunning heights when merger and acquisition activity is peaking near a market high. Check if company directors are active buyers or sellers of their own shares. A correlation exists between directors' dealings and subsequent market movements. *The Sunday Times* runs an 'Inside Watch' indicator, which shows that the stock market performs well when the directors' buy/sell ratio exceeds 2.5:1 and poorly when it falls below 1:1.

For further insights and clues, examine the top 10 companies you plan to buy. Check the offer (buy) prices against the 52-week highest and lowest prices, quoted daily in the *Financial Times*, to judge how current prices compare with recent highs and lows. Check the trend for the numbers of 52-week highs and lows across the whole market; a consistent trend of daily risers greater than daily fallers indicates an uptrend (see next table). Keep a record for a month or two, to detect the trend if any. Read the technical analysis section in the chapter on Level II before you act, as chart patterns can signal buying opportunities. Alternatively, continue with your paper portfolio until you reach Level II and have gained more experience in running it.

### RECORD OF TECHNICAL INDICATORS JANUARY/MARCH 1999

| Date | Rises | Falls | Unchanged | 52-wk high | 52-wk lows | FTSE 100 | Gain or loss |
|------|-------|-------|-----------|------------|------------|----------|--------------|
| 13 Jan | 312 | 1563* | 1108 | 36 | 82 | 5850.1 | −183.5 |
| 15 Feb | 767 | 712 | 1462 | 36 | 39 | 6023.2 | +72.5 |
| 16 Feb | 851 | 701 | 1390 | 41 | 47 | 6108.6 | +85.4 |
| 17 Feb | 522 | 949 | 1472 | 34 | 42 | 6078.4 | −30.2 |
| 18 Feb | 661 | 795 | 1488 | 31 | 39 | 6074.9 | −3.5 |
| 19 Feb | 710 | 670 | 1564 | 39 | 48 | 6031.2 | −43.7 |
| 22 Feb | 881 | 553 | 1509 | 43 | 43 | 6069.9 | +38.7 |
| 23 Feb | 1118 | 453 | 1376 | 70 | 37 | 6155.2 | +85.3 |
| 24 Feb | 890 | 596 | 1460 | 69 | 45 | 6307.6 | +152.6 |
| 25 Feb | 600 | 846 | 1500 | 57 | 37 | 6206.2 | −101.1 |
| 26 Feb | 683 | 744 | 1507 | 52 | 46 | 6175.1 | −31.4 |
| 5 Mar | 1163 | 437 | 1330 | 78 | 36 | 6205.5 | +104.1 |

*Note the massive number of falls on 13 January 1999.

Tread cautiously if market conditions seem uncertain. Buy your 10 holdings with a timed schedule over several months. To do this, list your prospective purchases with their current price on the first Monday in the month. Compare the prices a month later. Buy at least two holdings on a set date, over the next 5 months, to acquire all 10; do not buy just one or two and delay buying the others indefinitely as this could expose you to additional risks if one of the holdings suffered a sudden collapse. Buy those companies with fairly low current share prices compared with previous highs, before buying those where prices are high or in a trading range. By spreading your purchases, you gain more experience as you wait for prices to fall.

## The July 1998 Paper Portfolio

With constant changes, the top 10 you want to buy may differ from those you tracked on paper. Your Top Ten Portfolio is passive and automatically chosen, although with the reservations noted below. Have at least £15,000

**STEPS TO FOLLOW PRIOR TO BUYING YOUR PORTFOLIO**

1. Ensure you have savings worth £15,000 before you begin to buy your ten holdings.
2. Complete the checklist (page 75) to decide where the market cycle is now.
3. Read the technical analysis section in Level II as a guide on suitable buy points.
4. Examine the composition of the portfolio you are about to buy.
5. Compare the paper top ten with the current top ten companies you plan to buy.
6. Ensure your portfolio is well diversified, with at least six sectors, if possible.
7. If you are undecided on when to buy, continue with your paper portfolio while you read through Levels II and III to gain more experience with your paper portfolio.
8. Buy your holdings in groups of two or three, if market conditions seem uncertain.
9. Spread the timing of your purchases over several months if more appropriate, buying two holdings at one-monthly intervals over five months.
10. Decide on a stockbroker to make the purchases on your behalf.

capital before opening your portfolio with a minimum £10,000, leaving an emergency fund of £5,000. By investing at Level I, your capital starts growing, assuming you can time the cycle and buy your shares at reasonable prices.

**THE TOP TEN PORTFOLIO STARTED 20 JULY 1998**

| Rank | Company | Number of Shares | Price in (p) | Cost of Holding (£) on 20 July 1998 |
|------|---------|------------------|--------------|--------------------------------------|
| 1 | Glaxo Wellcome | 51 | 1884 | 986 |
| 2 | British Telecom | 118 | 820 | 993 |
| 3 | Lloyds TSB | 103 | 940 | 993 |
| 4 | BP | 113 | 862* | 999 |
| 5 | SmithKline Beecham | 124 | 786 | 1,000 |
| 7 | Shell | 232 | 420.5 | 1,000 |
| 8 | Barclays | 50 | 1949 | 1,000 |
| 9 | Diageo | 128 | 760 | 998 |
| 11 | Vodafone | 111 | 875* | 996 |
| 12 | BAT | 135 | 721 | 998 |
| 6 | HSBC[a] | – | – | – |
| 11 | Zeneca[b] | – | – | – |
| 13 | Unilever[c] | – | – | – |
| 14 | NatWest[c] | – | – | – |
| 15 | Halifax[c] | – | – | – |
| **Total Cost** | | | | **9,963** |
| Cash | | | | 37 |
| **Initial Capital** | | | | **10,000** |

(FTSE 100 at a peak: 6179)
[a] Passed over to avoid having 3 banks in the portfolio.
[b] Passed over to avoid having 3 pharmaceuticals in the portfolio.
[c] Next 3 largest as reserves.
* Prices prior to later share splits.

Market conditions for the *Investors Chronicle* portfolio illustrate the task. The FTSE 100 was in a trading range in August 1988 (see earlier table on page 68), recovering from the 1987 crash. Prices were moderate, and so this was excellent timing to buy. At the 10-year cut-off point in mid-July 1998, prices hit a peak of 6179. Good timing at both the start and end of the term boosted the gains. The paper portfolio used here (see page 72) begins at that July 1998 peak. We can compare this top ten with the original mid-1988 list, to discover the survivors ten years on. You will do this to compare your paper ten to the top ten you plan to buy.

## STEPS TO TAKE WHEN BUYING YOUR PORTFOLIO

Before buying your Top Ten Portfolio, complete a checklist to decide where you are in the current market cycle and to ensure you avoid investing at a peak. Check the companies in your intended portfolio to assess its composition and reduce your risk, as I did for the 20 July 1998 paper portfolio outlined above. Aim to hold companies in at least six sectors to reduce your risks, although this is not a priority while you follow the fortunes of the companies on paper. However, when planning your Top Ten Portfolio, pay attention to the numbers and types of sectors involved. Finally, you must choose a stockbroker before you can buy your shares (see later section).

A suitable checklist of 20 questions is shown on page 74, and do not worry if you cannot answer *all* the 20 questions. The checklist is simply a guide. The answers on your checklist may help you time buying your Top Ten Portfolio. If in doubt, continue monitoring events and repeat the checklist with new answers a few weeks later.

*'When visionaries muse on the subject of money, they imagine a perfect world that has no money in it.'*

*Kevin Jackson,* Ten Money Notes

## The Composition of Your Top Ten Portfolio

Buying a portfolio that is focused in a few sectors increases risk. Unfortunately, the FTSE 100 index became more concentrated during the 1990s. The largest British companies are in just a few sectors. As shown in the

---

**CHECKLIST ON WHERE THE MARKET STANDS AT . . . (DATE)**

1. What figure is the FTSE 100 at now?
2. How many months ago was the last high?
3. What was the highest daily closing figure this year?
4. How many points is the FTSE 100 below that high?
5. How many months ago was the last market low?
6. What was the lowest daily close this year?
7. Is the market currently in a trading range?
8. If so, how many points between the high and lows in the range?
9. How many times has the index hit the top of the range?
10. Are company directors buying or selling shares in their companies?
    (Directors have a good track record of actively buying shares in their own companies just before prices begin a sustained rise.)
11. Are most financial analysts and brokers making optimistic/pessimistic comments about the current market level?
12. Have brokers set higher/lower forecasts for the market by year end?
13. How many FTSE 100 companies are reporting higher/lower profits than forecast?
14. How many profits warnings/good trading statements are being made?
15. Are many companies announcing factory closures or job cuts?
16. Are many companies optimistic and announcing take-overs or mergers, or wanting to raise money in the market?
17. Is the financial press reporting bumper bonuses for City dealers?
    (When bonuses peak, it may indicate a stock market top, to be followed shortly by big job losses in the City.)
18. Have the numbers of new highs (for shares over the last 52 weeks) been larger than new lows each day over several weeks?
19. Have the numbers of shares showing rising prices been greater/smaller than lower prices each day over several weeks?
20. Do you know where the market is? Rising, falling or in a trading range?
    (If the answer to question 20 is, 'Don't know', it may indicate a trading range is in progress.)

---

paper portfolio discussed earlier, and analysed by sector in the table below, I bought only two of the three eligible banks. I omitted HSBC bank, ranked 6, because I did not want to hold three banks, even on paper. As HSBC has extensive trading links with Asia, which was in recession in 1998, that gave me further reason to avoid it. I took similar action in the pharmaceutical sector.

To judge the composition of your Top Ten Portfolio, compare the latest top ten companies with your paper portfolio. There are almost certain to be some differences between the two portfolios, as there are differences between the two used here. By comparing the mid-1998 paper portfolio with the original *Investors Chronicle* portfolio of 1988, we can work through the key issues you will face when buying your own portfolio. This comparison is part of the asset-allocation process covered more fully in Level III. We compare the companies in the two portfolios to see how they differ, starting with the 1988 *Investors Chronicle* portfolio.

## 'Sell your cleverness and buy bewilderment.'

*Jalal Ud-Din Rumi (1207–73), Persian mystical poet*

The 1988 portfolio contained eight sectors but by July 1998 BTR, Marks & Spencer, ICI, demerged British Gas and Hanson had lost their top ten rankings. There were no banks in the 1988 ten but by mid-1998 there were three. Banking is a highly competitive and risky business, especially during recessions; for a well-balanced portfolio, I decided against holding three companies in any one sector, either banks or pharmaceuticals. I therefore omitted Zeneca and chose BAT, ranked 12th. The composition of the July 1998 portfolio, covering 6 sectors, was as shown in the second part of the table.

### 1988/1998 PORTFOLIOS BY SECTOR

**Composition of Mid-1988 *Investors Chronicle* Portfolio:**

| | |
|---|---|
| 1 telecommunications company: | British Telecom |
| 1 retailer: | Marks & Spencer |
| 1 chemicals/pharmaceuticals company: | ICI (including Zeneca, floated off in 1993) |
| 1 pharmaceutical firm: | Glaxo (merged with Wellcome in 1995 to form Glaxo Wellcome) |
| 2 oil companies: | BP and Shell |
| 1 gas provider: | British Gas |
| 2 conglomerates: | Hanson and BTR |
| 1 tobacco company: | British American Tobacco (BAT) |

**Composition of July 1998 Top Ten (Paper) Portfolio**

| | |
|---|---|
| 2 pharmaceutical companies: | Glaxo Wellcome and SmithKline Beecham |
| 2 telecommunications companies: | British Telecom and Vodafone |
| 2 oil companies: | BP and Shell |
| 2 banks: | Lloyds TSB and Barclays |
| 1 alcoholic beverages company: | Diageo |
| 1 tobacco company: | British American Tobacco |

## The Long-Term Future of Your Top Ten Portfolio

Owning a portfolio with just six sectors is risky, and it is clearly better to spread your investment risks widely. By building up a tracker fund with your savings regime, you spread the risks. In later Levels we will check how the July 1998 portfolio is faring. Using this example, set up your own Paper Top Ten Portfolio and watch its progress while you continue reading *The Wealthy Investor*. Follow news items and results announcements for your 10 companies. Being the largest UK companies, they will feature constantly in the press. Keep a file of press cuttings relating to each company and write full notes of all the dividends that are declared, the amounts to be paid and the date when they will be paid. The table below shows how to do this.

#### DIVIDEND HISTORY FOR JULY 1998 PAPER TOP TEN PORTFOLIO

| Company | No of Shares | Amt (p) | Total (£) | Dividend paid on | Invested | Cash £37 |
|---|---|---|---|---|---|---|
| Glaxo Wellcome | 51 | 15 | 7.65 | 1.8.98 | 11.9.98 | |
| British Telecom | 118 | 11.5 | 13.57 | 1.8.98 | 11.9.98 | |
| Lloyds TSB | 103 | 6.7 | 6.90 | 1.8.98 | 11.9.98 | |
| BP Amoco | 113 | 6 | 6.78 | 1.8.98 | 11.9.98 | |
| SmithKline Beecham | 124 | 2.43 | 3.01 | 15.8.98 | 11.9.98 | |
| Barclays | 50 | 15.5 | 7.75 | 1.8.98 | 11.9.98 | |
| **Total** | | | **£46*** | | | |
| Add cash in hand | | | £37 | | | |
| **Total cash** | | | **£83 invested on 11.9.98** | | | |

*Rounded to nearest £

*'Why should I fatten up the brokers? I'm just going to buy and hold.'*

*Anne Scheiber (1894–1995), American private investor*

## What Can Go Wrong?

Launching any long-term project can create anxieties. So, right at the outset you should examine the possibilities that your plans will not work out as you hope. The whole essence of financial planning revolves around detailed preparation, which must include what precautions you will take if events turn against you. By thinking the unthinkable, that is, the chance of failure, you reduce that chance considerably. Knowing roughly what you would do if your plans go awry is part of your plan; it is a form of insurance policy.

Here are a few pointers on occurrences that may throw you off course, but your circumstances may be special. View every future eventuality carefully in the light of how it could upset your long-term plans.

## The market may collapse and not recover for years

This sorry event did occur in the early 1970s. Professional and private investors slowly sold out over a period of 30 months, until by Christmas 1974 the market had lost over 74 per cent of its May 1972 value. This proved to be the turning point. In January 1975 prices across the market leapt by around 50 per cent from that devastating low.

No one can know whether such a horrendous investment experience will recur. However, part of the process of acquiring sound investment skills is to learn how to deal with extreme events as well as the mundane repetitive ones. Knowing when to sell is a skill that can improve your investment returns. But ultra-long-term investors can ride out even these awesome declines, which is exactly what Anne Scheiber did for over 40 years. With hindsight, the winter of 1974 proved to be one of the few great buying opportunities of the century. And just as certain is the fact that very few investors were ready to participate in the 1975 rise.

## I do not have the time to devote to making a success of my investments

When you set out on a long-term project, you cannot plan the detail in sufficient depth to cover all eventualities. If you are buying a house on a mortgage, the loss of Miras tax-relief on interest payments in the March 1999 Budget transformed house purchase from a long-term investment into a financial burden to be eliminated as soon as possible. Learning how to make your investments grow could give you that vital additional fund of free capital to put your home purchase plans into a better perspective for wealth-creation during your working life.

## I already own some privatisation or demutualised bank shares

Put them away safely and proceed with the 5-Level Progression. After 2 or 3 years you will have gained enough experience to hold them long-term or sell and reinvest the proceeds.

## I lose interest in the project and find I do not want to continue

This may seem a big impediment to even setting out, but if you put sensible contingency plans in place, your confidence in a successful outcome is built on firm foundations right at the start.

If for one of these reasons or any other, you decide to discontinue the project, here is a plan on what to do. But 'Never say never' is a sound axiom for financial planning. At a future date, you may find you can pick up the threads from where you left off, so do not abandon your hopes of creating long-term wealth simply because you have problems running this project in the short term.

## How to Proceed if You Stay Passive in Level I

If you buy a Top Ten Portfolio but then decide to hold it indefinitely, remaining totally passive at Level I, aim to turn £10,000 into £50,000+ within about 10 years, depending on market conditions. Reinvest your dividends, any interest earned on idle cash plus accumulated savings once every year. Having decided to stay at Level I, try to equalise the size of your portfolio with other funds you hold, to diversify your assets.

The following example explains what to do. After two years in Level I, your portfolio is worth £15,000, your savings regime in a FTSE All-Share tracker is worth £5,000 and you have an emergency fund worth £7,500. If you now decide to hold your Top Ten Portfolio passively, rearrange your assets to achieve a balanced portfolio, not overweighted in equities. Currently, your equity-based assets are £20,000 within total funds of £27,500. It would be safer to hold half your funds in cash, perhaps in an ISA. You would therefore want cash funds worth about £14,000 with about £13,500 in equities.

How you arrive at this result depends on your attitude to risk. You could sell part of your Top Ten Portfolio, say two holdings worth £4,000 (£15,000 − £4,000 = £11,000) plus some units in your FTSE All-Share tracker, say £2,500 (£5,000 − £2,500 = £2,500). In total, your equities would then amount to £13,500 (£11,000 + £2,500 = £13,500). You then add the extra cash of £6,500 to a deposit or ISA account (£7,500 + £6,500 = £14,000). These steps are summarised in the table below.

### TOTAL FINANCIAL ASSETS (EXAMPLE)

| Action | Top Ten Portfolio (£) | Tracker Fund (£) | Cash on Deposit (£) |
|---|---|---|---|
| Initial Position | 15,000 | 5,000 | 7,500 |
| Sales Made | (4,000) | (2,500) | Nil |
| Total Sales | | | 6,500 |
| **Final Position** | **11,000** | **2,500** | **14,000** |
| **Total equities** | **£13,500** | | |
| **Total cash** | **£14,000** | | |

Having equalised your financial assets, you could stay indefinitely in Level I while you continue with your savings regime. At any later date, you could reverse the passive stance and begin to build additional capital by moving on to Level II.

*'Investors aiming at a specific retirement income should take note. You need not be a rocket scientist to realise that higher savings will probably be needed to compensate for substandard investment prospects in the years ahead.'*

David Schwartz, stock market historian

## CHOOSING A STOCKBROKER

When you move from a paper to your real Top Ten Portfolio, you need to choose a stockbroker to make the purchases for you. No stockbroker will make a fortune with you as a client, even when your assets are worth £500,000. As a long-term investor, you may only make two or three changes to your portfolio in any year.

For your first portfolio you will buy 10 sets of shares, but as each holding involves a modest £1,000, the costs for investing such small sums are disproportionately large. One of the cheapest routes is a postal purchase, from a bank or broker. Yet although the costs are low, the price you pay for your shares could be high and is out of your control. Visit the local branch of your bank or building society where you save or hold your mortgage; ask for a brochure on their stockbroking services. Because you know exactly what shares you want to buy, you do not need the expensive services of an **advisory broker**. Such brokers charge clients when advising them on companies they favour. Use an **execution-only broker**, who executes your order at cheaper rates because he will not give professional advice on what to buy or sell. Alternatively, explore the Internet, where new services are springing up every month. Search the Web to find the best deals. There is a summary of the choices you can make on page 80.

The next decision is whether to hold your own share certificates or use a **nominee account**. Shares held within a PEP or an ISA must use the manager's nominee account; there is no choice. Outside your PEP or ISA, by holding your own certificates you get dividend payments, annual and interim results and other information direct from the company. You may

---

**THE CHOICE FOR STOCKBROKERS**

1. A postal broker
2. Your local bank or building society branch
3. The Internet
4. An execution-only broker
5. An advisory broker

For names of brokers in your area, contact the Association of Private Client Investment Managers and Stockbrokers – Tel: 020–7247 7080.

---

have to tell the broker you want to hold the certificate in your own name when you buy. He may make a small charge to provide a certificate. Keep certificates safely as they are costly and time-consuming to replace: you need an indemnity statement to prove the loss. If you are planning to hold your shares for many years, direct shareholdings are beneficial. Difficulties arise with timing when you sell if you hold certificates as you must settle the deal within 5 days; ask the broker to allow you 10 days for settlement. Send the certificate plus a signed Crest transfer form together with the invoice section of the sales contract note by recorded delivery as non-delivery at the correct time incurs interest.

*'We can still make world leaders part of a long-term portfolio, via selective funds and some index tracking. Or you can gradually assemble your own, starting the easy way with the many quoted in London.'*

*Graham Seargeant,* The Times, *January 1999*

## PROGRAMME UPDATE

Whether you hold a real or paper portfolio, check your progress regularly to stay on target. The progress report below is a guide on planning a routine to monitor how you are faring. In the early stages, complete a 6-monthly report or do a yearly report as a minimum. Hold your paper portfolio for about one year and aim to reinvest all the dividends and cash, to keep it growing. If you do this routinely, you have converted your passive portfolio in to a semi-passive portfolio. After completing your first yearly report, do you feel ready to move to Level II? Aim to increase your savings, capital and net worth before you move. Feel comfortable with the progress of your Top Ten Portfolio, even if it is only on paper.

You might prefer to take a staged approach. Read through Level II to become familiar with the main ideas before moving on. Stream B and C investors should read the technical analysis section of Level II before buying their Top Ten Portfolio, and move to Level II only when they are confidently running their own Top Ten Portfolio. Stream A investors might remain with a paper portfolio while progressing through Level II and perhaps into Level III, so that they build their investment expertise while accumulating the £10,000 in cash ready to open their Top Ten Portfolio.

### Level I Progress Report

| Reading Schedule | Start Date | Finish Date |
|---|---|---|
| Read through Levels I & II<br>Re-read Level I | | |

| Net Worth Statement | Start Value (£) | Finish Value (£) |
|---|---|---|
| ASSETS<br>House<br>Pension funds<br>Insurance policies<br>Top Ten Portfolio<br>Savings regime<br>Other cash<br>Other assets<br><br>Total Assets | | |
| DEBTS<br>Mortgage<br>Bank loans<br>Credit card debts<br>Store card debts<br>Other debts<br><br>Total debts | | |
| **Net Worth in Level I** | | |

*'Fear loses its potency when the unknown suddenly becomes the familiar.'*

Philip Stephens, Financial Times

## LEVEL II – THE PASSIVE INVESTOR
## Settling In

*'As a fund manager, I depended a great deal on my emotions. That was because I was aware of the inadequacy of my knowledge. The predominant feelings I operated with were doubt, uncertainty and fear.'*

George Soros, the philanthropic financier, President of Quantum Funds

In Level II, as a passive investor, you settle in and start to pace yourself. You examine growth and value investment approaches and the roles of fundamental and technical analysis. Using FASTER GAINS, you create and run a paper portfolio for small growth companies, checking it regularly to follow the results. Watch small growth companies to find good stories. Stream A investors, with no starting capital, aim to accumulate £10,000 within 4 to 6 years, in order to run a Top Ten Portfolio. Stream B and C investors continue with the semi-passive portfolio of top 10 companies, begun in Level I. Dividends and interest earned are reinvested once a year. Look at software packages designed to follow the market and produce charts of promising companies. Aim to move to Level III when the FASTER GAINS Paper Small Company Portfolio shows consistent profits over 9–12 months.

Here is a summary of the action plan for Level II.

1. Learn about the differences between value and growth investing.
2. Learn the role of fundamental analysis for finding suitable companies to invest in.
3. Learn how technical analysis aids buy and sell decisions.
4. Learn the key concepts for profitable investing using FASTER GAINS.
5. Learn how to create and run a paper portfolio of small growth companies.
6. Learn to monitor the progress of your paper portfolio for best results while searching for small growth companies using FASTER GAINS.
7. Learn how to move from a passive to an active stance with the Top Ten Portfolio.
8. Examine software packages to follow the market and company shares.

## LONG-TERM WEALTH

Investors who remain at Level II face the same limitations as those staying long term at Level I. To build a fund of £500,000 in a passive Top Ten Portfolio may prove elusive, even over 25 years. Being totally dependent on the fortunes of your initial top 10 companies leaves the outcome in doubt. For a faster rate of progress within a reasonable period, you must learn to become an active investor.

Successful investment is an art rather than a science, but I am surprised that so many professional investors rely on just one analysis stance: value, growth, fundamental or technical, or a mixture of some or any of these. I think the debate over the best approach is misguided and detracts investors from their primary goal: to become wealthy. Unless you find these discussions useful, ignore them and focus on that objective.

I try not to slavishly follow any investment style. The advantages of 'belt and braces' is to look at every helpful issue when reaching a decision: buy, sell now or wait. I avoid drifting companies, and there may be hundreds of these. The companies to invest in are those where the business, and share price, will improve in the long term. I cannot see how this will happen unless a company is growing or has assets that another firm is willing to buy. In investment, if you are not moving forward, you risk drifting or falling back.

Promising companies will generally be either in growth or recovery situations, the latter being growth stories that develop when a company begins resolving earlier problems. They are covered in Level IV. Here, we look at the various investment styles, so you can see how to profit by adopting them. In the early stages, you may cautiously decide to follow proven routines, but in time your expertise and personal judgement will grow. You will become more adept at making investment decisions when you reach Level IV. You will then have many years of hard-earned experience to rely on. This is the essence of becoming a self-confident investor.

*'Growth is simply the calculation used to determine value.'*

*Warren Buffett, the greatest investor of the 20th Century*

## VALUE OR GROWTH?

A heated debate surrounds which route is best: buying value or growth companies. Naturally, smart investors who are searching for large gains always seek good value and avoid paying inflated prices. Yet clear differences separate the two approaches. Value investors want bargain-basement purchases that will not lose money; growth investors seek companies with a niche product or service capable of producing impressive streams of future earnings, and the price paid is not the key issue – they may pay more than the current 'fair value'. Calculating fair value is discussed below.

This summary is grossly oversimplified and ignores the details, but on many occasions value turns out to be a poor bargain and growth disappoints. A great divide separates good value and cheap price. Value may be there but remain hidden or unrecognised by the market. The company may be cheap because it faces intractable problems and then goes bankrupt. Some companies are good value but do not have an outstanding stream of future earnings, while some growth companies never fulfil their early promise: they hit serious setbacks and investors lose money.

The most famous value exponents were Benjamin Graham and his brilliant disciple, Warren Buffett. Graham recommended that novice investors buy undervalued blue-chip companies (similar to some in the FTSE 100 index) and hold them long term. For active investors, he had several key criteria for running an aggressive portfolio, with higher profit potentials. His criteria were very restrictive, in order to create a safety margin and strictly limit the risk of losing money through the selection process. Buffett accepted the strength of Graham's system but developed his own special brand of value investing while strongly maintaining that no gulf separates the two categories of value and growth.

For small investors with limited resources, value investing faces the problem that the market may take years to discover value in a company you bought. This will not matter once you reach your wealth targets but might delay that time for years. Again, some value shares are cheap in terms of assets or earnings and pay high dividends, yet may never be recognised by the market and languish indefinitely. This possibility became a stark reality during the 1990s market boom, when professional investors pursued growth and ignored value shares. Fund management groups, such as M&G and Philips & Drew, that favoured value underperformed the market for several years while growth investors prospered. In 1998, growth stocks outperformed value stocks by 22 per cent.

If you checked your investor type in Level I, you might know you prefer the value route and may be uncomfortable pursuing growth. As you gain more confidence to act, adjust your investment style and portfolio content to accommodate your personal attitude. Both routes can be profitable if you follow a winning system.

Growth investors focus on future prospects. Peter Lynch was the fabled fund manager from 1977 to 1990 of America's largest mutual fund, Magellan, run by the Fidelity Management Group – this was its greatest growth period. He searched tirelessly for 'ten-baggers'. Readers will see this as his hunt for money doubling. Ten-baggers increase your wealth tenfold while you hold them. Glaxo Wellcome, the only ten-bagger in the *Investors Chronicle* portfolio, turned £1,000 into £10,100 in ten years. Yet long-term investors in companies like Vodafone, Tesco or Lloyds TSB saw similar dazzling returns. The ten-bagger hunt, at the heart of growth investing, fits comfortably with my approach yet Peter Lynch was a value investor. Huge profits are possible by diligently searching for sound growth companies. For an added bonus, buy them at bargain-basement prices, when the market is weak. Such growth gems are scarce but the hunt is eminently worthwhile, justifying the time and effort spent. I believe the future lies firmly with growth companies, a point discussed in Level III.

*'I wouldn't do it if I didn't think we'd survive. That's what we're preparing for in training – we think of the worst-case scenarios and work out what we'd do, so that with luck we'll never have to face anything we haven't prepared for to some extent.'*

Richard Branson, on his round-the-world balloon challenge, December 1998

## Dividends and Growth

Many routes lead to growth; through new products, new markets, new managers, or simply by being a young, expanding company. Actively growing firms reinvest their profits (as **retained earnings**) to finance growth rather than pay cash out as dividends. Investors accept small dividends if they expect high earnings in future years and will pay a full price to own shares in strongly growing companies. Some investors willingly overpay: strong buying at market peaks confirms that. Growth companies command high prices precisely because investors anticipate big future returns. Great growth stories are rare, so when they emerge they quickly become investor favourites.

Many companies have steady rather than outstanding potentials. They may be in mature industries, like privatised utility companies, or lack new or high-value products. They may face problems or weak markets, be vulnerable to recession or a high sterling exchange rate. Companies with modest steady earnings do not command high prices. Therefore, the **yield** or return obtained from their dividends, will be higher, as the yield is the ratio of the annual dividend paid on a share divided by its current market price, expressed as a percentage (see below). Some investors want regular, high dividends, to supplement income. A low purchase price automatically ensures a higher dividend from the way the yield is calculated, although you can calculate the yield on either net or gross dividends.

$$\text{Yield} = \frac{\text{Net annual dividend paid} \times 100}{\text{Current market price of share}} \ \%$$

There are good reasons for buying value companies at lowly prices. If they are sound but temporarily out of fashion, they attract value investors, keen on the large dividend. Reinvesting large dividends improves returns. There is always the possibility that an unfashionable company will suddenly return to favour because the market **re-rates** its prospects and the price rises smartly over several months as new investors buy. Several reasons encourage a re-rating: the sector a company operates in may return to favour; the company may become a bid prospect; it may solve earlier problems; sterling may fall; or the company may begin to make larger-than-expected profits. When a major re-rating happens to a company in your portfolio, your funds enjoy a double boost: you obtain the growth in your capital plus the high dividend income.

When you choose a growth share, you ignore the current dividend, hoping to achieve long-term capital growth. The small dividend is irrelevant, although dividends in growth companies increase long term, raising your income and giving you handsome capital gains. How this works in practice is discussed below, but now we will look at the core qualities that constitute a growth company.

## THE GROWTH SHARE PROFILE

Ideally, investors want exciting companies whose fortunes start growing soon after they have bought their shares. Picking winners means finding companies with such attractive prospects, other investors decide to buy shortly after you. Future growth depends on the assets a company owns and its ability to create earnings on them for years to come. Such assets vary for each company so we will look at some examples. On privatisation, Railtrack had a large portfolio of undervalued property. Subsequently, investors recognised this future stream of earnings. The share price rose to reflect its value in excess of routine track revenue earnings. Information technology companies have human assets with great intellectual value (their highly trained staff), but they may manufacture niche products as software packages that promise future earnings for years ahead. Microsoft's operating software, with its phenomenal monopoly position, typifies the strength of such valuable assets. Yet so far Microsoft has not paid investors a dividend. In the UK when the market awoke to the value of ongoing service contract revenues for Sage Group, it re-rated the shares to reflect this secure income stream, even though Sage has large debts.

*'If the business does well, the stock will eventually follow.'*

*Warren Buffett*

Most successful growth companies have special, valuable assets that ensure future success. The hallmark of a growth share is its ownership of lucrative revenue-creating assets that are a driving force for decades of expansion. When you invest in such a company, you hope it will continue to earn strong revenues on its unique income-producing assets so as to eventually create a ten-bagger.

Since investors factor future growth into their forecasts, setbacks have a highly damaging impact on the company's share price. Rapid falls reflect abrupt disappointment, with the interruption of the much-heralded profits story. The regularity with which small growth companies fall from favour is an important reason for small investors to stop being stock-pickers and plan to be wealthy long-term investors. When you find a group of companies that you are happy to hold for years, you have reached Utopia for private investors. Unless you appreciate how precious this wonderful state truly is, you may sell some of the potential ten-baggers you were clever enough to spot.

Two of the small companies used as FASTER GAINS examples in *The Armchair Investor*, Medeva and Telspec, classically illustrate the difficulty of finding small companies that do not quickly disappoint. Their fall from grace emphasises the role of active monitoring, one of eleven factors in the FASTER GAINS formula. Medeva, a small pharmaceuticals company, suffered a run of bad news in 1997 and 1998 as competition hit its main market for methylphenidate, a drug for the central nervous system, and safety fears hit Ionamin, its weight-loss drug. From an all-time high of 329p in March 1997, the shares had fallen to 100p by December 1998. I made good profits and sold in 1995, before disaster struck. Telspec, a fledgling telecommunications group, was a sorry tale of a growth company with a huge order book but beset by problems. I sold my shares at 770p after the price fell from 1050p. Telspec had disruptive management changes and delayed orders. By December 1998 the price had shrunk to 32p, when the shares suddenly sprang to life as investors – besotted by stocks with Internet connections – recognised the Internet gadget Telspec makes to enable a telephone line to be used for Internet access and voice simultaneously. Aggressive buying shot the price up to 133p within eight weeks.

*'The market, like the Lord, helps those who help themselves.'*

*Warren Buffett*

## Future Earnings

There are many ways to value a company's potential prospects, but small investors should avoid being bogged down in accounting detail unless they find that helpful. For investors more intent on being wealthy than financial gurus, examining a company's broad-based possibilities should be sufficient to estimate future promise. Future earnings make a big contribution to share price behaviour, and so this needs close attention. Although some suggest it is an overused indicator, estimated earnings help investors compare values for different companies, as described later.

If investors greatly bid up a price, as happened to many high-technology companies (such as Sage Group during 1998 and again in 1999), that price is then high relative to forecast future earnings growth. This may not matter for companies that consistently produce 20 or 30 per-cent annual earnings increases; but if there are unexpected problems, the share price might plunge. If success continues, eventually the expected earnings emerge and the high share price falls relative to the company's expanding value. In time, young, aggressively growing companies mature and experience more difficulty in making a big impression on the share price by expanding earnings than when the company was fairly small. Earnings growth may slow to pedestrian levels unless new products are found to replace successful maturing ones. So there are several ways for growth shares to lose momentum: they may meet setbacks, mismanage growth, make acquisitions that cannot be properly integrated with current operations, saturate their markets, lose a major client on whose orders they are overdependent or fail to develop new replacements for maturing products.

Pharmaceutical firms perennially face this last problem, as drugs periodically go off patent. Analysts thought the proposed merger of Sweden's Astra and Britain's Zeneca, announced in December 1998, was a major cost-cutting exercise to wring more profits from a smaller cost base, driven by the future loss of key patents. The percentage of 1999 expected sales at risk from patent expiries was 58 per cent for Astra, 33 per cent for both SmithKline Beecham and US Merck, 31 per cent for Zeneca and 7 per cent for Glaxo Wellcome.

*'Our preferred stocks are drawn from a pool of companies benefiting from earnings clarity, strong balance sheets and robust cash flows.'*

*Jeremy Batstone, head of research at NatWest Stockbrokers*

## Valuing a Company's Future Earnings

To assess a growth company, you value its future earnings by examining its current and prospective share price in relation to its forecast future earnings. The share price related to annual earnings per share is the **price/earnings ratio (PER)**. It shows how many years (in earnings for that share) are required to recoup your initial investment. The price/earnings ratio on any share is calculated with the following formula:

$$PER = \frac{\text{Current price of share}}{\text{Annual earnings per share}}$$

For example, suppose the share you buy at 200p has a PER of 10: this means it will make 20p earnings this year (200p ÷ 10 = 20p) and you must wait 10 years to recoup the cost of buying it. The earnings per share figure is routinely watched as it gives clues about a company's future. The forward estimated earnings is central here, so the same price/earnings ratio calculation might be made three times: once for the current year, then to see how much earnings the current share price will buy next year compared with this, and again for the situation in two years hence.

To see this working in practice, we will calculate the price/earnings ratio for SuperStock, an imaginary company with terrific growth prospects that the market has overlooked. We will check the PER for this year (2000), next year (2001), and for two years hence (2002), based on a current share price of 800p (in 2000) and two years of forecast earnings per share. We would look in *Investors Chronicle* or *Company REFs* to find detailed information on earnings per share for any company we wanted to investigate further. REFs is a compendium of essential financial information on every company listed on both the main London Stock Exchange and the Alternative Investment Market (AIM). The hard copy version is available on quarterly or monthly subscription and there is a website (see page 242).

In our example:

> Present share price for SuperStock = 800p
> Actual annual earnings per share (2000) = 50p
> Estimated annual earnings per share (2001) = 100p
> (Note: the forecast rise in annual earnings is 100%)
> Estimated annual earnings per share (2002) = 150p

So we have:

> PER for 2000 (current year, i.e. 'historic PER') = 800p ÷ 50p = 16
> PER for 2001 (next year, i.e. 'prospective PER') = 800p ÷ 100p = 8
> PER for 2002 (two years ahead) = 800p ÷ 150p = 5.3

If the earnings double (grow by 100 per cent), the PER will fall by 50 per cent (from 16 to 8). If you buy at 800p and this forecast rate of growth occurred, by mid-2001 the market would be anticipating rising earnings for 2002, perhaps to 150p. A new PER calculation would make your purchase at 800p look very cheap, as it would now only take 5.3 years of earnings to recover your 800p investment. The prospective PER for 2002 reflects this valuation. This is almost one-third of its year-2000 PER of 16. If the price/earnings ratio stays at 16, anticipating the continuing high rate of growth, the share price should rise to 2400p (2002 earnings of 150p × 16 = 2400p). If this happens, your 800p will grow to 2400p and you will have a three-bagger share. Investors who did not spot SuperStock when you did will bid up the share price in 2001 and 2002 to provide your extra gains.

## Calculate Future Target Prices

Will the market view SuperStock's earnings growth like this? During a bull market, many investors become over-optimistic. They could bid the share price way above a 16-year earnings multiple. Perhaps they do not calculate the future earnings potential as described here. A forward price/earnings ratio of 20 is moderately low for growth shares in bull markets, but that rating would lift the price to 3000p (150p × 20 = 3000p). At the peak of the market, some investors might willingly pay 35 or 45 years' earnings to own shares in SuperStock.

Achieving your targets is harder if you buy highly rated companies. However, when you hold shares for the long term and they reach high multiples, you might prefer to coast along until the euphoria subsides. You may then decide to add to your holdings.

For SuperStock, we now have three prices: the current view, a target for 2001 and a target share price for 2002. Multiply the prospective 2001 earnings per share of 100p by the 16 years it will take the share price to recoup the 100p and you arrive at the first forecast target price of 1600p (100p × 16 = 1600p). If the share price rose from 800p to 1600p, you would have a money-doubling gain. For 2002, as we saw, the target price at a price/earnings ratio of 16 is 2400p (150p × 16 = 2400p), three times your outlay of 800p per share. To see this rate of return, either the market view of SuperStock will remain euphoric or the company will deliver this fabulous earnings stream over the next two years.

*'Life is short and so is money.'*

*Bertolt Brecht,* The Threepenny Opera

## Calculate Your 'Target Buy Prices'

The foregoing calculations explain why growth companies of any size with one or more successful products are so highly rated. Many investors willingly chase prices higher than caution suggests, especially during strongly rising markets. You will need great discipline to resist this temptation. Overpaying reduces the potential rewards. Calculate a future earnings stream relative to the current share price to judge the value of those earnings. You can grow your portfolio impressively by recognising the growth gems before the crowd.

How does this apply to our example of SuperStock? On the year-2000 estimates at a price of 800p, our investment might treble in about two to three years if the price reaches 2400p while we hold the shares. But suppose the price rises while SuperStock is in the *paper* portfolio or, having spotted it, we leave it on our 'watch' list? At 900p, the profit potential may still be around 167 per cent if the price reaches 2400p. But by delaying until the price is 1600p, we lose 50 per cent of our targeted gain. This may not be a total disaster if you hold a small growth share over many years and it rewards your confidence by rising steadily. However, it is better to have a large safety margin when you set your target buy prices and capture as much of that future growth as possible.

By year-end 1998, there were real examples to consider: Vodafone (before merging with AirTouch and making a 4 for 1 share split), at 974p. It had estimated 1999 earnings of 17.5p and was rated at a prospective (future) price/earnings ratio of 55.6. Logica, at 523p with 1999 earnings forecast at 12p, was trading on a prospective price/earnings ratio of 43.5. Sage, at 1570p with forecast 1999 earnings of 34p, was on a forward price/earnings ratio of 46. Shares with high multiples are anticipating a huge amount of future growth. Yet the purpose of owning such shares is to enjoy a large price re-rating as the hoped-for earnings finally come through. To benefit from owning Vodafone, Logica or Sage, you should have been considering their price/earnings prospects in 1995 and 1996, not in December 1998. Alternatively, wait for a market setback and buy your shares when or if they fall to lower target prices.

**CHECKLIST FOR FINDING SOUND GROWTH COMPANIES**

1. Is the PER high or low for this company, and how does it stand relative to others in its industry?
2. What is the percentage of institutional investors? The lower the better, as you want to buy your holding before they do.
3. Are directors buying the shares, or is the company buying back its own shares? This increases earnings per share; both are positive signs.
4. Check the earnings record over five years. Is it consistent or variable? Were there any negative years?
5. Check whether expansion is speeding up or slowing down.
6. Is the balance sheet strong?
7. Check the debt/equity ratio. How does the company rate for financial strength?
8. Check whether the company relies heavily on only one product. This is a negative factor if problems with that product arise.
9. Check whether the company can duplicate its success in more than one town or country to prove that expansion works.
10. Check whether the company still has sound growth potentials.

# ROUTES TO EARNINGS GROWTH

Successfully managing growth is one of the hardest tasks that small companies face. Their investors are exposed to extra risk. Forecasts of future earnings are precisely that: predictions, and hence unreliable. Yet earnings can grow – or fail to grow – in a variety of ways (see table below). New products can be created, a company can expand into new markets, sell more in existing markets, use more advertising, lower prices to sell more, or raise its prices. Few companies grow earnings each year by 20 per cent or more. This eliminates most of the quoted companies listed, greatly reducing the research effort.

**PROSPECTS FOR FUTURE EARNINGS**

| Ways to Increase Earnings | Causes for Lower Earnings |
|---|---|
| 1. Introduce a new product | 1. Failure of a product |
| 2. Expand into new markets | 2. Falling sales in recession |
| 3. Reduction in costs | 3. Increasing costs |
| 4. Increase prices | 4. Inability to raise prices |
| 5. Sell more in existing markets | 5. Sell less in existing markets |
| 6. Increase advertising | 6. Fail to handle expansion |
| 7. New management revitalises poorly performing assets | 7. Poor management decisions |
| 8. Niche products or markets | 8. Loss of orders or markets |
| 9. Monopoly products | 9. Very high levels of debt |

*'An investor cannot earn superior profits from stocks simply by committing to a specific category or style. He can earn them only by carefully evaluating facts and continuously exercising discipline.'*

Warren Buffett

## Fundamentalists . . .

Purists of one style or the other might hold rigid views and exclude the opposite camp. Yet on the central issue both groups agree: by studying a range of indicators (fundamental facts or technical signals) you find companies worth investing in because they show promising prospects.

Fundamentalists limit their analysis exclusively to data relating to a company's trading performance. They compare it across similar firms, first in just one sector of the market and then to all other companies, by examining a host of figures and ratios. These include such items as sales revenue, current earnings, profit margins, net assets, cash flow, shareholder funds, dividend yields, whether dividends are covered by earnings, debt and how **solvent** the company is, and whether it has enough earnings to cover the interest on its debt. This information is constantly being updated, and so analysts must continuously revise their forecasts. Twice yearly, the company announces results: interim and final. It reports to shareholders on current trading conditions at its **annual general meeting**. Occasionally it may announce exceptional news – perhaps a proposed merger or takeover, new large contracts, or a profits warning. By analysing all of this new information, fundamentalists make buy or sell decisions and may set target prices.

*'The idea that stock-jobbers have secret sources of information and . . . mark the prices of their wares up and down accordingly is, of course, moonshine. They take the same interest in public affairs as the rest of us, no more, no less, and have the same sources of information, which is usually the press.'*

Lawrence Jones, a merchant banker in 1914

## . . . Versus Technical Analysts

Fundamentalists sometimes decry technical analysis but in *The Edge of Chaos*, I explored the idea that financial markets are governed by the rules of **deterministic chaos**, the science of order within disorder in the physical universe. I think financial markets are classic examples of chaos behaviour in this strict scientific sense. At present, most of the evidence is anecdotal; we lack mathematical equations to tie financial market behaviour into the theory of chaos in natural systems.

From this research, I find technical analysis extremely helpful for detecting buy and sell signals, both for companies and the general market, using chart analysis of benchmark indices, such as the FTSE 100 or the FTSE All-Share index. I extensively covered chart and other technical signals in *The Armchair Investor* and *The Edge of Chaos*. Here, I include only a broad summary, but some suitable books are listed in the bibliography.

Essentially, the great divide between fundamentalists and technical analysts is in the way they gather information. Technical analysts ignore all the quantitative detail on a company. They view all trading activity in its shares as evidence of how investors collectively assess the potentials. Investors bidding up the share price register a vote of confidence. When they sell or ignore it, they register fears on future company problems. The Top Ten Portfolio, consisting of the most highly valued companies in the UK at the date it is set up, indicates how professional investors rate these companies. This is clearly not the most important issue for assessing future prospects; other factors possibly more relevant to success include the volume of sales revenues, profit margins, new products or services, global reach, and competitors. By learning to be an active investor, you can find truly great growth companies, rather than follow companies that institutions favour. None the less, a passive Top Ten Portfolio is an excellent place for inexperienced investors to begin. By definition, they buy shares in 10 of the companies that have the greatest support from professionals.

*'Market capitalisation is an effective measurement as it shows the value of a company as dictated by shareholders alone, and, because the top 100 firms remain highly liquid, shifts in investor sentiment can be detected in a company's value.'*

*Mark King, Money Observer, December 1998*

Technical analysts look at the impact of collective investor behaviour across the whole market, through price changes of the benchmark indices or total volume activity. They look at the level of support for one company by examining its price and the volume of shares traded, plus other technical indicators. This evidence assumes individual investors made buy, sell or hold decisions using fundamental factors. Hence, the major clues that technically minded investors use to find promising opportunities are found from studying what investors collectively are doing or have done, disregarding all fundamental details.

By far the most important technical tool is the share price chart, showing how the price of the particular stock has changed over various periods, from a few days or weeks to several years. Charts can refer to key indices, for judging the whole market's behaviour or an individual company's performance. Many other technical details are used to improve the depth of the analysis. The large range includes the following:

- Various patterns that prices make, 10 of which are detailed below, under List of Useful Chart Patterns.
- The behaviour of moving averages of the price, defined and explained below.
- Daily volumes of shares traded, for the total market or any one company, including days of exceptionally heavy volume. This may be linked to:
  ◇ a rising price (more buying);
  ◇ a falling price (more selling); or
  ◇ very little price change (implying collective investor indecision).
- Evidence for new highs and lows in the share price or an index.
- How the momentum of trading develops – is the price forming a trend?
- Evidence for more rising prices or falling prices across the market each day.

Fundamentalists insist that market movements are random, with no repeatable patterns; they think patterns exist only in the minds of observers. However, I have always found useful evidence for patterns in the charts and will illustrate some here so you can utilise this information when applying FASTER GAINS. The patterns are never exact repeats, but are often close enough for the discerning analyst to recognise when they reappear.

Evidence for patterns suggest order or structure in the market, which does not fit the idea of randomness. I think randomness is a red herring. It detracts investors from using the excellent technical tools available to their financial advantage. Critics who say different investors see different patterns are right, but this is irrelevant. Investment is not an exact science and false signals arise. This should not concern investors who use FASTER GAINS because technical clues are not an isolated tool. *Fundamentals come first*. You should never buy unless the fundamental facts support the purchase. Technical clues offer confirmation and can help you find an attractive buying price even if each investor interprets the patterns uniquely.

Chart patterns are **fractals**, and typical of chaos. A fractal in the stock market is a geometric depiction of a price time series or an index time series, mapped on to paper and displayed as a chart. The **time series** is a sequence of closing prices: daily, weekly or even monthly. Many important technical clues are detectable on a price chart. When you know what to look for, the charts reveal phases of chaos (disorder), structure (order) and ambiguity (investor indecision) in the market. The charts depict the continuous struggle between buyers and sellers. There is plenty of short-term pattern-less movement, but by choosing a suitable time span, patterns emerge and can guide your investment decisions. I use a scale of 4–5 years for the long-term view. The list of chart patterns briefly explains what they depict. The examples of structure gives guidance on appropriate actions when you spot an emerging pattern.

*'To make money in the market, recognise the order and invest when it appears'.*

## List of Useful Chart Patterns

Here are 10 useful chart patterns to look out for and use in your analysis of a company's performance.

1. *Base-building phase*. The price is held in a narrow range, with perhaps months or years of little movement. This is mainly seen with small rather than larger or blue-chip FTSE 100 companies, where there is usually plenty of price activity. The chart of Perpetual's share price (page 109), shows a long base-building phase from 1987 to 1992.

2. *Moving averages*. These are continually updated price averages over a specific interval. They can be short (5, 10 or 20 days), medium (30 or 50 days), or long (90 or 200 days) moving averages. The best signals come by using two or three moving averages in conjunction. A dead cross forms when the short, 20-day moving average cuts down below the medium 50-day moving average. It is a negative signal and indicates a possible sell. A golden cross forms when the short 20-day moving average cuts up through the medium 50-day moving average. It is a positive signal, and indicates a buy. A golden (or dead) cross can also form when the 50-day moving average cuts up (or

down) through the 200-day moving average. Moving averages are shown on the chart of the FTSE 100 (bottom figure on page 101).

3. *Support levels*. A support level operates when a price falls to a point to which more buyers arrive in force and drive the price up higher again. A support level and its opposite, a resistance level, are shown on the FTSE 100 chart (top figure on page 101).

4. *Resistance levels*. In Level I we saw a resistance level operating on the FTSE 100 at around 2400 in 1987 and 1989. Every time the price hit this level it ran into a surge of selling, which brought prices down again.

5. *Trends*. Strong up- or downtrends can develop that last for weeks, months or even sometimes for years. The most profitable opportunities arise from buying a share as a strong uptrend develops out of a base-building phase. You stay with that trend until it reverses decisively. An interesting feature of a good trend, either up or down, is that it rises, (or falls) consistently, just above (or below) the 20- and 50-day moving averages. Although this effect is obviously just an expression of the rising or falling moving average associated with a prolonged trend, it is a very promising signal when you spot it on a chart. An uptrend can be seen on the FTSE 100 chart (middle figure on page 101). A long term uptrend is also illustrated on the chart of Perpetual's share price shown on page 109.

6. *Channels*. When the trend is well established, it is often possible to join all the low (support) levels and the high (resistance) levels, to form a channel. If the price line falls below the lower line of the channel it signals a break in the uptrend. Conversely, if the price line rises above the upper level of the channel, it signals a breakout above the trend. A channel is drawn on the middle figure on page 101.

7. *Rectangles*. A rectangle is a prolonged trading range where there are definite, identifiable support levels that attract buyers and resistance levels at which more selling occurs. Rectangles, or trading ranges, can last for many months or years. A prolonged rectangle is another example of a base-building phase. A rectangle is shown on the top figure on page 101.

8. *Breakout*. This term describes precisely what happens when a price shoots out beyond the previous support or resistance levels. It can signal the end of a base-building phase, a trading range, a channel or a rectangle. Both a trading range and a rectangle are ambiguous phases; it is impossible to know how they will end. Once the breakout occurs, however, you have a buy signal if it is up, or a sell signal if it is down. If you feel uncertain, wait until the breakout is confirmed by a two-day consecutive close above the former resistance level, or when the rise is 3 per cent above that previous resistance level. This helps to avoid false breakouts (which do often occur). An example of a breakout is shown on the Medava chart, see page 120.

9. *Head and Shoulders*. This is a very conspicuous pattern with the appearance of

three peaks, the central one being the 'head' and a lower one on either side forming the shoulders. This pattern usually signifies a market peak but when it is inverted it can signify a market bottom. The Tokyo Nikkei index made a spectacular head and shoulders pattern during 1988 to 1991 (see page 102).

10. *Double/Triple tops*. Here the market peak is indicated by two highs of nearly equal size followed by a fall. Market double tops, or the inverted pattern of double bottoms, are more regularly seen on charts than head and shoulders patterns. See illustration on the Glaxo Wellcome share price chart on page 172.

## *'Avoid ambiguous phases: they are the most difficult to decipher and can produce losses.'*

The above descriptions of discernible chart patterns are summarised in the table below, together with an indication of your preferred actions as a result.

### EXAMPLES OF STRUCTURE IN THE MARKET

| Name of Pattern | Comment | Action |
|---|---|---|
| 1. Base-building phase | Ambiguous | *Buy* if it ends with a rise. |
| | | *Sell* if it ends with a fall. |
| 2. Moving averages (MA) | 20-day short | *Buy* when MAs form a golden cross. |
| | 50-day medium | *Sell* when MAs form a dead cross. |
| | 200-day long | |
| 3. Support levels | buyers arrive | *Buy* if support holds for 2 days. |
| 4. Resistance levels | sellers arrive | *Sell* if resistance develops. |
| 5. Trends | Draw trend lines | *Buy* when line hits 3 points. |
| | | *Sell* when price falls below line. |
| 6. Channels | Draw channel lines | *Buy* as the price turns up. |
| | | *Sell* if the base line is breached. |
| 7. Rectangle (Trading Range) | Ambiguous phase | *Do not buy or sell* until a decisive signal occurs, e.g. a breakout. |
| 8. Breakout | i) Buyers arrive | *Buy* if breakout is up. |
| | ii) Sellers arrive | *Sell* if breakout is down. |
| 9. Head and Shoulders | A complex pattern | Often indicates a market peak. |
| 10. Double/triple tops | A double/triple spike | Often indicates a market peak. |
| Double/triple bottom | A double/triple spike | May indicate a market bottom. |

The charts below illustrate some of these patterns. In Level I we examined a chart of the FTSE 100 index movements over 16 years. We can now identify some of the patterns on that chart.

## FTSE 100 Index showing support and resistance levels

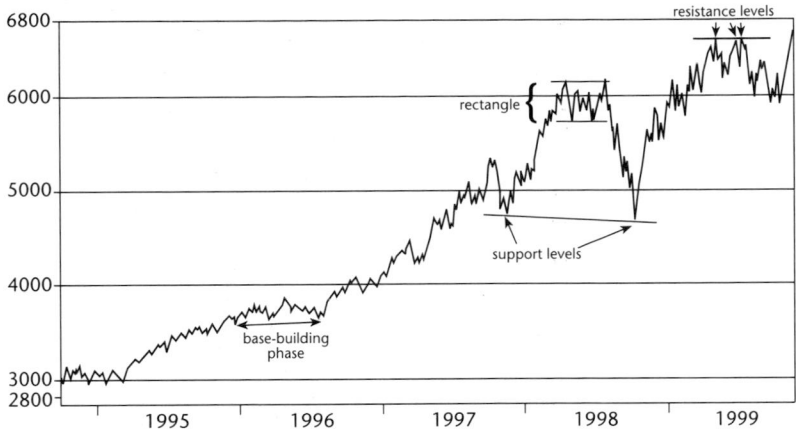

## FTSE 100 Index showing up and downtrends

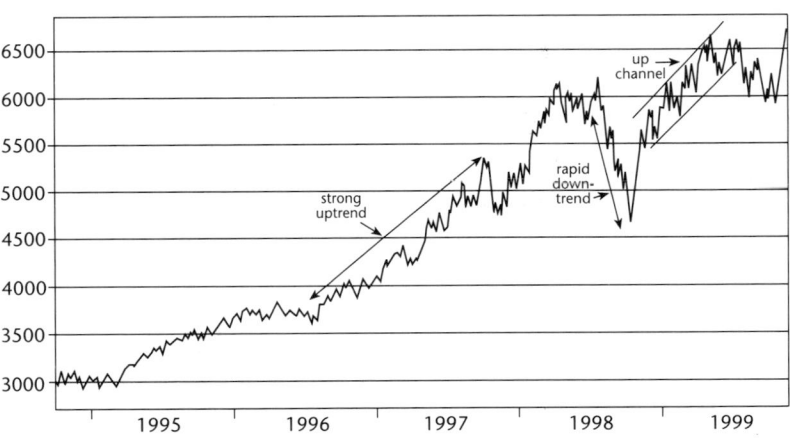

## FTSE 100 Index showing golden and dead crosses

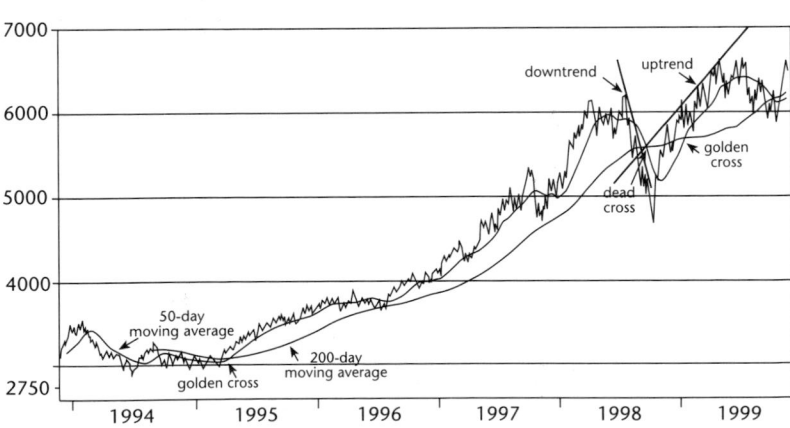

**NIKKEI 225 Average 1986 to 1993**

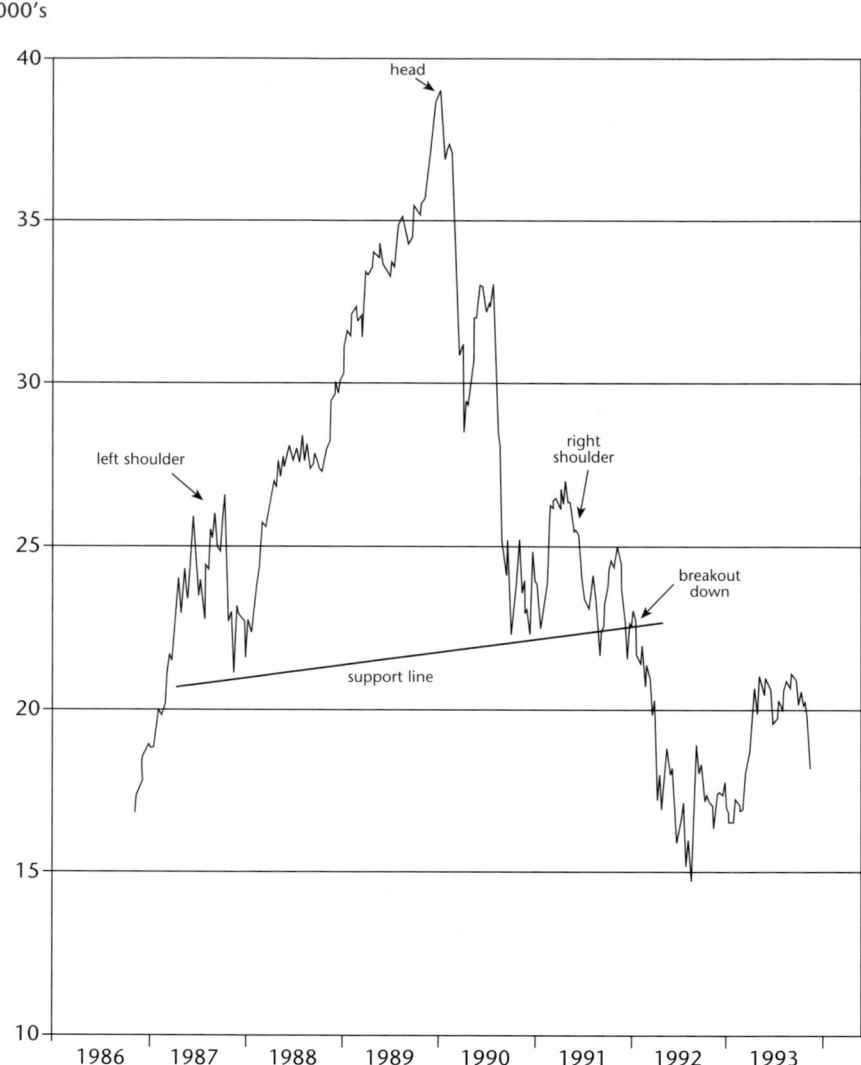

*No thing in use by man, for power of ill, can equal money.'*

*Sophocles (c 495–405 BC), Greek tragic poet*

## WHAT IS FASTER GAINS?

For finding promising companies, I want a detailed picture of the important information relevant to a wise choice. I achieve this with FASTER GAINS, my favourite stock-picking system. It is difficult to make sound investment decisions, but my system incorporates both fundamental and technical data. I call it 'belt and braces', but when I mentioned this to a financial journalist I was shocked to learn he thought this was investment jargon. 'Belt and braces' is definitely not jargon. It is simply a safety-first means of using as much available evidence and information as possible before taking a final decision.

FASTER GAINS examines 11 different criteria before deciding to buy, but finding a company that conforms to all 11 will be rare. In most cases, a compromise is necessary or you can wait for prices to fall back so that more companies fit the FASTER GAINS formula. The investment choice is wider and more attractive as recession ends. Most investors are then extremely pessimistic about prospects for the economy and share prices. To make super profits, this is precisely the right time to invest in great growth stories. William O'Neil says that the best profits are made in the first two years of a new bull market. Learn to recognise it and invest when it arrives.

FASTER GAINS grew out of my early reading to form my personal tailor-made version of stock-picking systems recommended by two gurus: William O'Neil, with his CAN SLIM formula, and Jim Slater, who has a set of criteria to find small growth companies with excellent prospects. FASTER GAINS spans some of the key issues you must consider for the early recognition of promising companies to buy. I introduced FASTER GAINS in *The Armchair Investor*, but as it is still my preferred stock-picking regime we will look at the typical portrait of a FASTER GAINS company.

Of the 11 separate pointers in the FASTER GAINS formula on whether or not you should buy, 4 cover company fundamentals, 3 are technical factors and the remaining 4 are on general items for added analysis. 'Belt and braces' provides a broad-based discipline when choosing shares. Relying on a wide spread of different factors reduces the risk of being wrong. The future earnings growth of a company is an important measure of its prospects, but it is only one within a cluster of key issues to consider when deciding between possible investments. While some of these 11 factors are obviously more crucial than others, we would lose the helpful mnemonic if we were to list them in order of importance. We look first at what the formula stands for, and then use examples to see how it works in practice.

## The FASTER GAINS Formula

**F: Fundamental Facts**. These provide an overview on the fundamentals surrounding a company. Many newsletters and company REFS give a variety of key statistics, including dividend yield, growth rate, return on the capital employed (ROCE) and profit margins as a percentage of turnover. Many fundamental facts appear in the weekly magazine *Investors Chronicle* for almost every company in the week after it announces interim or annual results. For additional information, contact the company directly for a copy of its latest annual report or use the free *Financial Times* Report Service.

**A: Annual Earnings per Share (EPS)**. The latest annual results should preferably show growth of around 20 per cent or more. As very few UK companies consistently achieve this rate of earnings growth this one factor eliminates a huge number of prospects to explore. If you know the current price and the forecast future earnings per share, you can calculate the price/earnings ratio for this year, next year and two years ahead. These calculations are only broad estimates based on forecasts by analysts or brokers, but they may help you decide whether, at today's price, a share is cheap in terms of its estimated future earnings growth. Target prices can be calculated for one or two years ahead, as described for the SuperStock example given earlier. This important statistic (EPS) appears in *Investors Chronicle*, *Company REFS* and *The Estimate Directory*. It is the second fundamental factor in the group of eleven.

**S: Supply/Demand Factors Governing the Share Price**. A small market capitalisation and strong demand encourages a rising share price. Strong demand can also benefit the share price in large companies. This is especially notable with large companies that do not attract high daily trading volumes, such as Sage Group, Reuters, Dixons and Railtrack. Strong demand occurs when market makers are short of stock or when a new FTSE 100 entrant is announced and tracker funds must buy it to achieve the proper weighting in their portfolios. This is a technical factor on the supply situation.

*'Respect the privilege of money and never forget that only real risk can provide true reward.'*

Matthew Harding, insurance tycoon and former director of Chelsea Football Club

**T: Technical Analysis.** Technical analysis gives clues on buy or sell decisions. It is the second technical factor. We saw above how chart patterns indicate buy or sell decisions; the volume of shares traded and numbers of shares rising or falling each day offer further guidance.

**E: Efficient Management.** Efficient management can squeeze more profits from the same amount of turnover, increasing earnings per share, which in turn helps a share price to rise. If companies hit a bad patch, the arrival of new managers can trigger increased buying as investors hope that new managers will solve the problems. Efficient management is a general factor but, in addition, it is useful to check whether the directors have either a sizeable shareholding or options in the company. If they own shares or the right to buy shares at below-market prices, they should be highly committed to growing the profits of the company.

**R: Rich in Cash.** I prefer investing in companies with no debt or who produce goods that generate plenty of cash to repay debts. When companies retain profits to fund further growth, they do not ask shareholders for more cash. If companies raise more cash from shareholders, they issue new shares. This dilutes the earnings per share of the existing shares. Increased numbers of shares are generally bad news unless the company expects future earnings to rise substantially, in spite of its fundraising actions, to compensate for the extra shares. I avoid companies with high debts as cash flow problems can increase during a recession. If cash flow dries up, bankruptcy may result. Information about a company's cash or debt levels appears regularly in company analyses provided by *Investors Chronicle* and *Company REFS* and in every company's annual report. 'Rich in cash' is another fundamental factor.

**G: Growth in Long-Term Earnings per Share.** Growth should show a doubling over 5 years. Such doubling is difficult to achieve, and so this factor alone eliminates about 80 per cent of the total list of quoted companies. *Investors Chronicle* and *Company REFS* provide this vital long-term indicator. It is another fundamental test for analysing company performance.

**A: Active Monitoring.** This activity is vitally important when investing in small growth companies. Like the proverbial angler who always bores his friends with tales of the huge catches he missed, I have a long list of investments that went horribly wrong either while I held them or after I sold. Always consider selling when a profits warning is announced, if there are unexpected setbacks or if the price chart suddenly makes a pattern that implies future trouble. Monitor a company's share price moves in your paper portfolio for a few weeks or months before you make a purchase. This is the second general factor.

**I: Institutional Support.** A little such support is good, but preferably after you have bought your holding. When several professional buyers emerge, they may force the share price higher. They raise the demand when there may be insufficient sellers around to fill these buying orders. Institutional investors buy in such large volumes that they improve share trading **liquidity**, the ability to buy and sell a security with ease. Yet to make 'super' profits, you must invest before all the expected good news is reflected in the share price. Examine the list of institutional investors who hold more than 3 per cent of a company's shares in either *Company REFS* or *The Estimate Directory*. The names may indicate whether value or growth managers are investors as some are renowned value-seekers, while others favour growth. This is the third key technical factor.

*'Things are never clear in the stock market and by the time they are, it is too late to profit from them.'*

*Peter Lynch,* One Up on Wall Street

**N: Something New.** This heading can cover new products, new management or new major contracts. It may be a niche market, conferring growth advantages, or a new high in the share price – perhaps a breakout, which is often a good buy signal. This is the third general factor.

**S: Stock Market Direction.** As noted in Level I, your portfolio will prosper if you time your major purchases close to the onset of a new uptrend. Timing is a tricky skill to master, but you can improve your success rate by following the stock market and learning about its mood swings. It is more difficult to make money in falling markets. Yet if you hold sound growth companies during a prolonged trading range, you may still make gains or at least conserve your profits. Tracking the market, to assess the current phase in the economic cycle, is one of the most profitable skills to acquire. This is the fourth general factor. We discussed it in Level I and will return to it again in Level III.

## THE SEARCH FOR FASTER GAINS COMPANIES

Finding a company that fits all 11 criteria simultaneously is not easy and becomes progressively more difficult as the market rises and share prices grow more expensive in terms of future price/earnings ratios. When you find that most of the companies you want to buy stand on very high P/Es of over 30, 35 or even 45, this alone is a useful sign that the market might be near a peak. Yet history shows very strong uptrends can last for months, perhaps even years. A prolonged uptrend in a share you are holding is a most exhilarating event; it is a proven route for acquiring faster gains and added wealth. When the market enters one of its periodic boom phases, retain your core holdings but do not buy more if the FASTER GAINS analysis shows most shares are expensive.

If your choice does not fulfil all 11 criteria, you may take a majority verdict. One or two factors can be ignored if most indicate a buy and you are comfortable about that. However, some factors I never ignore. Stock market direction is most important, as is earnings per share and the 5-year history of earnings growth. I may buy companies with high debts, but only if their products generate substantial cash – Glaxo Wellcome, SmithKline Beecham, Sage Group and Vodafone AirTouch all have high debts but their products generate large cash flows. Institutional support and supply/demand factors are less crucial, especially for large companies, as is active monitoring. I work through each factor and only buy when most evidence suggests exciting long-term potentials. Some chart patterns give guidance on *when* to buy a share you have followed on paper.

So how does FASTER GAINS operate in action? We will look at Perpetual and Logica to demonstrate this.

*'There is no shame in losing money on a stock. Everyone does it. What is shameful is to hold on to a stock, or, worse, buy more of it, when the fundamentals are deteriorating.'*

*Peter Lynch,* One Up on Wall Street

## Perpetual's Great Growth Story

**F: Fundamental Facts.** Perpetual is a fund management group. In 1998 it had a portfolio of 20 unit trusts and 4 investment trusts. The engine for its great growth period stemmed from carefully crafted PEP products in the early 1990s. It began operating as a fund management group in 1976 and floated as a public company early in 1987, a few months before the October crash. This was poor timing, as private investors were soon nursing horrendous losses from their shareholdings. Yet after a period of consolidation, small investors recognised the value of buying tax-free PEPs, and Perpetual duly benefited. Growth was greatly enhanced by excellent performance for many of Perpetual's funds, with regular high appearances in fund tables and numerous awards for performance and administrative service to clients. These successes were soon evident in the share price. Although by 1998 it could be argued that Perpetual was a mature company, its long-term prospects for growth still seemed intact.

**A: Annual Earnings per Share (EPS) for the latest year should show growth of about 20 per cent**. Perpetual's EPS grew 18.8 per cent in 1998, but were forecast to fall by 2.5 per cent in 1999, with a rise of 23 per cent in 2000. This erratic performance reflects the high market level in 1998, with a recession forecast for 1999. From an opening price of 100p early in 1987, with no share splits, by December 1998, eleven years on, the price at 3062p had grown nearly 31 times, a superb illustration of excellent long-term growth.

**S: Supply/Demand acting on the share price**. Perpetual is one of the quoted companies where volumes of shares traded were not disclosed, either daily or weekly until late in 1999. This lack of information was annoying but not greatly important for long-term investors in Perpetual. The share price is very high at around twenty to thirty pounds, but it simply reflects the fact that there have been no share splits since flotation. By December 1998 there were still only 28.4 million shares in the company, but its market capitalisation had grown from about £2.8 million in 1987 to £870 million.

**T: Technical Analysis**. The long-term chart for Perpetual (page 109) shows many classical features. Although the price fell from 100p to below 50p by year-end 1990, a long base-building period lasted from 1987 to late 1992. Then the market noticed Perpetual's exciting growth prospects and the share price began a prolonged uptrend of over 1,000 per cent, from a low of 45p in 1990 to 4538p at its July 1998 peak. In 1998, chart analysis proved extremely helpful for timing a purchase. From the summer peak, the price fell back dramatically, because investments in fund management groups serve as a proxy for the whole market. During a major boom, share price rises reflect the underlying growth in the economy and fund management

**PERPETUAL showing extended uptrend**

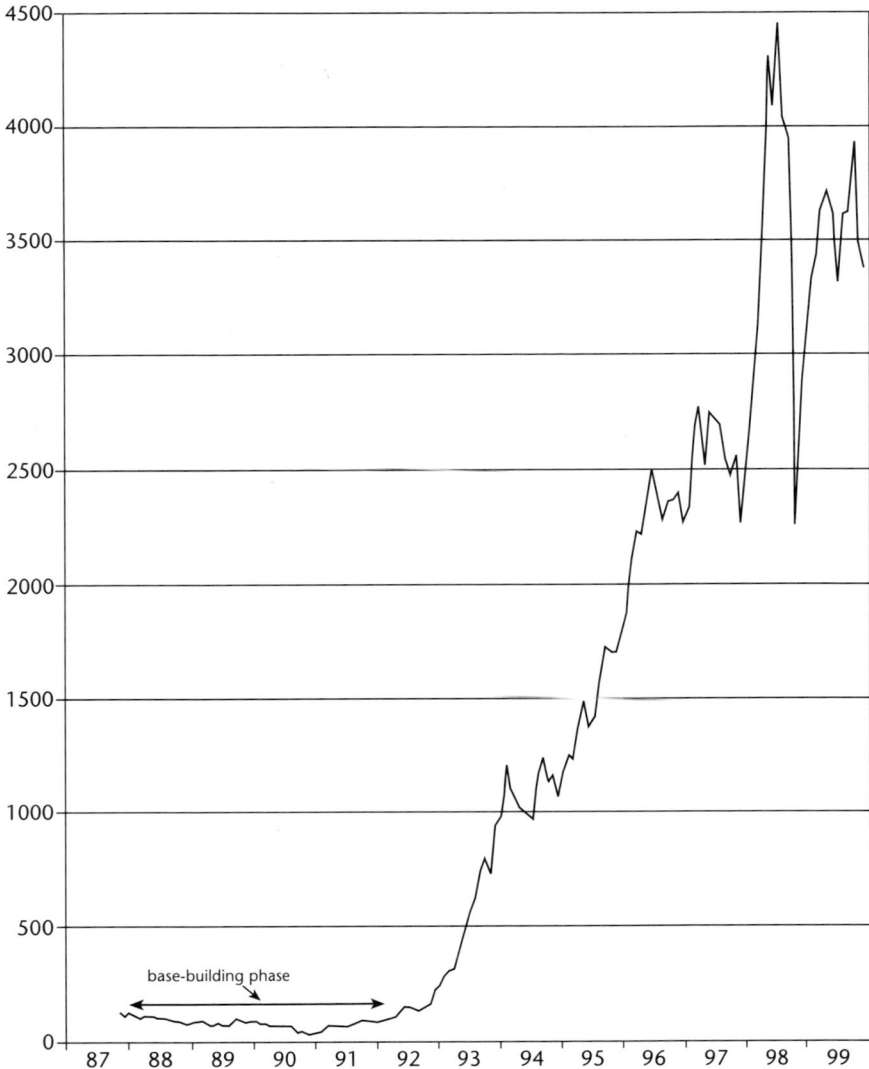

groups prosper; if recession threatens, the business will suffer and the share price anticipates that. In autumn 1998, an international crisis erupted and share prices fell globally. Among the worst-hit sectors were banks exposed to capital losses on suspect loans, and fund management groups, which make lower profits in a recession. Perpetual's share price plunged nearly 51 per cent to an October low of around 2225p, the price it had been in early 1996. Yet at that time, forecast earnings for 1999 were 166p and so Perpetual was trading on a low prospective price/earnings ratio of 13.4 (2225p ÷ 166p = 13.4). For 2000, forecast earnings of 200p gave a price/

earnings ratio of 11 (2225p ÷ 200p = 11). The fall seemed excessive and represented a buying opportunity for long-term investors.

*'I didn't care to provide for my old age, for I didn't think I'd have one.'*

James Buchan, The Psychology of Money

**E: Efficient Management**. Perpetual's management team have a proven track record for excellence in serving their huge client base. The company is highly recommended by independent financial advisers for clients seeking a good fund manager to handle their funds. In November 1998, Perpetual had £9.8 billion under management. Most revenue derives from annual fees earned by managing those funds. Perpetual forecast a loss of growth from its profitable PEP revenues as ISAs replaced new PEPs in April 1999, but it planned to enter the personal pensions market and was optimistic that move would compensate for lower ISA and PEP revenues.

**R: Rich in Cash**. Perpetual has a consistent record of high cash reserves. They were over £42 million in 1998.

**G: Growth in Earnings Per Share**. Over the long term, this shows Perpetual's rapid growth. In 1993, earnings per share were 39.1p, up 213 per cent on the EPS of 12.5p for 1992. By 1998, EPS were 140p, a rise of 258 per cent in 5 years. In January 1993, funds under management were £846 million, the share price was 236p and the market value was £62 million. By December 1998, funds under management were approximately £10 billion, the share price was 3062p and the market capitalisation was £870 million.

**A: Active Monitoring**. This has not been of major importance to long-term investors, although this share price tends to mirror stock market setbacks, which indicate a downturn in the general economy. Perpetual does best when private investors are actively seeking to invest in the stock market but this flow of funds dries up whenever harsh conditions are forecast. In that context, therefore, the result of −4 per cent for EPS in 1995 following the market downturn of 1994, and the forecast fall of −2.5 per cent for 1999 due to an expectation of recession in 1999, reflect this close relationship.

**I: Institutional Support** for Perpetual was strong during 1998 at around 40 per cent of the shares. As the directors owned nearly 15 per cent, this only leaves 45 per cent, or 12.8 million of freely available shares, from the total 28.4 million shares in issue.

**N: Something New** for Perpetual in 1999 was the anticipated introduction of ISAs in April of that year. There was no way of knowing how successful ISAs would be, but as the government hopes to encourage more saving among the population, successful fund management groups should spearhead that activity. Another positive development was the plan to launch personal pensions in 1999. Bid prospects became another 'new', when Prudential Corporation paid a massive premium to buy M&G, the biggest unit trust fund manager, in March 1999. Ironically, investing in fund management groups has frequently proved more profitable than buying their funds.

**S: Stock Market Direction** is an important issue for Perpetual's future prospects and share price. As we noted, the steep decline in the share price in the autumn of 1998 forewarned of an expected recession. But for long-term watchers, Perpetual has been a superb small growth company. Any plunge in the share price could therefore be a good buying opportunity. From the October low of 2225p, the price rose to end 1998 at 3062p, a rise of 37.6% in less than two months.

*'If you sell in desperation, you always sell cheap.'*

*Peter Lynch,* One Up on Wall Street

## Logica for Long-Term Growth

**F: Fundamental Facts.** Logica is one of Europe's leading software and computer services groups. It specialises in systems integration, consultancy, project work and market-reusable software, providing IT (information technology) solutions for complex systems, such as trading electricity, and covers high-growth areas, including banking and telecoms. There is added-value through 'outsourcing' – that is, taking on IT work for other companies. This gives higher margins for contracts like installing and managing a bank's settlement system, rather than solving the notorious millennium bug or running call centres. Logica's software seems 'tailor-made' but most of it is recyclable for other clients, reducing costs. In December 1998, Logica announced an upbeat trading statement. Orders, sales and profits for the first five months of 1998 were well ahead of the previous year. Logica wins contracts in rewarding areas in Britain and abroad, and has a higher rate of earnings growth than many companies in the highly rated technology sector.

The shares were a star performer during 1998 and 1999. I bought my holding at an average price of 1087p during December 1997, but in November 1998 at a price of around 1950p, they underwent a five-way split, dropping the price to around 400p. My holding was then bought at the corresponding figure of 217.4p, and given that the shares ended 1998 at 520p, my stake grew by one and a third times in twelve months. By 11 November 1999, the share prices had more than doubled again to 1164p and Logica finally entered the FTSE 100 index on that date, ranked 74th in the list.

**A: Annual Earnings per Share (EPS) growth** in 1998 was 8.5p, 38.9% higher than in 1997 and way over the 20 per cent growth we want. Estimated EPS at 10.3p for 1999 was 21.2 per cent higher, with 22.3 per cent earnings growth of 12.6p forecast for 2000. We can project forward targets based on these estimates to assess future prospects. In December 1998, at 520p, with estimated earnings per share of 12.6p, the prospective price/earnings ratio for 2000 was just over 41 (520p ÷ 12.6p = 41.2). This seems excessively high but Logica's rate of growth had been exceptional. In January 1993, the share price was 33p, earnings per share were 1.4p and the market value £101 million, compared with £1,945 million by December 1998 and £4,220 million on 6 November 1999. The share price during the autumn of 1999 was boosted by tracker fund buying in the expectation that Logica would soon enter the FTSE 100 list. This astonishing rate of growth took 7 years. If Logica continues to win major new contracts to boost growth, another 5 years of 25 per cent EPS growth could produce earnings of 39p in 2004. At 520p with earnings of 39p for 2004, the prospective price/earnings ratio would be 13.3 (520p ÷ 39p = 13.3). A price/earnings ratio of 41 looked high for 1999 but continued strong growth over the next 5 years could keep the price/earnings ratio at around 40, to lift the share price to 1560p (39p × 40 = 1560p). This is almost three times the 1998-year-end price of 520p. During 1999 high-tech stocks became hot market favourites and price/earnings ratios grew even more inflated, to 50 or 60 times current earnings.

**S: Supply/Demand** for Logica shares was transformed after the four-for-one bonus issue to shareholders in November 1998. For every one share held, another four were received, triggering a five-way split on all the vital statistics, including the share price, the EPS and the dividends per share. The shares in issue rose from 73.8 million to 369 million (73.8 × 5 = 369). On a daily basis, the numbers of shares traded rose from around 400,000 to about 1.5 million to reflect this split.

**T: Technical Analysis** for the Logica share price shows a similar long-term pattern to Perpetual's. During 1991 and 1992, the share price was round 40p in a prolonged base-building phase. It then began a slow climb to another year-long base-building phase at 60p in 1994. Early in 1995, it started rising more rapidly, to form an up channel into 1997. There was a sharp correction of about 33 per cent within four months. From mid-1997, the price rose steeply in an amazing uptrend. However, I did not buy my Logica holding on chart signals.

*'Even the most noble causes are pursued one day at a time.'*

Mark Bryan and Julia Cameron, The Money Drunk

**Logica showing uptrend from 1994 to November 1999**

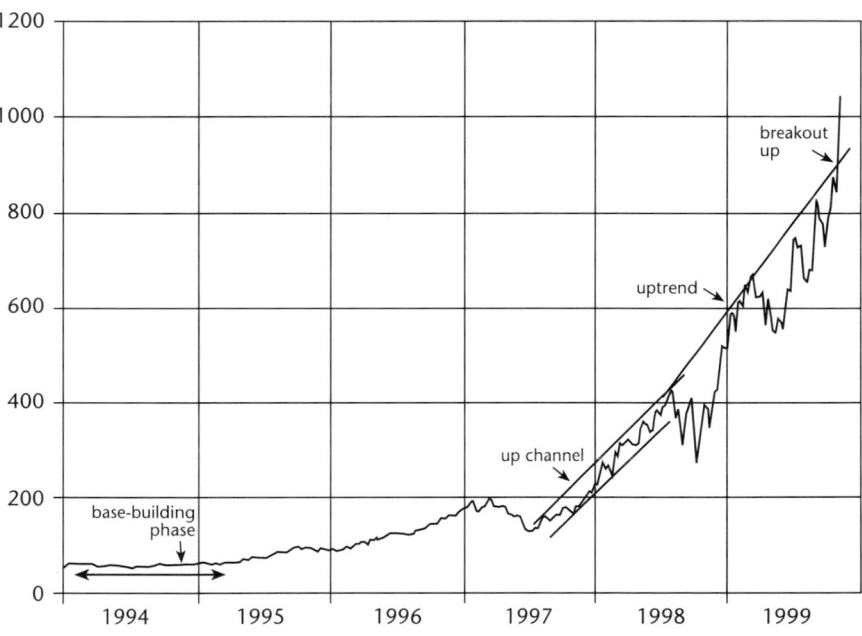

I used fundamental analysis to buy Logica in December 1997. I followed the action for a few months and then read comments on future prospects by brokers in the Stock Market Report in the Companies and Markets section of the *Financial Times*. With the share price at 210p, some analysts set a target price of 320p within a year to December 1998. I could not buy at 210p because there was great share price activity in response to these upbeat comments. But I thought the long-term prospects looked very strong. If the price reached 320p within a year, my holding would have grown 47 per cent.

**E: Efficient Management**. The managers at Logica seem highly capable of securing lucrative contracts for the IT products. The recycling side of their software is excellent for reducing costs.

**R: Rich in Cash**. Unlike many high-technology companies, Logica is cash-rich with about £54 million during 1998. This position compares favourably with other large IT companies, including Misys, Sema and Sage, the last of which has large debts.

**G: Growth in Earnings per Share** over the long term are excellent. EPS in 1994 was 2.77p, reaching 8.46p by 1998, a growth rate over the 5-year period of 205 per cent.

**A: Active Monitoring** is very important for high-technology companies. In 1997, a sudden plunge in the share price occurred when the company announced it might have difficulties recruiting trained staff. This alarmed investors because IT companies rely on a highly skilled workforce. The shares trade on such a high price/earnings ratio, even a whiff of any bad news can send the price diving.

**I: Institutional Support** for Logica is not unduly high at 20 per cent of shares in issue. As the directors hold less than 1 per cent, there are at least 295 million shares freely available. If the growth story continues, more institutions might buy a declarable holding of 3 per cent. This is exactly what I always hope will happen, if I can buy ahead of the crowd. In 1999, Logica became a candidate to join the ranks of the elite FTSE 100 index. This was the first time I had chosen a small growth company, valued at £874 million in December 1997 (rank: 188) and then held it until it reached FTSE 100 status.

**N: Something New** for Logica is the constant updating of its product range of major software packages. During December 1998, there was a breakout in the share price, first above its previous high of 463p, to a new high of 530p just before Christmas and on again to 660p in January 1999. In late October 1999, another breakout shot the price up from 850p to 1200p in under 4 weeks.

**S: Stock Market Direction** is important for growth shares. A severe downturn might affect companies in the highly rated IT sector more than most. They trade on such high price/earnings ratios that these can be vulnerable to adverse news items. If one of the main companies in this sector hit trouble, Logica's price might also fall. Yet at Christmas 1998, other information technology stocks were far more highly rated: London Bridge Software had a price/earnings ratio of 60 (1200p ÷ 20p = 60) and the price/earnings ratio for Sage was 55.9 (1565p ÷ 28p = 55.9). In November 1999, the London Stock Exchange launched a technology sector with two new indices; a FTSE techMARK 100 and FTSE techMARK All Share index. An exuberant surge in the US high technology Nasdaq index took it to an all time high of over 3000 at this time, sending most high-tech stocks soaring in a possible 'bubble'.

*'New readers must trade on paper for a few months before exposing themselves to the stress of using real money.'*

The Options Trader, Investors Chronicle

## The Search For Promising Small Growth Companies

Try using FASTER GAINS when searching for small growth companies to create and run your own paper portfolio. Setting up your paper FASTER GAINS Portfolio is the main task in Level II but, in addition, Stream B or C investors should continue to run the semi-passive Top Ten Portfolio. Stream A investors should run two paper portfolios simultaneously: the Top Ten and the FASTER GAINS, while building up £10,000 to begin investing.

Watch promising candidates and monitor their progress on paper. Early in 1999, the small-companies sector was almost in crisis; many were neglected and trading on very low price/earnings ratios because fund managers focused on FTSE 250 and 100 shares. The numbers of under-valued small companies was larger than usual. Yet some might not recover their popularity even when the threat of recession passes. Analysts thought some might be forced to delist and go private for lack of investor support. However, when the economy returns to growth, many small companies will have sound prospects, or will be recovery situations. Sectors severely hit that may have held promising recovery stories include construction and engineering, the media and leisure sectors, retailing and oil exploration, the last of which includes many small firms.

Pursue all the avenues to find good growth situations before the market notes their future promise. The *Financial Times* Companies & Markets section covers some companies every day. In the London Stock Market Report, analysts and brokers often give reasons for favouring a company and suggest a target price. This is a starting point for further research. The business section of *The Times*, the *Telegraph* and the *Guardian* include company analysis and results. *The Sunday Times*, the *Sunday Telegraph* and the *Observer* are additional useful sources. *Investors Chronicle*, *Money Observer*, *Company REFS*, *The Estimate Directory* and *Bloomberg Money* are extra hunting grounds, as are investment newsletters. Some are listed in the bibliography. Join an investment club or attend classes and conferences; this may alert you to companies you have missed. Resist the temptation to take tips from friends, magazines or newspapers. There is no substitute for following a sound formula, but if you get a tip from a friendly stockbroker or a colleague with sound research skills, it could be worth pursuing.

---

**HOW TO FIND SMALL GROWTH COMPANIES**

1. Companies & Markets section in the *Financial Times* (broker recommendations).
2. Broadsheet newspapers, daily or on Sunday.
3. *Investors Chronicle, Money Observer, Bloomberg Money*.
4. Newsletters you buy on subscription.
5. *Company REFS* and *The Estimate Directory*.
6. Investment clubs, classes or conferences, or money shows.

---

## The Progression of Your Paper and Actual Portfolios

Creating the Paper Small Company Portfolio follows the steps taken in Level I to set up the Paper Top Ten Portfolio. Begin a separate portfolio record in your workbook, personal organiser or personal computer, to operate in conjunction with, but separate from, your Top Ten Portfolio, whether that is on paper or an actual portfolio. Keep separate records for each portfolio and never mix paper with real transactions or you will get hopelessly muddled. Avoid confusion by never having more than two paper and two actual portfolios at any time. First, start your Top Ten Paper Portfolio in Level I and convert it to a real portfolio when £10,000 is available or market conditions seem right. In Level II, set up your Paper Small Company FASTER GAINS Portfolio and convert it to a real portfolio after 12–18 months. When that is running profitably, start converting your semi-passive Top Ten Portfolio into the active New Millennium Portfolio using paper positions. Finally, in Level V, you can merge the Top Ten and Small Company Portfolios to create your active

New Millennium Portfolio. This progression, from Level I to Level V, is summarised in the table below.

## THE PROGRESSION OF PAPER AND ACTUAL PORTFOLIOS

| Portfolio | Opened in: | Closed in: |
|---|---|---|
| 1. Paper Top Ten Portfolio | Level I | Level I or II |
| 2. Top Ten Portfolio | Level I or II | Level V (converted to active) |
| 3. Paper Small Company Portfolio | Level II or III | Level III or IV |
| 4. Small Company Portfolio | Level III or IV | Level V (merged) |
| 5. Paper New Millennium Portfolio | Level IV | Level V |
| 6. New Millennium Portfolio | Level V | Hold for the long term |

## Set Up Your Paper Small Company (FASTER GAINS) Portfolio

Start with a stock watch-list of 8–10 prospects while you decide which to buy. From your 'paper fund' of £10,000, invest £2,000 in each of at least 5 companies. Follow the others on your list, in case you decide to sell and reinvest in another candidate later. Allowing £30 for commission and stamp duty costs gives you £1,970 to invest in each of your 5 companies. Record the details of each purchase: the date, company name, number of shares you bought, price paid per share and the total cost. Lay it out as a table, for ease in updating the portfolio value at any time. Follow the layout of the July 1998 Paper Portfolio (page 72).

Use the **mid-price** (quoted in newspapers). This is a price set between the buy (**offer**) and sell (**bid**) **price**. Buy at the close of business, to establish a regular working system. When you have more experience, follow your paper companies realistically and buy or sell them during working hours because when you actually buy a share it can be impossible to obtain the price you set on paper. Be scrupulously honest in your paper dealings – the only person you will cheat if you are not honest is yourself.

If at first you cannot find 5 companies that fit all the FASTER GAINS factors, delay starting your paper portfolio while you prolong your search, or try a compromise. You might buy your companies over a few months, as you continue your search. Or choose companies that only comply with some of the 11 criteria. You might include a company with high debts but strong cash flow; it may have an extremely high P/E relative to forecast earnings. You may select a company with less than 20 per cent growth in its latest annual earnings per share, or one that did not double EPS growth over the past 5 years. You might act on a tip without checking the fundamentals or use a chart signal without checking if the fundamentals support the buy decision. Compromises in selecting companies on paper can add to your knowledge about the market as you watch how share price changes unfold. In Level III, we will cover further ways to expand the field for finding small growth stocks.

The action you should be taking on your paper portfolio is summarised in the box below. Item 10 is discussed further in the next section.

---

**CREATE A FASTER GAINS SMALL COMPANY PAPER PORTFOLIO**

1. Prepare a worksheet in your personal organiser or PC to record your portfolio.
2. Allocate £10,000 to your paper portfolio.
3. If possible, list 8–10 suitable candidates.
4. Select 5 using FASTER GAINS, taking several months if necessary, or choose compromise companies.
5. Record every transaction on your portfolio worksheet so you can calculate its value at any time.
6. Keep a separate full record of every purchase and sale made.
7. Enter the details for dividends due and 'paid' so you can reinvest these dividends at least once a year.
8. Follow your 5 chosen companies plus those still on your stock watch-list with press cuttings.
9. Keep changes of sales and repurchases to a minimum.
10. Monitor the portfolio's progress regularly, and value it at least once a month.

---

*'If a business is worth a dollar and I can buy it for 40 cents, something good may happen to me.'*

Walter Schloss, a Buffett contemporary and fellow Benjamin Graham disciple

## MONITOR YOUR RESULTS

With the portfolio established, you should monitor news items and annual results for your companies plus those on your watch-list. Keep a file of press cuttings for each company. Record every transaction and note dividends due and 'paid' so you reinvest dividend cash regularly, perhaps once a year. If you sell a holding, update the list of remaining shares. Avoid too many changes: each sale and repurchase costs about £55 (sale commission of £25, reinvestment commission plus stamp duty of £30), and overtrading damages the portfolio's performance. Calculate its value regularly to judge whether your paper wealth is growing. Be realistic. I met an investor whose paper portfolio, begun with £1 million, was making profits. He was surprised when I asked him if he had £1 million to invest. As the answer was 'No', he was running a fantasy, not a paper, portfolio. This is not a realistic test of investment skills.

## Dealing With Losses

Active monitoring is essential when running a small company portfolio. Gain the maximum benefits with a paper dry-run before risking your own money, and learn how to limit losses if one of your companies disappoints. Immediately after buying, prepare a plan of what you will do if the share price falls rather than rises. Set a limit on what size loss you will take – perhaps when the price is 15 to 20 per cent below your buying price. Be ready to sell quickly on adverse news announcements such as shock bad results or a profits warning. Sell if the story changes or if the chart shows a sell signal.

In summary, consider selling a stock:

- when the price hits your pre-set stop-loss point, perhaps 15 to 20 per cent below your buying price;
- on an adverse announcement or a major profits warning;
- if the growth story falters;
- when you spot selling signals on the chart, such as a dead cross, the price falling through a previous support level, the end of an uptrend or the price dropping below the lower line of a channel.

Suppose you watched Medeva for a few months on paper and decided to buy 1,000 shares. On 27 January 1997, the mid-price hit an all-time high of 293.5p (See point A on the Medeva chart on page 120). (The offer, or buying, price would be a few pence higher, perhaps around 295p.) As this was a new breakout, let us assume that you bought 1,000 shares for a total cost of £2,995 (£2,950 + £30 [commission] + £14.75 [stamp duty] = £2,995). By 13 May 1997 the price had fallen to 264p (B on the top chart of page 121), showing a loss of £355 on your purchase, excluding selling costs. You have only held the shares for sixteen weeks, and so you make no decision. By 19 May, as the share price has recovered to 298p (C on the top chart of page 121), you breathe a sigh of relief and do nothing. But if you look closely at that chart you will spot that on 13 May the share price had fallen below the 200-day moving average before recovering rapidly. Yet by 19 May the price still lay below the 50-day moving average, which had by then turned down decisively. So what will the price do now?

On 13 June 1997, with the price at 290p, a dead cross appeared (D on the middle chart of page 121). This is a negative signal. The holding showed a small loss after four and a half months. Selling, perhaps at a bid price of 285p, would crystallise a £175 loss (£2,850 − £30 [selling commission] = £2,820 − £2,995 (costs) = −£175). The chart shows the dead cross coincided with a dramatic share price collapse, beginning in June and continuing into July. This drop created a much larger loss. Should you sell on 20 August at a mid-price of 236p (bid price then about 230p)? The loss is 24 per cent or £725 (£2,300 − £30 = £2,270 − £2,995 = −£725). Or should you wait? Two days later the mid-price fell to 222p. Selling on 22 August at a bid price of 218p increases the loss to £845 or 28 per cent. (£2,180 − £30 = £2,150 − £2,995 = −£845). Selling after only seven months is difficult; it implies you made a bad choice with Medeva in January at 295p. Investors hate admitting – even to themselves – that they showed poor judgement or timing, especially with such a quick move. Lost pride accompanies the financial loss and is sometimes tougher to swallow. Yet some losses are inevitable and must be philosophically accepted.

Although £845 is a cruel loss to take so rapidly, the down channel was securely in place by August 1997 and the unfolding disaster continued. After one year, the share price had shrunk to 140p, and the loss on a bid price of 136p would then have been a thumping £1,665, or 56 per cent (£1,360 − £30 = £1,330 − £2,995 = −£1,665). Poor fundamentals must have prompted this downward re-rating, but the charts tell the whole story.

**Medeva 1995 to January 1997**

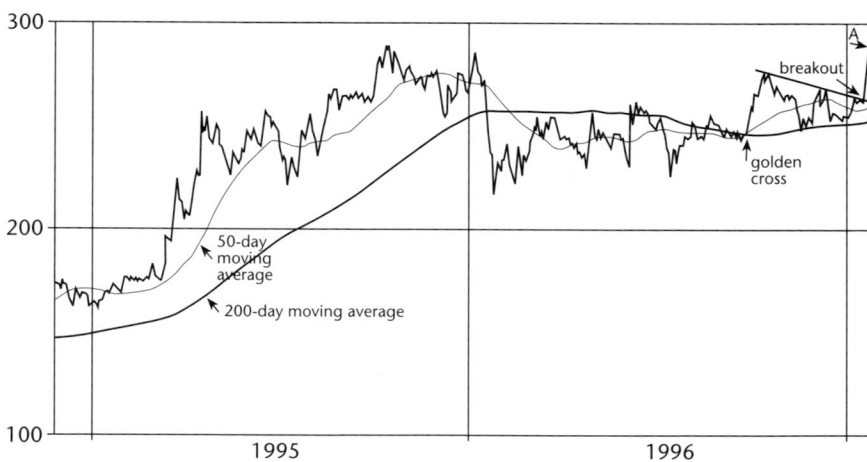

**Medeva July 1994 to May 1997**

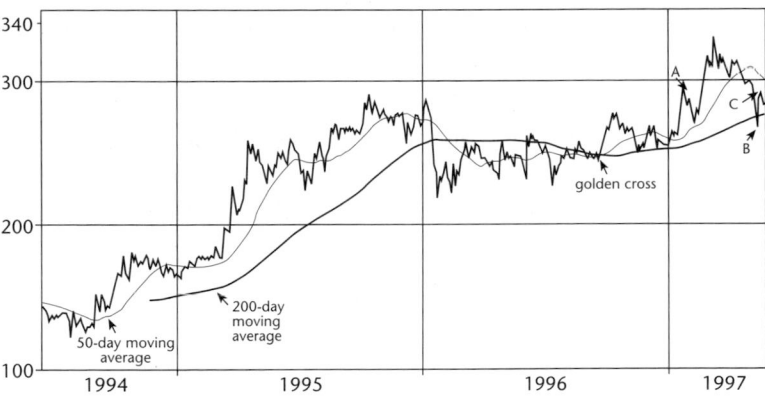

**Medeva July 1994 to July 1997**

**Medeva March 1994 to November 1999**

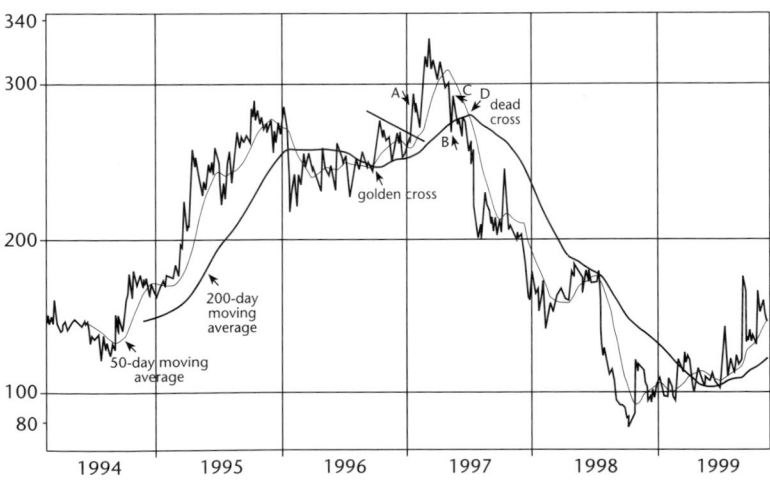

Follow the fortunes of your small growth shares on paper so that when you begin to own some in your FASTER GAINS Small Company Portfolio, you know exactly *what* to do and *when* in order to avoid such nasty losses.

*'If you approach the whole process with an attitude of optimism, the results will be far better in the long run.'*

Richard McCall, martial arts expert and author of The Way of the Warrior-Trader

## Review the Progress of Your Top Ten Portfolio

We set up the Paper Top Ten Portfolio in Level I. While there, some investors may have bought their own passive Top Ten Portfolio. We will look again now at the July 1998 paper portfolio so you can see how to make changes in your own paper or real Top Ten Portfolio and become more active. Being an active investor is crucial in order to ensure you reach your wealth targets within a reasonable time, and so it is important to make a start. The example below outlines the stages involved. If you are nervous, carry out your changes first on paper and watch the results for a few weeks to see how events unfold. Novices might prefer this approach, for a preliminary 'dry run'.

The July 1998 portfolio had six sectors: two pharmaceutical companies (SmithKline Beecham and Glaxo Wellcome, with Zeneca ranked 11th and excluded); two oil companies, (BP and Shell); and two telecommunications companies (BT and Vodafone); two of the three eligible banks (Lloyds TSB and Barclays); one alcoholic beverages company (Diageo); and one tobacco company (British American Tobacco). A summary of the portfolio and its value as at 11 September 1998 is reproduced in the table below.

## START TO BECOME AN ACTIVE INVESTOR

While writing *The Wealthy Investor*, I was astonished at the hyperactivity of some FTSE 100 companies. Within months, rankings switched, and mergers or profits warnings were announced; there was continuous change.

By September 1998, major moves had transformed the July 1998 portfolio's structure. The international global crisis had decimated bank share prices, justifying my caution for holding only two. BAT left the top ten by demerging its insurance interests and simultaneously remerging

**PROGRESS OF THE JULY 1998 TOP TEN PORTFOLIO AS AT
11 SEPTEMBER 1998: FTSE 100: 5118.5**

| Rank | Company | Number of Shares | Price (p) | Value (£) |
|------|---------|------------------|-----------|-----------|
| 1 | Glaxo Wellcome | 51 | 1745 | 890 |
| 2 | British Telecom | 118 | 786 | 927 |
| 3 | Lloyds TSB | 103 | 652 | 672 |
| 4 | BP Amoco | 113 | 793 | 896 |
| 5 | SmithKline Beecham | 124 | 691 | 857 |
| 6 | Shell | 232 | 358 | 831 |
| 7 | Barclays | 50 | 1117 | 559 |
| 8 | Diageo | 128 | 550 | 704 |
| 9 | Vodafone | 111 | 767 | 851 |
| 10 | BAT[a] | 68 | 454 | 309 |
| 11 | Allied Zurich[a] | 67 | 655 | 439 |
| **Total** | | | | **7,935** |
| Dividends plus cash | | | | 83 |
| **Total** | | | | **8,018** |

[a] Change arising from BAT share split

them with Zurich Insurance, a Swiss financial services firm. Each BAT share was split into two. The new combined group, Allied Zurich, began trading on 8 September 1998, ranked 24 with BAT ranked 35.

On 11 September BAT plus Allied Zurich were worth £748. The bank sector was reeling from the global crisis. I decided to be an active investor and reshuffle the portfolio. It is sensible to do this if your 10 companies change as dramatically as happened that September. On paper, try running the two portfolios in tandem, to check whether your changes prove more or less profitable – which we shall do later. Barclays, at 1117p, showed a nasty loss of 44 per cent. I sold BAT and Barclays, reinvesting the proceeds in Zeneca but keeping the 67 Allied Zurich shares. The portfolio still held 10 companies, but only one bank, one insurance company and three pharmaceuticals. Hence, there were still only 6 sectors. The paper transactions plus reinvested dividends and cash, worth £83, worked out like this:

| | |
|---|---:|
| Sell 50 Barclays at 1117p = £559 – £20 (costs) | £539 |
| Sell 68 BAT at 454p = £309 – £20 (costs) | £289 |
| *Add* dividends plus cash (£37 + £46) | £83 |
| Total | £911 |
| Buy 39 Zeneca at 2240p (plus £25 costs) | (£899) |
| **Cash balance** | **£12** |

*'Later Marx was to recall his mother's shrewd words, "If only Karl had made capital instead of writing about it."'*

Edna Healey, Wives of Fame *(on Jenny, wife of Karl Marx)*

To begin the Paper Top Ten Portfolio, I deliberately chose 20 July 1998 as the start date because it marked a market top. I hoped to illustrate what an expensive error buying at a peak can be. Searching for the bottom is incredibly hard, but it is still better to buy at lower prices than at a top. Therefore, although the bottom of the autumn correction occurred in the first week of October, we can compare the fortunes of a second paper portfolio set up on 11 September 1998 (the date of the first reshuffle) and the original July 1998 portfolio. The September portfolio excluded BAT, Allied Zurich and extra banks (although Halifax was at 11th place), including instead food manufacturer Unilever, placed 12th. The rankings and composition of the portfolio are as set out in the table below.

### SECOND PAPER TOP TEN PORTFOLIO (SET UP ON 11 SEPTEMBER 1998)

| Rank | Company | Number of Shares | Price (p) | Cost (£) |
|------|---------|-----------------|-----------|----------|
| 1 | Glaxo Wellcome | 56 | 1745 | 1,000 |
| 2 | British Telecom | 124 | 786 | 1,000 |
| 3 | BP Amoco | 123 | 793 | 1,000 |
| 4 | SmithKline Beecham | 141 | 691 | 999 |
| 5 | Shell | 272 | 358 | 999 |
| 6 | Lloyds TSB | 150 | 652 | 1,003 |
| 8 | Vodafone | 127 | 767 | 999 |
| 9 | Zeneca | 43 | 2240 | 988 |
| 10 | Diageo | 177 | 550 | 999 |
| 12 | Unilever | 181 | 539 | 1,001 |
| **Total** | | | | **9,990** |
| Cash | | | | 10 |
| **Total** | | | | **10,000** |

Note Companies 7 and 11, HSBC and Halifax respectively, were deliberately excluded as they were other banks.

## Compare the Two Portfolios

We can now compare the values of the two paper portfolios as at 30 December 1998. Again, several companies had changed their rank, as shown in the next two tables.

## PROGRESS OF THE JULY 1998 TOP TEN PORTFOLIO AS AT 30 DECEMBER 1998 (AFTER 11 SEPTEMBER 1998 RESHUFFLE)

| Rank | Company | Number of shares | Price (p) | Value (£) |
|---|---|---|---|---|
| 1 | Glaxo Wellcome | 51 | 2068 | 1,055 |
| 2 | British Telecom | 118 | 905.5 | 1,068 |
| 5 | Lloyds TSB | 103 | 855 | 881 |
| 3 | BP Amoco | 113 | 897.5 | 1,014 |
| 4 | SmithKline Beecham | 124 | 840 | 1,042 |
| 7 | Shell | 232 | 369.25 | 857 |
| 10 | Diageo | 128 | 684 | 876 |
| 8 | Vodafone | 111 | 976 | 1,083 |
| 20 | Allied Zurich | 67 | 896.5 | 601 |
| 9 | Zeneca | 39 | 2617 | 1,021 |
| Cash | | | | 2 |
| **Total** | | | | **9,500** |
| | | | | **(loss of £500 or 5%)** |

## PROGRESS OF THE SEPTEMBER 1998 TOP TEN PORTFOLIO AS AT 30 DECEMBER 1998

| Rank | Company | Number of shares | Price (p) | Value (£) |
|---|---|---|---|---|
| 1 | Glaxo Wellcome | 56 | 2068 | 1,158 |
| 2 | British Telecom | 124 | 905.5 | 1,123 |
| 3 | BP Amoco | 123 | 897.5 | 1,104 |
| 4 | SmithKline Beecham | 141 | 840 | 1,184 |
| 5 | Shell | 272 | 369.25 | 1,004 |
| 6 | Lloyds TSB | 150 | 855 | 1,283 |
| 8 | Vodafone | 127 | 976 | 1,240 |
| 9 | Zeneca | 43 | 2617 | 1,125 |
| 10 | Diageo | 177 | 684 | 1,211 |
| 12 | Unilever | 181 | 674 | 1,220 |
| Cash | | | | 10 |
| **Total** | | | | **£11,662** |
| | | | | **(gain of £1,662 or 16.6%)** |

The July 1998 portfolio was still showing a loss because it was bought at the summer peak. On 30 December 1998, the FTSE 100 was 5882.6, 296 points or 4.8% below its July 1998 high of 6179. The July 1998 portfolio still trailed by 5% – but the portfolio begun on 11 September was in profit by a thumping 16.6 per cent. A few months, however, is far too short a period to judge performances. We shall update the two paper portfolios in Level V.

Work through similar changes while holding your paper portfolio, and if you hold it for a year, reinvest the dividends and cash to keep it growing.

Most investors should then be ready to buy their own Top Ten Portfolio and make the necessary changes as they crop up to eliminate companies that fall below 10th position. As a first step to being active, eliminate these laggards at the time you reinvest cash from your dividends. You might buy a software package, to track your portfolio, to which we will now turn.

*'Grace is given of God, but knowledge is bought in the market.'*

*Arthur Hugh Clough (1819–61), English poet*

## SOFTWARE PACKAGES

When I began investing, like a trappist monk, I did everything manually, including preparing charts to follow the market and shares I was watching. I do not recommend this route to anyone now that so many useful software packages are available at modest prices. You can buy a complete portfolio manager that will keep all your records, update your portfolios at the click of a mouse, and provide a full budgeting programme to run your savings regime.

Unless you are a highly sophisticated computer buff, buy a simple package. Software is intended as an aid to improve your investment performance. Only buy items that earn their keep. A software package is not a standalone device; it should operate as a support system to help you reach your targets. Information on, and advertisements for, investment software appear regularly in financial sections of newspapers and in *Investors Chronicle*.

## STAY ON TRACK

During Level II you should have saved enough capital to close the paper portfolio and begin running a real Top Ten Portfolio. Continue with this as a semi-passive portfolio of FTSE 100 companies, described in Level I, while running your Paper Small Company Portfolio. Keep separate records for them both and consider moving to Level III when you feel confident or when the Paper Small Company Portfolio is showing paper profits of 15–25 per cent. This may take 12–18 months, depending on market conditions. As we saw, the September 1998 Top Ten Paper Portfolio was 16.6 per cent ahead after only 17 weeks because it began with the benefit of improved timing, although not at the lowest point of the autumn correction in early October. By following the market, you do not need the benefit of hindsight to judge when it is high and likely to fall. With growing experience, you become more in tune with the market's mood.

If you uncover a share with a promising growth profile, you might buy a holding for perhaps £2,000 and add more if the growth story continues. I did this in March 1991 when buying Airtours, the tour operator. It was an exciting early success, doubling in value within six weeks of my purchase. I paid £1,860 for 1,000 shares (4,000 after a later share split). When they hit £3,600 I was keen to bank the gain. I sold them in three blocks of about 1330 shares but within a few months I bought them back. Look for an appropriate buying opportunity with a chart signal – perhaps a breakout or golden cross on the moving averages. Increase your gains by buying more shares on each new breakout because buying more shares on a new buy signal, known as **pyramiding**, is a proven route to growing your wealth as you are backing winning companies. I did this during 1998 with my core holdings.

## PROGRAMME UPDATE

Check your progress regularly to stay on target. Complete another progress report (see below) when you start and finish Level II to help your monitoring routine and show how well you are doing. If necessary, make adjustments to improve your performance. Preferably, try to complete a report every 6 months but do at least one yearly report.

Investors who remain at Level II should continue to reinvest dividends, interest and accumulated savings once a year. If you decide to remain a passive investor, ensure you are not too heavily exposed to equities. Rearrange your assets to achieve a balanced portfolio, holding at least half your total funds in cash, perhaps within an ISA. Follow the steps outlined in Level I. You might turn your initial £10,000 into £60,000+ in 10–12 years, depending on the markets. Later, you may decide to continue building your capital. Recalculate your net worth, spend a refresher period in Level II, and then move on to the higher levels.

When considering whether to move up a level in the 5-Level Programme, calculate by how much you have increased your savings, capital and net worth before the move. After completing the Level II progress report (see below), you may feel ready to move. Read through Level III to become familiar with the main ideas. Try to feel relaxed about the progress of your portfolios, both for the semi-passive Top Ten Portfolio and the Paper Small Company FASTER GAINS Portfolio.

### Level II Progress Report

| Reading Schedule | Start Date | Finish Date |
|---|---|---|
| Re-read Level I<br>Read Level II | | |

| Net Worth Statement | Start Value (£) | Finish Value (£) |
|---|---|---|
| *ASSETS*<br>House<br>Pension funds<br>Insurance policies<br>Top Ten Portfolio<br>Savings regime<br>Other cash<br>Other assets<br><br>*Total Assets* | | |
| *DEBTS*<br>Mortgage<br>Bank loans<br>Credit card debts<br>Store card debts<br>Other debts<br><br>*Total debts* | | |
| **Net Worth in Level II** | | |

*'Keep paying attention to the near-term realities that will affect growth in earnings.'*

*Peter Lynch,* One Up on Wall Street

## LEVEL III – THE ACTIVE INVESTOR

## Begin Relying on Your Own Expertise

*'None of the six Tempus new year tips for 1998 ended the year in the black and all underperformed the benchmark FTSE All-Share index.'*

*Tempus column, The Times, 30 December 1998*
*[The Times 1998 Tempus tips were as follows:- Laporte, Next, Billiton, Bass, F&C Pacific and Beazer Group. The FTSE All-Share index rose 10.9 per cent on the year and the FTSE 100 rose 14.5 per cent. Early in 1999 Tempus picked BATM Advanced Communications as one of its tips. This was a fantastic winner in 1999.]*

In Level III, as an active investor, you are ready to take a more active role. Change your perspective and success then looks achievable. You learn to understand how economic business cycles affect the stock market, which issues move markets and how to identify the onset of recession. You examine four elements for portfolio-building with PAYS (an add-on to FASTER GAINS). You start following large-value stocks to find growth stories while continuing with the semi-passive Top Ten Portfolio. Stream A investors, having saved £10,000 during Level II, should close the Paper Top Ten Portfolio and open a real portfolio, to join Streams B and C. You run a paper portfolio of small, fast-growing companies using FASTER GAINS, as explained in Level II. Aim to move to Level IV when this paper portfolio shows consistent profits. We discuss more tools, for checking real-time prices, and stock market newsletters, to follow companies you are watching.

These steps become the action plan for Level III, as follows:

1. Learn how the business cycle relates to the stock market cycle.
2. Recognise the major market movers.
3. Identify the onset of recession and recovery.
4. Learn PAYS – the four elements in portfolio-building.
5. Search for big- and small-capitalisation companies with growth stories.
6. Continue running the Paper Small Company FASTER GAINS Portfolio.
7. The Paper Small Company Portfolio can be closed after a period of about 12 to 18 months during which it has made consistent profits and a real portfolio can then be opened.
8. Consider additional tools to use in order to obtain real-time stock market prices plus newsletters to find small growth companies.

## A BACKGROUND OVERVIEW: 1944–1999

Knowing how events unfolded in the past is constructive for understanding markets. Because cycles are recognisable but irregular, some events recur but the sequence and details are different each time. As Heraclitis, the Greek philosopher, said: 'You can never step into the same river twice.'

To understand market behaviour we shall view events on two planes: first, the historical overview, to set our present time in a longer context; and, second, the local view, for the impact of the recent past. Together, they create a panorama of the past to reveal how global events affect the markets. The overview is a framework, spanning 55 years, allowing a longer perspective so you can exploit fluctuating markets. It looks simplistic, but we can see the main thrusts, while the local view adds detail on recent events. The long view provides valuable insights on the over-riding trends. These trends are like motorways, forging straight ahead. They drive the tenor of events by sweeping the past up into the present to roll it on into the future. This view identifies the seminal megatrends that shape our world, while avoiding the clutter of examining too much confusing detail. Recognise the megatrends to be in tune with the future.

## A Half-Way Point

I was introduced to the world of fast-moving, unpredictable financial events in 1971. Although I was a busy working mum, Friday afternoons were special as I visited my father to watch him making money in the markets. I did not realise it then, but he was my role model, the first successful armchair investor I knew.

As the markets surged in 1971, he used a narrow system based on rising markets. He was optimistic both about the future and his system because Britain was pursuing policies to safeguard full employment and expand the Welfare State. These policies promote economic growth and a rising stock market. If his system failed, he reasoned, the world we knew would have fallen apart – and, sadly, that is precisely what then happened. However, he had sold all his UK shares well before the disastrous collapse of 1973 and 1974 unfolded.

## Lost Global Stability

The stability of the world trading system, excluding the Communist bloc, rested on the American dollar–gold standard, set up in 1944 as the Bretton Woods international monetary agreement. It replaced the pre-war gold standard that Britain first adopted in 1871. After the war, America emerged as the strongest capitalist nation, ousting Britain, by then financially crippled with huge debts incurred in defeating Hitler's Germany. Vast swathes of Britain, continental Europe and Japan lay in ruins, but reconstruction was aided by American loans. Under the dollar–gold standard, the US dollar was freely convertible into gold, and during the post-war recovery period it stabilised the global economy.

The standard was inherently flawed, however, because confidence in the dollar depended on America's economic performance. As the primary importing nation, she accumulated huge trade deficits. In August 1971, the system collapsed. Dollar convertibility abruptly ceased, in recognition of the dollar's declining value. Ripple effects of adverse consequences followed: floating exchange rates, rising global inflation, and a massive rise in oil prises. These tumultuous shocks rocked the entire global economy to its capitalist foundations throughout the 1970s.

Crucial political and economic influences converged to generate massive disruptions in the international trading system. In October 1973, the Opec oil-exporting countries of the Middle East raised the price of their oil fourfold. Oil was the lifeblood of industrial economies, growing more strongly then after years of strenuous reconstruction. The suddenness of the move and the Opec monopoly on oil recycled global cash flows on a monumental scale. Money poured out of the main oil-importing nations – Japan, Western Europe and America, all of which were overdependent on Opec oil – and into the bulging bank accounts of Arab producers. Since the importing nations were forced to pay vastly higher sums for vital oil supplies, a deep global recession ensued. (A recession exists when there is a contraction during at least two consecutive quarters in national output or **Gross Domestic Product (GDP)**, which measures total goods and services produced in the economy over one year.) Money previously allocated for other spending was diverted to buy oil. Drastic spending cuts were abruptly imposed to reduce huge sums owed to oil producers. In 1979 a second big oil price-rise was imposed, delaying into the 1980s the massive adjustment processes then underway.

Among the early responses was a frantic search for oil around the world, to break the Arab stranglehold. Ultimately, important new sources, in Venezuela, the Gulf of Mexico and the North Sea, created a glut. When this coincided with a global recession and reduced demand, the oil price fell dramatically during the late 1990s. Eventually, this price fall led to a series of megamergers among giant oil companies. In 1998, America's Exxon agreed to take over Mobil in the world's biggest industrial merger to that date, of $75.4 billion. Britain's BP agreed to merge with Amoco of America, and Total of France confirmed it would take over PetroFina of Belgium, creating Europe's third-largest oil group by production and reserves. A merger reduces costs and overheads, to squeeze more profit from operations when internal growth is limited. Eliminating duplicate services produces extra profits. In November 1998, with these mergers occurring, world oil prices languished at about $10 a barrel, below the levels of £20 a barrel or more during the 1970s oil-price crisis and cheaper in inflation-adjusted terms than pre-1973 levels. Gasoline in America was cheaper than Coca-Cola; and Saudi Arabia was amassing such vast debts that it borrowed £6 billion from its neighbour, Abu Dhabi.

*'The quadruple rise in the price of crude oil at the end of 1973 had detonated the world's trading system, and money was streaming into Saudi Arabia as nowhere and never before, trailing its usual baggage of power and influence.'*

James Buchan

## The 1973 Political Watershed

These were substantial effects, but the greatest response was in Western political reaction. The 1973 oil price rise marked a political watershed. The economic policies that were centred on full employment and government spending to boost economic growth had dominated the post-war era. These 1960s ideas grew from lessons learned following years of economic suffering during the 1930s. The post-war policies, relying on increased government activity in economic life, became unsustainable. Expansion of the Welfare State and low unemployment were impossible with rapidly rising fuel and wage costs. Two huge rises in oil prices within six years introduced fundamental instabilities in the West's economic programmes.

By 1979, policies promoting 'sound money' and less government debt brought Margaret Thatcher to power in Britain. Ronald Reagan became President of the United States in 1980 proposing similar policies. High interest rates were imposed, to squeeze out inflation. These were crude measures for people facing economic, political and social chaos. Harsh monetary policies were like a dose of 'cold turkey' for the Japanese, Western European and US economies. But after the pain and severe disruptions, the path was set for success during the enterprising eighties, which duly emerged.

Spoiling tactics by the British unionised workforce were curbed and firms were forced to manage more aggressively to protect profits. Japan had no domestic oil supply, yet despite the massive added costs of importing it all, it was one of the first industrial nations to recover from this major dislocation. In America, the 'sound money' idea of balancing the budget ran headlong into the costly buffers of defeating Ronald Reagan's hated enemy, the 'evil empire' of Communism. While US government spending mushroomed, American companies drastically reconstructed themselves, as leaner and more profitable, to match super-successful Japanese competitors. The job losses from this 'downsizing' were more than offset by millions of new jobs in emerging industries. Intense restructuring, coupled with the extraordinary growth in information technology, laid the groundwork for an amazing American economic renaissance and prosperity.

In 1990 and 1991, draconian constraints of uniform exchange rates, dictated by the EU from Brussels, led to Britain's most severe post-war recession. Success in the 1990s sprang from abrupt ejection from Europe's Exchange Rate Mechanism (ERM) in September 1992. Freed from this inappropriate policy, the economy recovered rapidly and galloped ahead, while the European Union suffered slow growth and high unemployment, expensive labour costs and restrictive social regulations.

The broad sweep of economic events in the early 1980s revealed both Britain and America coming to terms with new economic realities through a drastic reshaping of economic life. By tackling the painful issues early, both economies grew fitter and stronger and many companies on both sides of the Atlantic literally reinvented themselves to benefit from the changed climate. The United States enjoyed the longest period of economic growth for the twentieth century; the expansion entered its 107th month (and the history books) in February 2000; growth exceeded 3 per cent in 1996, 1997, 1998 and 1999. These effects were less dramatic in Western Europe, until the concept of a European Union – and then the single currency – generated more momentum to conform to the proven formula that worked such successful transformations in America and Britain.

*'Do not weep; do not wax indignant. Understand.'*

*Baruch Spinoza (1632–77), Jewish philosopher*

## THE EQUITIES CENTURY

The twentieth century was generous to equity investors. Over the shorter term, the FTSE-100 ended ahead in 14 of the 17 years from 1978 to 1995 (the exceptions being 1979, 1990 and 1994), showing an average annual return of just over 12 per cent. The long-term picture is even more impressive. In its 1998 annual equity–gilt study, Credit Suisse First Boston showed that excellent returns from equities spanned 80 years (1918 to 1998): An investor who put £100 into a broad spread of shares in 1918 was a millionaire by December 1998, with a portfolio worth £1,000,351. The real value of this nest egg, after inflation, was £48,290. Yet £100 invested in gilts in 1918 only grew to £13,315 (a paltry £643 after inflation), while in short-term US treasury bills it grew to £7,038 (only £342 after accounting for inflation). The long-term history of inflation partly explains this result. The index of UK prices tripled between 1694 (when the Bank of England was founded) and 1948, but it rose by almost 20 times from 1948 to 1994. This finding was reported by two Bank of England economists, H. McFarlane and P. Mortimer-Lee, in the Bank of England Quarterly Bulletin of May 1994 in an article entitled 'Inflation over 300 years'.

---

**LONG-TERM RETURNS FROM DIFFERENT ASSET CLASSES HELD OVER 80 YEARS (£100 INVESTED FROM 1918 TO 1998)**

|                   | Equities £ | Gilts £ | Treasury Bills £ |
| ----------------- | ---------- | ------- | ---------------- |
| Before Inflation  | 1,000,351  | 13,315  | 7,038            |
| After Inflation   | 48,290     | 643     | 342              |

---

Studies by Barclays Capital, on returns of asset classes, showed that UK shares outperformed gilts and cash over the century, by 6 per cent a year. The outperformance, or equity premium, was remarkably consistent over all but the shortest periods. Research for America produced a similar result. The premium exists because risk is the essence of capitalism. Hence equities yield more than cash or gilts and should be better rewarded. Performance improved between 1980 and 1999 and price/earnings ratios soared. Michael Edesess, an economist with Lockwood Advisers, compared price/earnings ratios from 1933 to 1997 with the subsequent 10-year earnings growth. He found the market was right in raising share prices to above-average multiples in 77 per cent of cases. The P/Es rose in the 1990s because investors had more company information and realised that owning shares had become less risky so the equity premium fell as compared to gilts.

This poses a paradox. If equities outperform safe assets, the risk of holding them for any 10-year period should be negligible. But there are two causes for pessimism. First, a minority of investors – those who are luckier or better informed – enjoy superior returns. When everyone thinks shares are the best investment, no one makes exceptional gains. This problem could arise in America where over 35 million people own equities directly. A whole generation of British adults – perhaps 34 million of them – have yet to discover the wealth-creating equities bonanza, and so the opportunity profits for informed investors should continue for many years. Second, if the twentieth century was special, the excellent returns may be unrepeatable. The unique effects included secular economic growth trends, the transition to post-industrialism, decades of higher-than-expected inflation, and the growth in numbers of listed companies. There was high productivity growth and a rise in knowledge-based industries developed by private entrepreneurs. Equities were re-rated as institutional investors switched from fixed-interest assets into shares, thereby boosting prices. With low commodity prices, falling interest rates and low inflation, however, there will be lower growth and gilts might again become more popular.

The main reasons favouring equities during the twentieth century are given in the box below.

---

**SPECIAL FACTORS FAVOURING EQUITIES IN THE TWENTIETH CENTURY**

1. Major secular economic trends.
2. The move to post-industrialisation and the rise of the service industries.
3. Decades of higher than expected inflation (destroyed the purchasing power of cash).
4. Greater prominence of public companies in national life.
5. Transition by institutional investors out of fixed-interest investments (due to losses from high inflation) and into equities.
6. Re-rating of equities by investors with this move by the professional investors.
7. Higher rates of productivity growth.
8. Explosive rise of knowledge-based new industries: computers, mobile telephones, biotechnology, Internet companies, in the hands of private entrepreneurs.

---

*'An unstable exchange rate undoubtedly presents difficulties but they are nothing compared with a rate that is wildly overvalued as ours was when we joined the ERM. At least then we were able to escape.'*

Roger Bootle, author of The Death of Inflation

Do these special factors explain the consistent outperformance of equities in the twentieth century? Underlying growth in the global economy has underpinned this great performance. Britain had only four serious recessions since 1945 (see table below); during the post-war period economies were growing rather than contracting. With economic growth positive in almost nine years out of ten, growth is generated among most of the firms that comprise the economy. A massive dislocation in global events would be needed, as occurred in 1973, to disturb this long-term picture. We cannot know when – or, indeed, whether – a huge disruption will halt the equity outperformance. In 1982, when two financial economists, Mehra and Prescott, first noted the high equity premium puzzle, the world was poised on the brink of its longest bull market ever.

## THE PEAKS IN PAST BUSINESS CYCLES

| Economic Peak | UK Stock Market Peak | Major UK Post-war Recessions |
| --- | --- | --- |
| 1958 | 1958 | 1958 |
| 1972 | May 1972 | 1973–1975 |
| 1979 | June 1979 | 1979–1982 |
| 1988 | July 1987 | 1989–1993 |

By understanding the links between the economy and markets, you do not need to know how events will unfold: with your growing expertise, you can exploit profitable opportunities wherever and whenever they arise. One advantage of being an active investor running your own New Millennium Portfolio is that if the global scene turns unfavourable, you will have the expertise to react and be better placed than most to protect your growing nest egg.

## Megatrends

By looking at the underlying global events that shaped the world since the 1940s, we can see how crucial global changes set Britain and America on a fast-growth track. From January 1996 to January 1999, FTSE 100 companies rose on average 70 per cent, while those in the Dow Jones Industrial Index doubled, reflecting the emergence of America's longest peacetime expansion of the century. Yet longer-term, Britain is sinking down the wealth league in a decline reaching back to the 1880s when the British Empire was 'the workshop of the world'. By 1999, Britain ranked 16th in the table of GDP, or output per head, down from 1st place in 1900. But more recently, with tough political and economic decisions, a new climate has evolved and the economy has flourished, although this has taken many years to bring about.

I feel optimistic about the future, when setting current events into this long-term picture. I think a flexible system for achieving personal wealth, based on the 5-Level Learning Progression, will continue to work, although it may become increasingly driven by European or American markets rather than being focused solely on London. My optimism is grounded on evidence for megatrends that seem almost unstoppable. They are forcing the top-class companies in Western nations to think and act globally, inspiring a rising tide of cross-border megamergers. Deals worth $2.4 trillion in 1998 looked set to be comfortably exceeded in 1999. Some mergers were defensive, to bolster profits in declining industries such as oil, defence, motors and banks; but others sprang from aggressive growth potentials in industries such as Internet services and telecommunications that were experiencing explosive growth.

The cult of a world-class élite of companies was another megatrend. About 200 multinationals account for about a quarter of world output, with companies in this premier corps blazing their trail internationally. The UK can claim no more than 25 members of this club, but investors who follow the fortunes of the FTSE 100 Top Ten are almost bound to be investing in the *crème de la crème* of Britain's most renowned and profit-generating companies. Such companies were excellently placed to exploit the beneficial economic fundamentals prevailing in the 1990s. In an environment of low inflation and low interest rates they will undoubtedly continue to prosper, perhaps increasingly through additional mergers.

Yet even if the long-term trend is highly positive, there could be detours or setbacks ahead. One such detour may be a bout of global deflation, not seen since the 1930s. Deflation is bad news for equities because prices, and therefore profits, consistently fall. Modern economies are strongly resistant to falling prices, so a deeply rooted deflation may be avoided. But if you stay alert and in tune with the great sweep of history, I believe you can profit from the overriding megatrends as they unfold.

## THE EFFECT OF GLOBAL ECONOMIC EVENTS

Having set the global scene, we turn to our local universe of events. Scanning the recent trends for the British economy, we observe the business cycles that stock market movements have reflected. Quoted companies operate in the real economy, and so events that affect their ability to thrive and prosper will impact on the price at which their shares are freely traded. Britain experienced four main post-war recessions (see earlier table), grounded mainly in the overexpansion of a preceding boom and its attendant high level of inflation. Each recession led to lower growth and rising unemployment.

The first recession in 1958, following the Suez crisis, centred on Middle East oil; and the next two, in 1973–1975 and 1979–1982, stemmed mainly from oil price rises. The 1989–1993 recession was rather special: it followed Britain's entry into the European Exchange Rate Mechanism at too high a rate. In these UK recessions output fell by a cumulative average of 10 per cent, and they were just as severe as the inter-war recessions of 1920–1921 and 1929–1932.

At a time when the economy in the 1980s was recovering from two deep recessions, major North Sea oil revenues were filling the UK government's coffers. These rising revenues coincided with and underwrote the Conservative experiment with 'sound money' by taking firm control over public spending. The FTSE 100 rose during 1984 and 1985 (see chart on page 66). During the trading range in 1986 the oil price was collapsing and, in February 1987, finance ministers of the G5 nations (the Group of Five – America, Japan, Britain, France and Canada) decided to support the dollar by buying dollars with their reserves. Their intervention increased global **money supply** (which measures the amount of money in the economy). The rise was equivalent to a financial boost of $100 billion and generated a massive boom in bonds, property and stock markets. Share prices rose to unsustainable heights by late 1987.

Increasing the money supply encourages people to invest in the stock market through their pensions or **unit trust** holdings. Savings decisions that divert money to financial institutions, boosting their cash (or liquidity), can trigger a new market uptrend. Professional investors enter the market as it is rising strongly, because they know holding cash in a rising market is a certain recipe for fund underperformance. When the major institutions hold plenty of cash, prices rise as they invest it. Conversely, when they have low cash holdings and less free money to push up prices, the market may hit a peak. High levels of institutional liquidity may not lift prices if professional managers are worried about the condition of the underlying economy. High liquidity did not lead to high prices during 1988 because investors were recovering from the October 1987 stock market crash. In summer 1998, as the FTSE 100 fell by 25 per cent, pension funds held 6.8 per cent of their assets in cash, the highest proportion since 1990, when base rates were 15 per cent compared with 7.25 per cent in summer 1998.

The rapid recovery from the October 1987 crash was as unexpected as the suddenness of the crash itself, but stock markets can foretell events up to about two years ahead. By late 1989, conditions were unsettled and the Japanese market had reached an all-time peak. The London market moved in a broad trading range, reflecting the uncertainties. During 1990, the global event that undermined investor confidence was the Gulf War threat, underlining yet again the central role that oil supplies play in the economic life of industrial nations. This uncertainty held the market back in 1990, but entry to the European Exchange Rate Mechanism in October 1990, originally welcomed by the market, ushered in a very severe recession.

*'Stock markets like a situation where the monetary authorities will keep money very easy and interest rates low because the outlook for growth looks so uncertain.'*

Roger Nightingale, economist

## The Impact of Interest Rates

In the depths of recession, between January and September 1991, shares in London rose 30 per cent while the gloom deepened. The early rise stemmed from instant relief when the Gulf War proved short-lived. Yet by late 1991 the problems of membership of the European Exchange Rate Mechanism were exposed. It was the second-worse year in terms of declining GDP since the 1940s, the worst being 1980. The London stock market rose over several months as base rates fell in a series of small cuts, from 14 per cent in January 1991 to 10.5 per cent in September of that year. Small incremental falls keep the market rising, anticipating more cuts.

During the winter of 1991–1992, with rates becalmed at 10.5 per cent, the market entered a lengthy trading range, searching for Chancellor Norman Lamont's celebrated 'green shoots of recovery'. The uncertainty ended abruptly with the UK's famous withdrawal from the Exchange Rate Mechanism in September 1992. Politicians and the public were stunned by this disaster, but it merits a closer look, because the stock market thought differently. The government and Bank of England officials saw withdrawal as the total failure of the economic policy for closer integration with Europe. They were convinced that the UK economy would resume its errant path of high inflation and low growth outside the constraints of the European system. The market knew better. Expulsion meant sky-high interest rates to stay in the system could be discarded. Lower rates would hasten the arrival of a much-needed recovery. The recovery began in 1992, but not until 1993 did most businesses – and then most families – become aware of it, because pessimism persists long after the trend has turned.

As we see, therefore, a series of declines in interest rates move the market. On previous occasions, as in early 1987, 1993 and in 1996, they triggered large stock market uptrends. Interest-rate-driven price rises can occur even when the outlook for company profits is unfavourable, as happened in October and November 1998, when globally surging markets on London, Wall Street and continental Europe rallied by over 20 per cent in 8 weeks, from the October lows caused by the global financial crisis. This rally was prompted by falling base rates in early October 1998 and was sustained by a large series of cross-border mergers between multinational companies.

*Rising* interest rates are unwelcome news for the markets and produce the opposite result. In February 1994, Alan Greenspan, Chairman of the US Federal Reserve, the country's central bank, raised US interest rates by a minute 0.25 per cent. This tiny rise triggered a sharp 5 months' decline in bond and share prices, because investors realised it represented the first of many rises and a change in direction for interest-rate policy. Falling prices were responding to that wider scene – an expected series of interest rate rises – before they happened. Conversely, when Alan Greenspan cut rates unexpectedly in October 1998, in response to a looming international credit crisis, the US markets surged back to the high levels they reached in July 1998, despite continuing profits warnings from several major American companies.

## THE MAIN MARKET MOVERS

In several ways, therefore, underlying events shape major market movements. Changes in the direction of interest rates are among the most important, as they signal an attempt to alter the direction of the economy, either from recession to recovery, or to slow down an excessive boom. When rates fall, people save money on interest for loans and mortgages, giving them extra to spend on goods or services. A boost to personal spending is the antidote to recession, and interest-rate falls indicate that the government wants consumer spending to rise and revive economic activity. Investors recognise this link and anticipate the recovery, often by many months, thereby driving prices higher.

Increasing the money supply (i.e. putting more money into the economy) is often a consequence of a series of interest-rate falls and is another key contributor to rising stock markets. Investors may react swiftly to major global events, such as the threat of war or an international financial crisis. The behaviour of Wall Street exerts a powerful influence on global investors: they rejoice when Wall Street rises and rush to sell when it declines sharply. Another notable market mover is reaction to government policies that affect economic activity. Policy changes may involve interest rates, but might also be errors, as with Britain's joining of Europe's Exchange Rate Mechanism at the wrong rate. Again, markets respond positively to an important bout of international merger activity, hoping for rising profits from subsequent restructuring, but they naturally abhor the announcement of profits warnings, as these indicate lower returns.

---

**THE MAIN MARKET MOVERS**
........................................

1. Changes in the direction of interest rates.
2. A series of interest rate moves, either up (bad news) or down (good news).
3. Rising amounts of money in the economy (increased liquidity).
4. Major global incidents, including the threat of war in strategically important regions.
5. Following Wall Street, which represents 40 per cent of global stock market value.
6. Government policy changes.
7. Heightened merger activity or unexpected profit warnings.

---

*'People rarely recognise recessions until they've already begun.'*

David Mackie, chief UK economist at J. P. Morgan

## RECOGNISE THE ONSET OF RECESSION
............................................................................................

The whole economy is interconnected, and so bad news in one area soon spreads to others. Every month, key indicators published by government or other organisations are reported on television and in the press. The jargon is obscure and you may not understand what the figures imply. To understand the market, it helps to know how the economy is faring. Gross Domestic Product (national output) is reported quarterly. The Chancellor of the Exchequer makes future GDP forecasts in his budgets and budget statements. Falling GDP can tip the economy into recession. The Office for National Statistics (ONS) releases monthly figures on industrial production. They show the percentage change in output on the previous month, which depends on consumer demand – if that falls, so will output.

The index compiled by the Chartered Institute of Purchasing Managers is updated monthly and covers over 300 manufacturers. An index reading below 50 implies the sector is shrinking. By late 1998, while the service sector seemed unaffected, the manufacturing sector was in a deep recession due to the high level of sterling – it was contracting at the fastest rate since 1991. The index fell for 8 consecutive months, and by November 1998 it was 41.1 compared with 41.4 in October. In addition, the Chartered Institute of Purchasing & Supply reported the first monthly fall in services activity in November 1998 since it started tracking the sector in July 1996.

Such surveys help investors keep in touch with changing economic activity as it happens.

Sales figures, published monthly, express the percentage rise or fall in consumer spending on the previous month. The British Retail Consortium produces regular surveys, which then reflect rising pessimism during recession. Consumer spending, at over £500 billion a year or 63 per cent of the UK's GDP, plays a pivotal role; in America, consumer spending is 70 per cent of GDP. If spending falls, the economy slows, manufacturers have fewer orders, their stocks rise and retailers report lower sales. Government may reduce interest rates to stimulate demand. History shows inventory cutbacks can cause recession. In three periods during the 1980s and 1990s, stocks were run down: 1979–1981, 1989–1991 and 1996. On the first two occasions, recession followed.

The most influential survey is produced quarterly by the Confederation of British Industry (CBI) to assess confidence among UK companies. The November 1998 survey revealed business optimism at its lowest level since 1980. More firms were cutting export prices than at any time since 1945. Official employment statistics are reported monthly, as a percentage increase or decrease on the previous month. Job losses rise as recession begins.

Inflation can spread through the whole economy, to retail and house prices, wages and the stock market. The UK government set a target of 2.5% inflation for the Bank of England to meet by monitoring interest rates. If consumer demand rises, companies raise prices and the cost of living (measured by the **Retail Prices Index – RPI**) rises. Workers trigger a price rise spiral by demanding higher wages to keep pace with rising prices. With more money, people spend more and the economy booms. Rising prices can bolster rising house and stock market prices. If wage inflation matches the RPI, firms can control prices and sell more, improving their profits. But if wages rise faster than productivity, inflation grows and interest rates may have to rise in order to curb wage inflation. High interest rates boost sterling, so exports suffer and the economy slows.

The onset of recession is not an isolated event. It occurs in step with the demise of a bull market and a booming economy. Some adverse factors that may play a prominent role in stoking the boom include a loose monetary policy that encourages speculation on the stock market and rampant house-price rises. At such times, the economy is highly unstable, but there may be obvious indications of the boom's imminent end. For example, astonishingly high first-day rises for new companies floated on the stock exchange or a sudden increase in merger activity or **rights issues**, when companies ask their shareholders for money to fund expansion or pay off debts.

## HOW TO RECOGNISE A LOOMING RECESSION

| Key Indicators to Watch | Surveys, Indicators and Figures |
| --- | --- |
| 1. Growth across the economy | Gross Domestic Product (GDP) |
| 2. Growth in the industrial sector | Industrial production figures |
| 3. Consumer spending | Sales figures by British Retail Consortium |
| 4. Business confidence | Confederation of British Industry (CBI) surveys |
| 5. Unemployment statistics | Monthly government figures |
| 6. Inflation in prices | Retail Prices Index (RPI) |
| 7. Wage inflation | Government figures on average earnings |
| 8. Stock market performance | FTSE 100 & All Share benchmark indices |
| 9. House prices | Figures by Royal Institute of Chartered Surveyors or Halifax Housing Survey |
| 10. Public confidence | GFK, a research firm for the European Commission |

*'There has been much talk recently of an impending recession and the message appears to have had a significant effect.'*

Tony Lees, director of consumer research, NOP Research

## The Public Mood

Public confidence is another key indicator, widely reported in the press. If people feel financially insecure, they cut their spending and worry about job losses.

Small swings in confidence can produce dramatic changes in peoples' savings patterns. In the mid-1970s, when, as we saw, world affairs rapidly turned hostile, savings peaked at 15 per cent of incomes. Experts predicted that high inflation would prompt less saving, as the value of money declined; in fact, the opposite happened. Faced with the declining value of their savings, people saved more. By the peak of the 1988 boom, the savings ratio had plunged to 5 per cent, with people perhaps relying on the massive appreciation in the value of their homes to provide savings nest eggs. The overall effect of public confidence is a mixture: fears about job insecurity, global crises and inflation. Add them all together and the result is reflected in savings patterns.

Although most people rarely give a thought to stock market movements, public mood swings of optimism and pessimism mirror how stock market investors behave. So we should not be surprised if the public, *en masse*, can predict a threatening recession. In November 1999, members of the Bank of England's Monetary Policy Committee, which advises the Governor on future interest-rate levels, acknowledged that they were focusing more on surveys in addition to official data, as surveys are forward-looking and a good test of consumer and corporate psychology.

A checklist of items to watch for in recession is set out below.

*'I like buying companies that can be run by monkeys – because one day they will be.'*

*Peter Lynch,* One Up on Wall Street

---

**CHECKLIST FOR THE ONSET OF RECESSION        DATE . . . . . .**

1. Has Gross Domestic Product been falling/rising for the last six months?
2. Are industrial production figures lower or higher over the last 6 months?
3. Was the last Chartered Institute of Purchasing Managers' report negative or positive on manufacturing output?
4. Are recent consumer sales higher or lower than last month?
5. Is the latest Confederation of British Industry Survey pessimistic or optimistic about future prospects for business?
6. Were the latest unemployment figures boosted by recent job losses?
7. Is the Retail Prices Index (RPI) under control at the target 2.5 per cent level?
8. If not, is the RPI higher or lower?
9. Do government figures on average earnings show rising or falling wage inflation in the economy?
10. Is the stock market rising, falling or in a trading range?
11. Are house prices rising, falling or static as announced by recent reports from the Royal Institute of Chartered Surveyors (or Halifax figures)?
12. Are there many/few house boards with sale notices in your area?
13. Do newspaper reports suggest the public is gloomy about economic prospects and their jobs, or are people confident?
14. Are people in your street, office, factory losing their jobs?
15. Are brokers and traders in the City receiving huge bonuses because trade is booming?
16. Are analysts, financial journalists or brokers optimistic/pessimistic about future prospects?

*'The rewards of risk-bearing are so high as almost to eliminate the risk itself.'*

John Kay, Peter Moores director of the Said Business School at Oxford University

## RECOGNISE THE ONSET OF RECOVERY

The importance of recognising the onset of recession is central to investors' decision-making skills. As an economic boom ends, stock market prices are near a peak. This is not a sensible time to buy. Any action that enhances your investment timing will improve the potential growth in your portfolio. Follow the business cycle and watch the economy fall into a recession. Wait to time your share purchases until the seeds of the forthcoming recovery are more visible.

The recovery usually unfolds in three phases. When the worst of the financial crises are over and interest rates are falling, the economy may stop contracting. During this early phase, demand will stop falling, corporate debts should begin to decline and the overstretched banking system will haltingly begin recapitalisation, as bad-debt levels finally come under control. In phase 2, there is a widespread return to profitability. Initially, it is achieved by cost-cutting and the elimination of spare capacity. During phase 2, there is finally evidence for the emerging recovery and canny investors will already be fully invested, waiting for the arrival of phase 3. When it begins, phase 3 marks the return of growth in demand. The recovery is fully established and visible to all, but overshooting on the upside can then generate an unsustainable boom, in which the seeds for the next recession are slowly being sown. These three phases are summarised in the table below.

### THE PHASES OF RECOVERY

| Phase | Investment Action |
|---|---|
| 1. The economic crisis abates; interest rates are falling. | Begin to invest. |
| 2. There is a widespread return to profitability. | Be fully invested. |
| 3. The return of growth in demand is clearly visible. | Take some profits or ride out the next recession. |

## BUILD YOUR PORTFOLIO

For the small investor, success can be significantly improved by building a carefully planned portfolio for the long term. You may think all investors are portfolio-builders but this is not necessarily so, as is revealed by the way institutional investors have changed their portfolio balances.

During the 1980s, small growth companies were firm favourites, considered the lifeblood of a thriving economy. Top performers each year were tiny firms, largely unknown to most investors but keenly followed by the growth school. A dramatic change of strategy in the 1990s saw institutional investors ignoring small companies. Most of these companies manufacture products rather than provide services, and they operate in sectors dominated by manufacturing, which struggle when sterling or interest rates are high. Small companies, in engineering, construction, textiles, distribution, paper and packaging, and house builders, are mainly oriented domestically; they serve the home market, in retailing or service industries, and so high interest rates reduce their profits. For exporters, a high sterling exchange rate in the late 1990s decreased profits. The global financial crisis of summer 1998 heightened investors' aversion to risk, particularly in areas involving smaller companies, where extra risks are inherent. During the crisis, investors shunned smaller companies: their prices failed to recover with the main market in November and December 1998. For all these reasons, small companies lost favour with professional investors. Institutional support is a key criterion for FASTER GAINS. When they neglect the sector, share prices can languish for months or years.

Evidence suggests that smaller companies may be falling behind in the real world of the marketplace. According to research on smaller companies dating back to 1955 by Professor Paul Marsh of the London Business School, they outperformed the equity market by about 6 per cent a year from 1955 to the end of the 1980s. During that time, UK small companies increased their dividends at double the rate of the rest of the market; but during the 1990s, their dividends lagged behind. Global events offer an economic backdrop to these facts. In 1989 the Berlin Wall came down; then, the European single currency arrived; and, throughout the 1990s, information technology was learning how to turn the global market into commercial reality. Small companies were poorly equipped to gain from these developments. This, then, was the other side of the decline in institutional interest.

During the long 1990s economic boom, many fund managers adopted a global perspective for balancing their portfolios. Some industries – banks, telecommunications, pharmaceuticals, software, aircraft manufacture and computers – were ideally placed to exploit the new world order. Share prices of world-class multinational companies dramatically outpaced their smaller brethren: FTSE 100 companies grew 70 per cent through 1996 to December 1998 while the small company index rose about 10 per cent. When fund managers face investment uncertainties, buying stakes in large companies is less risky than buying into smaller firms. In time and effort, it may take almost as long to research a company worth £100 million as to cover one worth £100 *billion*. Yet much larger stakes can be invested in multinational giants. If the giant prospers, so will the gains. Sudden buy decisions also favour larger companies as bigger sums can be invested quickly.

Throughout the 1980s and 1990s, the world economy grew faster than the major economies of Europe and North America. World-class companies have branded products that enjoy high profit margins and are better geared to capture that extra growth, with lower risks to investors, making them doubly attractive to fund managers. In faster-growing periods, companies like Glaxo Wellcome, Vodafone AirTouch, BP Amoco and Diageo thrive, either directly through exports or through local operations. Efficient management are motivated by large share options in the success of their companies; effective management helps these companies to maximise their potential.

The superb gains made on multinationals may not last indefinitely, although their prospects will remain favourable while the global economy enjoys low interest rates and inflation. This is an ideal background for thriving growth companies. Ultimately, some small companies should return to favour. Truly great growth stories retain a loyal following and defy the rest by rising even in unfavourable market conditions.

## Wealth Creation Through PAYS

You can enhance your success by building a well-constructed long-term portfolio around a group of fast-growing companies. By Level V, this will become your actively managed New Millennium Portfolio. Our mnemonic here is PAYS; it covers the four key elements to ensure you are targeting wealth-creation. So let us look at each item in turn.

*'Only the fittest and most innovative global firms can survive in today's deflationary, technology-dominated world.'*

Guy Monson, *chief investment officer, Sarasin Investment Management*

**P: Portfolio-building.** Portfolio-building is an integral part of the 5-Level Learning Progression. At first, investors create a Paper Top Ten Portfolio to watch the progress of the 10 most valuable UK companies, before buying their own portfolio of them in due course. By learning core investment skills, the investors move on to create an active New Millennium Portfolio. Throughout the programme, investors always hold a portfolio of 10–15 companies, rather than a random collection of shares chosen by applying a set formula.

While stock-picking is a vital and necessary skill for big gains, the skills required for portfolio-building are slightly different as it takes a different perspective (see table on page 150). Stock-pickers search constantly for companies with large profit potentials, even though the risks of sudden disappointments or profit setbacks are high. The share price of a small company that announces a profits warning, a delay in a key order, or the abrupt departure of a manager, can be decimated within hours or days.

One major problem that all small companies must tackle is managing growth. Some take over another company and fail to successfully merge the two groups together. This dismal fate befell photocopier distributor Danka Business Systems, which paid £438 million in 1996 to acquire Kodak's photocopier business. The deal doubled Danka's size but by 1998 the merger was proving intractable. A similar disaster struck MAID, the on-line information provider. Growth prospects slumped after it bought the bigger Knight-Ridder information business, renamed itself Dialog, and then hit unmanageable problems integrating the acquisition into existing operations. By December 1998, Dialog was worth far less than the £285 million paid for Knight-Ridder. Repeated setbacks hit Telspec, the telecoms manufacturer, with the shares falling dramatically over three years, while Microfocus, another small IT company, met hard times in 1998 after some years of profitable growth. In retailing, the list of companies unable successfully to manage growth is dauntingly long: Body Shop, Laura Ashley, Next, Tie Rack and Filofax. We saw in Level II with Medeva, how quickly losses emerge if you stay invested in shares facing sudden adversity, hoping for recovery that is indefinitely delayed. Evidence shows that when small companies hit a bad patch, more setbacks can follow. By merely holding on, hoping for a resumption of growth, your optimism may be misplaced.

*'The big money is made in the first two years of a bull market.'*

*William O'Neil,* How to Make Money in Stocks

In autumn 1998, profit warnings from small companies occurred almost daily. Share prices fell across the small-company sector as institutional investors sold, worried about abrupt market falls, when selling small company shares is more difficult. (Only a few market makers make prices in each small company's shares. When bad news is announced, they are as reluctant – as both you and I would be – to increase their holdings. They slash prices drastically to discourage sellers and so reduce their risk of having to buy in more stock.) More market makers cover large companies, giving greater dealing liquidity. You could easily sell 5,000 Tesco shares, even in a falling market. But trying to sell 5,000 shares in a small firm, like Cirqual, the engineering group, or Black Arrow, the office equipment provider, in a falling market produces a lower price than selling only 500 or 1,000 shares. Such technical factors influence professionals in uncertain markets, and so they reduce their holdings in smaller companies in order to protect portfolios from the necessity of being forced into sudden selling decisions.

### STOCK-PICKING AND PORTFOLIO-BUILDING COMPARED

| **Stock-picking** | **Portfolio-building** |
|---|---|
| 1. Relies on a constant search for companies with strong gains potential. | 1. The search is for companies with ultra-long-term profitable potentials. |
| 2. Takes a shorter time view. | 2. Takes a longer time view. |
| 3. Faces the problem of replacing a poor performer with another showing better prospects. | 3. Avoids the problem of continually replacing failed choices with those showing better prospects. |
| 4. Risk of losses if the new choice does not live up to its early promise and is sold at a loss. | 4. More latitude for riding the dips as history shows it is more profitable to stay invested for the long term. |
| 5. Expensive on dealing and commission charges. | 5. Cheaper on dealing costs and commissions because there are fewer deals. |

*'There's an old saying that bull markets don't die of old age, it's the Fed that kills them.'*

*Rupert de la Porter, Hill Samuel Asset Management, North American desk*

Another difference between stock-pickers and portfolio-builders is their investment time horizons. When a stock you are following suffers a setback or reaches a high valuation that you think may be unsustainable, you might consider selling. But then you face the problem of finding yet another small growth company with promising potentials, for reinvesting your proceeds. Each time you sell and reinvest, you increase your level of risk, because during the changeover period you can never be sure that your new choice will prove to be a winner. Portfolio-builders invest for the long term and are psychologically more willing to ride out the dips. They avoid the continuous difficulty of searching for new growth stories to follow. Long-term investors save the additional costs of buying and selling commissions with each change, and the risk of choosing a company that does not perform as well as they expected.

Undoubtedly, all portfolios benefit from including a few small growth companies because of the potential rewards. But how many should you hold and for how long? Essentially, they should be in the minority. Plan a portfolio around a majority of high-capitalisation companies with strong future profits potential. Buy them when they fall along with the whole market. Hold the few smaller companies you add as long as the growth story stays intact. If you hold about 15 different sets of shares, at least 10 should be in large companies listed in the FTSE 100 or 250 indices, with a value of £1,000 million or more. The remaining 5 shares may have small market capitalisations of around £100 million. Shares in small companies can remain static for months, making it difficult to buy on a fall, but shares in the largest companies constantly change hands, so you can take advantage of falling prices. Sometimes, even if the whole market falls, small company shares stay unchanged; but if you are watching a larger company, having set a target buy price, this might suddenly appear, as good companies sometimes suffer share prices falls along with those with poorer prospects.

### *Your Investment Family*

Private investors should consider themselves as controllers of their own investment funds. If you do this, your portfolio-building will be completely different from how institutional investors create a balanced portfolio. Small investors should plan what I call a 'family of investments'. As the active manager of all your financial assets, with a long-term plan to build wealth, this includes a range of assets: buying a house on a mortgage, accumulating a pension fund for retirement, buying life assurance to protect vulnerable family members from the breadwinner's sudden death, and long-term savings plans that are less volatile than equities. Your financial health depends on creating a balanced portfolio to cover all such eventualities. While it is possible to build wealth with a portfolio of equities alone, it is more prudent to diversify risk with a broader asset spread. Within this financial family, however, your growing portfolio of company shares commands centre stage. It is the powerhouse of your growing wealth.

## Your Investment Family

1. Buy your house on a mortgage.
2. Accumulate a pension fund for retirement.
3. Buy life assurance protection for your family.
4. Use long-term savings plans to finance major family events, like paying for university education or a daughter's wedding.
5. Build your New Millennium Portfolio of self-selected company shares.

*'The art of good management is to anticipate the difficulties and to react to a changing environment.'*

*Dr Tom McKillop, chief executive designate of AstroZeneca, January 1999*

**A: Asset Allocation.** How you allocate your assets within your total funds is yet another key aspect of portfolio-building. It covers the way that you distribute your funds between different asset classes and usually means diversifying your resources across such areas as cash, property, bonds, foreign equities and UK equities. If you are buying your home on a mortgage, inevitably a disproportionately large slice of your future wealth will be tied up in that one purchase. Notwithstanding this large commitment, your principal focus centres on a specific goal: to meet set targets and create wealth. Home ownership is one desirable element in these long-term intentions, but it remains only one part of the overall scheme. With only limited financial resources but an infinite willingness to learn, over any 10-year term the best returns should come from equities. Yet even if you hold most of your wealth in equities, do not neglect the main prudent measures required to improve your finances. Always keep a sensible amount of cash as an emergency fund and build a sizeable pension fund for retirement – if your pension is inadequate, your portfolio will have to provide for extras. This may affect your ability to choose the best potential companies if you are unduly worried about the income potential of those choices. Through the 5-Level Progression, pension-building is another plank in your planned programme, again using equities or tracker funds for their long-term growth prospects.

Mark Capleton at HSBC found that, given a choice between UK equities, conventional fixed-interest gilts, index-linked gilts and overseas equities, an optimal portfolio based on returns since 1986 would contain only UK equities and cash. However, this may not be a suitable asset split for a portfolio to cover 20 or 30 years. Professionals plan a well-diversified portfolio, with a range of assets classes. This is a prudent route for them, but for private investors a highly focused portfolio of equities plus cash works well when set within the outlines of owning a sensible investment family.

A portfolio of equities plus cash is risky if you remain a passive investor in the long term. If you decide on that, adjust your assets as described in the chapter on Level I in order to reduce the risks. However, a portfolio of equities plus cash is far *less* risky if you become active and closely follow the fortunes of the companies whose shares you own. Over time, you improve your capital growth by selling poorly performing companies and staying long term with the best-performing shares.

Modify the composition of your portfolio if one of the companies you hold falls below its uptrend on the chart. From your reading, can you tell if there are short-term reasons for the poor performance? Alternatively, you may find after 5 or 6 years that your Top Ten Portfolio is quite unbalanced. Some holdings will be worth far more than others, even though they were all originally bought at around 10 per cent of your starting capital. We can see this operating by examining the value of the July 1998 portfolio on 5 November 1999. On 4 January 1999 the BP–Amoco merger was complete and BP Amoco became the largest FTSE 100 company by market capitalisation. A possible merger between Vodafone and AirTouch of America (subsequently clinched on 15 January 1999) plus huge excitement over telecoms growth and future mergers had lifted Vodafone AirTouch from 10th to 2nd position. In the table on page 154, the rankings of the portfolio are shown, with HSBC at number 6 still excluded. The changing fortunes of the Top Ten Portfolio show plenty of action. BP Amoco, Vodafone AirTouch and BT had ousted Glaxo Wellcome from top slot down to 4th place. Lloyds TSB had fallen from 3rd to 8th rank, Diageo was 12th, and SmithKline Beecham was at 7th. Merger activity had lifted AstraZeneca to 6th place. Barclays was lying at 10th place. BAT, demerged from its insurance interests, stood at 37th – although in January 1999 a merger with America's Rothman was announced.

*'Success comes from focusing in on what you really like and are good at – not challenging every random thing.'*

*Bill Gates, Chairman and co-founder of Microsoft*

### PROGRESS OF JULY 1998 TOP TEN PORTFOLIO AS AT 5 NOVEMBER 1999*

| Rank | Company | Number of Shares | Price (p) | Value** (£) |
|---|---|---|---|---|
| 1 | BP Amoco | 226[a] | 541 | 1,223 |
| 4 | Glaxo Wellcome | 51 | 1,856 | 947 |
| 3 | British Telecom | 118 | 1,102 | 1,300 |
| 7 | SmithKline Beecham | 124 | 880 | 1,091 |
| 8 | Lloyds TSB | 103 | 852 | 878 |
| 9 | Shell | 232 | 442.5 | 1,027 |
| 2 | Vodafone AirTouch | 555[b] | 317 | 1,759 |
| 6 | AstraZeneca | 39 | 2818 | 1,099 |
| 12 | Diageo | 128 | 596.5 | 764 |
| 25 | Allied Zurich | 67 | 777.5 | 521 |
| Cash | | | | 2 |
| **Overall Total** | | | | **10,611** |

\* FTSE 100 on 20 July 1998: 6179. FTSE 100 on 5 November 1999: 6356.6.

\*\* Figures rounded up or down to the nearest pound.

[a] BPAmoco share split in September 1999: 113 shares became 226.

[b] Vodafone AirTouch had a 4 for 1 share split in October 1999: 111 shares became 555.

The portfolio had only been running for 15 months but the range in values spread from £521 for Allied Zurich to £1,759 for Vodafone Air-Touch. Allied Zurich originally cost £500, as it was split out of BAT in September 1998. By November 1999 I was disenchanted with the banks. The portfolio was showing four main laggard areas, oil (Shell but not BP Amoco), alcoholic beverages (Diageo), and banking (Lloyds TSB) (both Diageo and Lloyds TSB were below their purchase prices). The fourth disappointing sector was the pharmaceuticals: Glaxo Wellcome and SmithKline Beecham, although AstraZeneca was purchased with £899 from the sale of Barclays and BAT and was therefore showing a profit. Three star performers were BP Amoco, Vodafone AirTouch and BT. The original balance was gone, but I rarely sell the best performers as they indicate investor confidence in continued growth. I always stay with the winners. During the summer of 1999 the pharmaceutical sector was hit by adverse news flows on new drug approvals. Glaxo Wellcome even issued a mild profits warning. When evaluating the performance of your Top Ten Portfolio you should try to stay with all the companies within the top ten long term while reshuffling those companies that have fallen decisively and have then stayed below no. 10.

On 5 November 1999 the FTSE 100 (at 6356.6) was 2.9 per cent above its mid-July 1998 high of 6179 but the Top Ten Portfolio was in profit by 6.1 per cent, worth £611 more than it had been at the start.

The Paper Portfolio begun in September 1998 was ahead by 25.9 per cent at 5 November 1999. Nine of the shares were showing a profit but on 5 November Unilever produced exceptionally weak quarterly figures and the shares lost over 13 per cent, £49 billion off its market value on the day (see table). Between 11 September 1998 and 5 November 1999, the FTSE 100 index rose 24.1%. The Paper Top Ten Portfolio had exceeded this and I would be inclined to continue with it for a further 6 months to see if Unilever recovered. However, on 9 November Diageo shares fell to 552p on concerns over flagging spirit sales.

### PROGRESS OF THE SEPTEMBER 1998 TOP TEN PORTFOLIO AS AT 5 NOVEMBER 1999

| Rank | Company | Number of Shares | Price (p) | Value (£) |
|---|---|---|---|---|
| 1 | BP | 246[a] | 541 | 1,331 |
| 4 | Glaxo Wellcome | 56 | 1856 | 1,039 |
| 3 | British Telecom | 124 | 1102 | 1,366 |
| 7 | SmithKline Beecham | 141 | 880 | 1,241 |
| 8 | Lloyds TSB | 150 | 852 | 1,278 |
| 9 | Shell | 272 | 444.5 | 1,204 |
| 2 | Vodafone AirTouch | 635[b] | 317 | 2,013 |
| 6 | AstraZeneca | 43 | 2818 | 1,212 |
| 12 | Diageo | 177 | 596.5 | 1,056 |
| 20 | Unilever | 181 | 466.5 | 844 |
| **Equities Total** | | | | **12,584** |
| Cash | | | | 10 |
| **Overall Total** | | | | **12,594** |
| | | | | **(gain of £2,594 or 25.9%)** |

FTSE 100 on 11 September 1998: 5118.5.

FTSE 100 on 5 November: 6356.6

[a] BP Amoco share split in September 1999. 123 shares became 246.

[b] Vodafone AirTouch had a 4-for-1 share split in October 1999: 127 shares became 635.

## 'Investors must beware – this year's fashion can quickly become next year's tank top.'

*Justin Urquhart Stewart, Barclays Stockbrokers*

We saw, in the *Investors Chronicle* Portfolio for 1988, a short-term out-performance of the FTSE 100 top ten occurred from mid-1988 to mid-1998. During 1997, while many FTSE 100 companies traded sideways or declined, the prices of the largest rose faster than the rest. Relative to the rise in the

FTSE All-Share index, the top 10 outperformed the next 90 companies in the FTSE 100 by 17 per cent. This escalating rise is not explainable in terms of forecast profits performance of the top 10 stocks because analysts were predicting an average 6 per cent *decline* in profits for the 1998 results. The companies' PERs were hugely inflated by share price increases. By November 1999, the prospective P/Es were almost 34 for Glaxo, 38 for SmithKline Beecham, 30 for AstraZeneca and 64.5 for Vodafone AirTouch. Can these stocks make further headway or will they drop precipitously? A drastic fall did occur in the United States in the 1970s among a group of major corporations. Dubbed the 'Nifty 50s', they included many that are still global household names: Citicorp, Coca-Cola, Disney, General Electric, IBM, Sears Roebuck, Johnson & Johnson, McDonald's, Polaroid and Xerox. In the late 1960s and early 1970s, they made amazing returns but their share prices (for all the nifty 50s) then suffered a huge de-rating. PERs fell by almost 80 per cent.

Looking back to the turbulent seventies, with more knowledge, we can set this incident into perspective. There was a major crisis of confidence in Western capitalism then, due to the abrupt oil-price shocks and unprecedented levels of global inflation. Anne Scheiber, and other long-term investors, still received dividends, while waiting for the international turmoil to abate. Yet many of the late-1960s nifty 50s remain great American companies. Investing in world-beating companies should be a highly profitable experience, but only when you are patient and invest long term.

## 'High average returns are only earned as a compensation for risk.'

*Professor John Cochrane, University of Chicago*

Why should the Top Ten Portfolio outperform the FTSE 100? Undoubtedly, the top 10 companies are the cream of British business excellence. Despite the UK's relative decline as an international trading nation, it remains a world leader in some industries. The FTSE 100 rankings reveal these industries as banks, oils, telecommunications (both fixed line and mobile), pharmaceuticals and alcoholic beverages, plus world-class companies in the tobacco and aerospace/defence industries. They have proved their excellence over decades of outperformance: they are well worth supporting over the long term.

In addition, the relative size by market capitalisation of the top 10–15 companies operates in their favour. In mid-January 1999 the total value of

2,500 listed companies on the Stock Exchange, by market capitalisation, was about £1,415 billion, of which £1,146 billion represented the FTSE 100 companies. In principle, therefore, the FTSE 100 dominates the value of firms in the UK economy, with another 2,400 together worth only about £270 billion. After the January 1999 merger, BP Amoco alone was worth about 8 per cent of the FTSE 100, and on completion of the AstraZeneca merger in April 1999 that combined company represented more than 3 per cent of the index. Meanwhile, the Vodafone–AirTouch merger created a mobile telecoms company worth £98.4 billion by 5 November 1999, putting yet another two super-sized companies into the index. The top 10 companies by value are worth about 47 per cent of the total market capitalisation of the FTSE 100. Therefore, when you focus on these companies you encapsulate within your portfolio around half the value of the entire 100. You boost your portfolio by following the fortunes of the largest, most highly prized UK companies. It sounds risky, but on a 15–20-year view most of these companies should prosper. Invest long term!

By becoming an active investor, can you improve this performance by looking further down the list of FTSE 100 or even 250 companies to replace portfolio laggards? For investors managing their own financial funds, asset allocation takes on a new dimension: it means ensuring your portfolio consists of a widely spread group of growth companies – primarily in the FTSE 100 or FTSE 250 categories – plus a few even smaller companies. Investing in overseas markets – the United States, Japan, Latin America or Asia – will be optional although, as discussed in Level V, you might eventually allocate 10–20 per cent of your funds to other areas to try to improve overall portfolio growth. Yet *staying focused* offers the greatest chance of hitting your long-term targets. Concentrate on the UK, and, increasingly, on continental Europe plus the UK. As the new euro experiment beds in, European companies will receive greater analytical coverage. Integration within the eurozone will ultimately lead to more consolidation and mergers, encompassing UK companies as well as those based in Europe. To illustrate this trend, in October 1999, an agreed bid by Germany's Mannesmann conglomerate for UK mobile phone operator, Orange, indicated how rapidly consolidation of European companies might occur. Within weeks Vodafone AirTouch launched the biggest hostile bid to date for Mannesman, emphasising this trend.

**Y: Yields.** Small growth companies often retain profits to fund growth. Investors committed to growth willingly pay high prices for it even when the yield – the return obtained – is low. Dividends will be low in the early years, but organic growth within the company is eventually reflected in dividend increases. A strongly growing company ultimately provides capital growth plus a rising income through increased dividends. The rising dividends follow the growth story because the dividend is paid from earnings, after payment of interest, taxes, and two other key items: **depreciation**, or funds set aside for replacing plant, fixed assets and variable assets, like cars and computers; and amortisation, which covers exceptional items and the goodwill involved in buying assets or other companies.

One way to assess the rising value of your dividends is to see how they grow by holding your shares over the long term. The original price you paid will later reflect the fact that you bought your shares when the company was relatively undervalued, that is, ahead of the crowd. The growth you hoped for was duly realised, making the company more valuable than when you bought your stake. A growth story may take many years to unfold, but that is the essence of searching for soundly based growth stocks: your low buying price automatically ensures your rising dividend from the way the yield calculation is made:

$$\text{Yield} = \frac{\text{amount of dividend paid} \times 100}{\text{price of company share on purchase}} \%$$

As the earnings stream materialises, the dividend rises, as shown in the following example. Suppose that in 1996 you bought 1,000 Glaxo Wellcome shares at 1080p when the **net** (after tax) annual dividend was 34p. The yield is 3.1 per cent (34p ÷ 1080p × 100 = 3.1 per cent). With the dividend at 40p in 1999 and a share price of 2100, the current yield for new buyers is only 1.9 per cent (40p ÷ 2100p × 100 = 1.9 per cent). But *you* would earn a dividend of 40p on 1080p (the price you paid in 1996) for a yield of 3.7 per cent (40p ÷ 1080p × 100 = 3.7 per cent). If, by 2002, Glaxo Wellcome's dividend reached 50p, the yield on your dividend would rise to 4.6 per cent (50p ÷ 1080p × 100 = 4.6 per cent). On your 1,000 shares, the dividend would have grown from £340 in 1996 to £500 by 2002, a rise of £160 or 47 per cent in 7 years. If, on the other hand, the Glaxo Wellcome dividend remained unchanged at 34p, the yield might still fall for new buyers if the share price rose, but in total you would have received £2,380 in dividends (£340 × 7 = £2,380). And if the dividend continued rising over the 7 years, the estimated total dividends received would have been around £2,810 (actual [£340 + £350 + £360 + £400 = £1,450] + estimated [£420 + £440 + £500 = £1,360] = £2,810).

*'It is not enough to stop spending foolishly. We must now begin spending wisely. Spending wisely means acknowledging our wants as well as our needs, our dreams as well as our obligations.'*

Mark Bryan and Julia Cameron, The Money Drunk

### YIELD ON 1000 GLAXO WELLCOME SHARES (BOUGHT AT 1080p) WITH A RISING DIVIDEND

| Year | Dividend paid (p) | Total Dividend (£) | Yield on Purchase Price of 1080p |
|------|------|------|------|
| 1996 | 34 | 340 | 3.1% |
| 1999 | 40 | 400 | 3.7% |
| 2002 | 50 | 500 | 4.6% |

### RISING DIVIDENDS ON A GLAXO WELLCOME HOLDING OF 1000 SHARES, 1996 TO 2003

| Year | Dividend paid (p) | Total Dividend (£) | Purchase Price of 1080p |
|------|------|------|------|
| 1996 | 34 | 340 | |
| 1997 | 35 | 350 | |
| 1998 | 36 | 360 | |
| 1999 | 40 | 400 (estimated only) | |
| 2000 | 42 | 420 (estimated only) | |
| 2001 | 44 | 440 (estimated only) | |
| 2002 | 50 | 500 (estimated only) | |
| **Total Dividends** | | **£2,810** | |

### How the Market Re-rates Company Shares

The rise or fall of a share price consists of two parts: a change in its earnings and a change in the multiple (PER) that investors are willing to pay for those earnings. A change in the multiple produces a share re-rating: up, with improving prospects, or down, when prospects worsen. To see a re-rating at work, look again at Glaxo Wellcome. In 1996, at a price of 1080p, the earnings were 56.6p for an historic (the actual rather than future or prospective) price/earnings ratio of 19. This was a reasonable PER for a pharmaceutical company with a good line of new drugs in development. During 1997, the share price ranged between 894p and 1455p, but earnings fell to 52.2p. Clearly, the price rise reflected a re-rating for the shares. Can we calculate the full extent of the re-rating between 1996 to 1998? In mid-January 1999, Glaxo's share price stood at an all-time high of 2288p and prospective estimated earnings for 1999 were 55.6p. This is 1.00p or 1.8 per cent lower than in 1996, but the share price had more than doubled, from 1080p to 2288p, a rise of 1208p or 112 per cent. For Glaxo Wellcome, investors were clearly willing to pay a high price for future earnings growth.

Similar calculations can be made for the whole market over short or longer time-scales. Over 17 years, the market grew 842 per cent from January 1982 to year-end 1998. The rise breaks down roughly into an 80 per cent increase in the market multiple (PER) and a quintupling of corporate earnings. This earnings growth in Britain was higher than in Germany, America and Japan, showing how well British companies were growing compared with their principal international competitors.

### Growing Your Dividends

In Level II we saw the rapid earnings growth for Perpetual in the 1990s. The shares were never split, and so measuring the growth is easy. Dividend increases accompanied the expansion, lifting the payment from 4.8p in 1992 to 75p for 1998, a rise of 1,463 per cent. For 1999, the forecast dividend was 80p, giving a yield of 3.6 per cent at a price of 2225p. If the dividend reached 100p by 2002, the yield at 2225p would be 4.5 per cent. I mentioned earlier how, by 1998, my friend's pharmaceutical investment was receiving £12,500 as dividends on an original 1963 investment of £3,000. This is a return of 316 per cent on the initial stake purely in dividends, without adding in the magnificent capital gain seen after 35 years of holding shares in this one drugs firm.

In the Introduction, we discussed drawing unearned income of £50,000 from a portfolio worth about £1 million. In your New Millennium Portfolio you can calculate the yield, and hence the income, for the whole portfolio. Suppose by year 8 of the planned programme you had paid £250,000 to buy shares in 15 companies and in the first full year you received £7,000 in dividends. The yield on your total portfolio, calculated as for any one company, is 2.8 per cent (£7,000 ÷ £250,000 × 100 = 2.8 per cent). If your portfolio doubled over 7 years, to £500,000, with no changes, by year 15 of the programme the dividends might be 75 per cent higher at £12,250 [(£7,000 × 75 ÷ 100) + £7,000 = £12,250]. The yield would now be 4.9 per cent (12,250 ÷ £250,000 × 100 = 4.9 per cent). Extending the example another stage, suppose you only succeeded in choosing 13 companies in the first 10 years of the programme and spent an extra £50,000, so that your outlay on a portfolio of 15 sets of shares rose to £300,000. When the portfolio doubled to £600,000, annual dividends might be £18,500, giving a yield on the portfolio cost of 6.2 per cent (£18,500 ÷ £300,000 × 100 = 6.2 per cent). Left unchanged, with rising capital and dividends, when the portfolio reached £1 million, dividends might be £33,000, for a yield of 11 per cent. This example shows the logic behind the buy-and-hold philosophy to achieve a high yield over the long term.

*'One of the most robust laws of experimental psychology is that individuals are wildly inconsistent in the way they rank rewards over time, and place a heavy emphasis on rewards in the present.'*

*Will Hutton,* Playing the Game – The Takeover

The *Financial Times* includes daily figures in the Companies and Markets Section that show the historic price/earnings ratio of the benchmark indices and the actual dividend yield. On 5 November 1999 the FTSE 100 PER was 28.56 and the actual **dividend yield** was 2.22 per cent. Another popular measure is the **earnings yield**. This is the inverse of the price/earnings ratio, namely the amount an investor would receive if a company paid out all its attributable earnings each year. However, interest, taxes, depreciation and amortisation are deducted from earnings before paying dividends. The earnings yield is a reciprocal of the price/earnings ratio; it expresses the income generated by the company relative to the price of one of its shares. But since investors receive income as dividends – which vary in unit value considerably from earnings per share – the dividend yield (as defined earlier) is a more usual way of expressing the income return on a share.

$$\text{Earnings yield} = \frac{1}{\text{PER}} = \frac{\text{earnings}}{\text{current share price}}$$

**S: Sector Analysis.** We looked briefly at sector analysis in Level I when comparing companies in the two Paper Top Ten Portfolios begun in mid-1988 and mid-July 1998. They differed in numbers and types of sectors covered. I adjusted the composition of the July 1998 portfolio to avoid exposure to too few sectors in order to reduce investment risk.

Sector analysis is a useful guide to allocating cash among the companies you plan to hold. It should be reviewed every time you are considering adding another company to your portfolio.

### The Emerging Services Era

When we discussed prospects for the continuation of the great equity bull market that occurred over the last quarter of the twentieth century, we saw there were strong reasons for optimism. In advanced nations, growth might be increasingly global and strongly weighted towards service industries. By 1998, the manufacturing sector in Britain was visibly in decline. It had shrunk to less than a quarter of economic output but, while it was in a deep recession, services seemed relatively unaffected, highlighting a growing split between services and manufacturing as they start travelling along separate paths. A similar separation has become evident within the economies of all the developed nations. Britain is in the vanguard of the growth in services, being the second-largest exporter after America. The UK share of global trade in services was over 6 per cent in 1998, higher than for Germany, France or Japan.

Evidence suggests that consumer spending patterns in Western countries are shifting increasingly to services – entertainment, travel, Internet access, software and mobile telecommunications – with less spending on consumption of durable goods. While spending on luxuries declines during recession, when the economy recovers it revives rapidly. Manufacture of products and consumer goods is moving to Asia and other developing regions because companies in the West, paying higher labour and social costs to their workforce, cannot compete on price. They will increasingly rely upon distribution, branding, marketing and after-sales support to increase profits. Purchasing a service is more personalised than buying goods off a shelf, and consumers become more discerning and critical of any failings they meet. As the global economy gravitates towards a services-dominated era, the companies who will benefit will be those who successfully exploit the service elements within their product range.

*'The most successful companies will recast the whole of their sales and order process as a benefit to consumers, not a chore.'*

*Peter Martin,* Financial Times

Some companies recognise this potential. The huge rise in Sage Group's share price from 1997 to 1999 followed the perception by investors that its facility to sell recurring items, like computer sundries and stationery, to its database of software customers would generate reliable profits for years ahead. Similarly, Internet stocks, such as Amazon.com (an Internet bookseller) and CDnow (an online music store), offer easy access to cater for customers' needs by targeting niche markets. Such companies help customers navigate their way effortlessly through an infinite range of available purchasing possibilities. Investors set astronomical values on them when they recognised this user-friendly approach. More companies must grasp this necessary realignment to benefit from the opportunities a services-dominated stance presents.

Increasingly, growth stories centre on companies alert to these priorities. Most are young firms with huge start-up costs, low revenues and no profits. If you buy them at inflated prices, you are buying promises that may never materialise. Finding companies with sound prospects is daunting, and so it is useful to know which market sectors offer the best hunting ground, especially for small companies. With changing technologies, new future growth sectors should arise, but certain market sectors provide a larger-than-average group of candidates with exciting prospects. Start by focusing on them.

Many growth firms are in high technology industries. This covers telecommunications (both land-based and mobile), information technology providers of software packages and hardware, plus outsourcing companies, which provide services in non-core areas for other firms to buy-in rather than perform in-house. Outsourcing is a fast-growing area, employing highly qualified personnel to cater for other companies' needs in IT, building services, project management, etc. Another burgeoning area is that of Internet providers and e-commerce, which some analysts predict will transform shopping habits. Other possible candidates include: mobile telecommunications operators, catering for business or retail customers; optical-fibre cable-laying companies, servicing the telecommunications needs of the corporate sector; and manufacturers of high-technology component parts.

Another major growth sector and hugely successful UK industry is pharmaceuticals. The top 10 FTSE 100 includes three world-class pharmaceuticals companies. The sector also covers biotechnology research companies. They proved a huge disappointment to investors during the 1990s, but some could be huge successes in the future. The transport sector, brought into favour by UK government plans to reduce private car usage, includes many growth candidates, with exciting potentials. They cover bus and coach services, airports, railways and ocean-transport companies. The small company sector was a proving ground for growth companies, but in the late 1990s institutional investors ignored their possibilities. This neglect could abruptly end, with the emergence of the next major uptrend when small growth companies often get maximum attention from analysts and professional investors.

*'But there is no doubt but money is to the fore now. It is the romance, the poetry of our age.'*

William Dean Howells, US novelist and critic, editor of both Henry James and Mark Twain

### Using Sector Information Through a Business Cycle

Our goal is to create an active New Millennium Portfolio, holding 12–15 shares in about 8 sectors. If we choose successful companies to buy and hold, little active management is needed apart from routine monitoring. Sectors rotate in and out of favour with the economic cycle but our search is narrower, being targeted primarily on growth. Bargains arise for shares in sectors temporarily ignored, and so it is useful to know how different sectors behave at the onset of recession or when boom conditions return.

**Defensive sectors** cover industries where consumers always spend money so that they have reliable income. Examples are food and beverage producers, food retailers, utility and transport providers, and tobacco and pharmaceuticals companies. As a recession ends and recovery seems possible, institutional investors forsake the defensive sectors and move into **cyclical sectors**, those areas that thrive in boom conditions. These sectors cover the major consumer goods and services areas, including leisure, media, restaurants, hotels, alcoholic beverages, banks and financial services, general retailers and computer retailers; as a recession ends, these sectors will be replete with unloved value bargains. When the recovery strengthens, engineering and construction companies return to favour. Towards the cycle peak later on in the cycle, air transport, paper and packaging, textiles, commercial property and house building gain support, plus a host of special situations. The variability of sector demand, depending on where in the business cycle the economy stands, is summarised in the table below.

### VARIABLE SECTOR DEMAND THROUGH THE BUSINESS CYCLE

| Sectors | Phase of the Cycle | Companies |
|---|---|---|
| 1. Defensive (all low risk) | Recession | Utilities, (water, electricity, power generators), food & drink producers, food retailers, tobacco, transport, bus and train companies, pharmaceuticals. |
| 2. Cyclical | Onset of recovery | Engineering, construction, consumer goods, media and leisure, banks and financial services. |
| 3. Late | Economy at a peak | Air transport, paper & packaging textiles, house-building, property. |

*'Money was, as ever, a problem. Harassed by their creditors, Jenny and Karl pawned their belongings and, finally, Marx wrote to his mother asking for a loan.'*

Edna Healey, Wives of Fame *(on Jenny Marx, wife of Karl Marx)*

Investors wanting to hold growth shares over the long term might acquire them at modest prices when the professionals abandon the defensive sectors for the cyclicals as recovery begins. You can time when this mass migration might occur because a combination of rising bond yields and economic recovery can trigger the move to value stocks. Examine a host of issues, looking for 'yes' answers, as they indicate that the time is ripe to switch to value and defensive companies. The list, produced by Merrill Lynch the brokers, appeared in *Investors Chronicle* and is reproduced in the box below. The answers, supplied by financial commentators will crop up in your reading of the daily press.

---

**CHECKLIST FOR TIMING THE SWITCH TO VALUE SHARES**

1. Are oil prices rising?
2. Are commodity prices rising?
3. Are bond yields rising?
4. Is an upward-sloping yield curve emerging?
5. Is the spread between corporate bond and government bond yields narrowing?
6. Are equities outperforming bonds?
7. Has the OECD's leading indicator turned around?
8. Is manufacturers' pricing power returning?
9. Are manufacturing orders outpacing output growth?
10. Is global trade growth increasing?
11. Is there an increase in earnings upgrades?

---

Source: Merrill Lynch as shown in *Investors Chronicle*

As we noted, the FTSE 100 index became more concentrated in the 1990s: by January 1999, the top 6 companies represented 30 per cent of it. Sector distribution has changed dramatically in the 15 years since it was launched. Initially, there was no utilities sector; the Conservative government of 1979–1997 created that by privatising major public utilities, starting with BT in 1984. The flotation of major building societies increased the financial sector from 18 per cent in 1984 to about 27 per cent by early 1999. As the consumer goods sector shrank, the services sector expanded greatly, indicating the future dominance of the service-driven era for UK companies. The change in composition from 1984 to 1999 is shown in the table below.

### FTSE 100 COMPOSITION BY SECTOR

| January 1984 | | January 1999 | |
|---|---|---|---|
| Financials | 17.9% | Financials (includes 0.33% for investment trusts) | 27.6% |
| Oils | 15.5% | Resources | 9.4% |
| Capital Goods | 18.2% | General Industrials | 8.8% |
| Other Industrials | 10.0% | Services | 29.4% |
| Consumer Goods Investment trusts | 34.6% | Consumer Goods | 17.9% |
| Plus Others | 3.8% | Utilities | 6.9% |
| **Total** | **100%** | **Total** | **100%** |

## FOLLOW THE BIG- AND SMALL-CAPITALISATION GROWTH STORIES

Earlier, when discussing the composition of the FTSE 100 paper portfolio, we noted that the top UK companies are clustered in just a few sectors. Initially, I decided that holding shares in 3 bank or pharmaceutical companies was risky, even on paper. Yet I later reconsidered on the drugs companies; although during 1998 they seemed overvalued, their long-term prospects look positive. When you set up a portfolio, pay as much attention to paper purchases as you would if you were actually buying shares. Then you avoid ill-judged or reckless decisions. Naturally, you pay close attention to the make-up of your real Top Ten Portfolio by checking the latest group of top 10 and comparing prices with those you hold on paper which were 'bought' several months earlier. Review the composition of your portfolio every time you change a company, to check the distribution of sectors you hold.

*'The markets are the same now as they were five or ten years ago because they keep changing – just like they did then.'*

*Ed Seykota, futures trader*

Use the reading sources outlined in Level I to discover large or small growth companies with promising stories. Search the sectors mentioned above and follow your selections on paper before buying. Finding ideal large companies to invest in is almost more difficult than finding small growth companies; some compromises on the 11 FASTER GAINS criteria may result. Yet following their activity is easier as they receive fuller coverage in the financial press. Often – as when both Vodafone and Glaxo began their meteoric growth phases – the true potential only emerges after some of the earliest price rises have occurred. To assess promising long-term FTSE 100 growth shares, we will look at two using FASTER GAINS. Railtrack was ranked 46th on 17 January 1999; the price was 1441p and market capitalisation was £7,305 million. Glaxo Wellcome was ranked 2nd on that date; at a price of 2165p, it was valued at £78,416 million.

## Railtrack Set For Growth?

**F: Fundamental Facts**. Railtrack, privatised in May 1996, controls the tracks on which other companies run Britain's train services. Track and train operators were formally part of British Rail, a government-run utility. At privatisation, Railtrack became a public company, quoted on the London Stock Exchange. It is regulated to ensure it does not make exceptional profits. Utilities are defensive companies, having safe, regular revenues regardless of the business cycle. However, they are free to expand into non-regulated areas where returns – and consequently risks – should be higher.

This potential proved valuable to Railtrack. It was floated with a large portfolio of station properties, whose collective values were incorrectly calculated in the balance sheet. Part of the business consisted of under-valued freehold properties able to provide a high stream of regular rental income. While in opposition, the Labour party was vehemently opposed to rail privatisation and committed itself to renationalisng the entire network at the initial flotation price when re-elected. This promise alarmed prospective investors, concerned at no compensation when returning Railtrack to the public sector. These threats influenced the Tory government's decision to sell the whole company at a low initial price with one launch date rather than using two separate sales tranches – a second tranche at a later date would have given taxpayers the financial gain of a rising share price once Railtrack was a successful private enterprise.

At privatisation, therefore, instead of being just another boring utility, answerable to a rail regulator, the market rapidly awoke to the embedded profit potential of the large portfolio of property assets beyond Railtrack's routine rail revenues. In November 1998, the price hit a high of 1768p, from the partly-paid launch price of 190p. But two further uncertainties then arose. The first, in December 1998, was the harsh pricing regime recommended by the regulator, due to operate from the next review period in April 2001; if this regime were to be instituted, Railtrack's revenues would be severely reduced. The second uncertainty was whether the Labour government would award Railtrack the contract to run the largest part of the London Underground system. This contract would greatly reduce reliance on the regulated business that accounted for 90 per cent of Railtrack's turnover. Involvement in the Underground project would improve future prospects. A declining share price reflected market concerns on these uncertainties.

Some analysts thought that ministers might be forced to rely on Railtrack to sort out the rail system's enormous problems, including updating the London Underground system, and that ministers would block the regulatory regime if its terms were too onerous. At 1441p, they thought these uncertainties were already in the price. Involvement in the Underground could lift Railtrack's share price to 2000p, a rise of almost 39 per cent. In the light of these background factors, how did Railtrack rate as a growth stock in January 1999 using FASTER GAINS?

**A: Annual Earnings Per Share (EPS)** should show 20 per cent growth. For Railtrack, EPS for 1999 were forecast to grow by 22.5 per cent, from 61.7p in 1998 (before deducting the one-off surcharge) to 75.5p. (The 1998 figure was distorted due to the government's one-off surcharge.)

**S: Supply/Demand.** Supply and demand acting on the share price is an interesting feature of Railtrack's price performance, because the number of shares traded on a daily basis is small compared with other FTSE 100 shares. Often, 1–2 million shares change hands compared with over 10 million routinely traded for Vodafone AirTouch or SmithKline Beecham. When there is a lower level of share activity, as for Railtrack, a major news item can shoot the price up or down significantly over a matter of a few days.

**T: Technical Analysis.** Technical analysis proved extremely helpful when I was deciding whether to buy Railtrack. I was alerted to the growth potential by a sudden explosion in the share price after excellent results were announced in November 1996. The shares were trading in their **partly paid** form, with the second payment due in June 1997. I read the press reports on the interim profits and then examined the movements on a chart. The price pattern, together with positive trading fundamentals, indicated continuing support. I thought the share price was halfway through a **flag formation**. This characteristic chart pattern consists of a pronounced two-staged move separated by a short pause or slight drop, lasting from a few days to about a month. Both moves are in the same direction, either up (with heavy buying) or down (when selling dominates). Shares such as Railtrack, with low daily volumes, are more likely to make flags when sudden news is announced. The flag pattern, marked A, is seen on the chart below.

**Railtrack showing flag formation in November 1996**

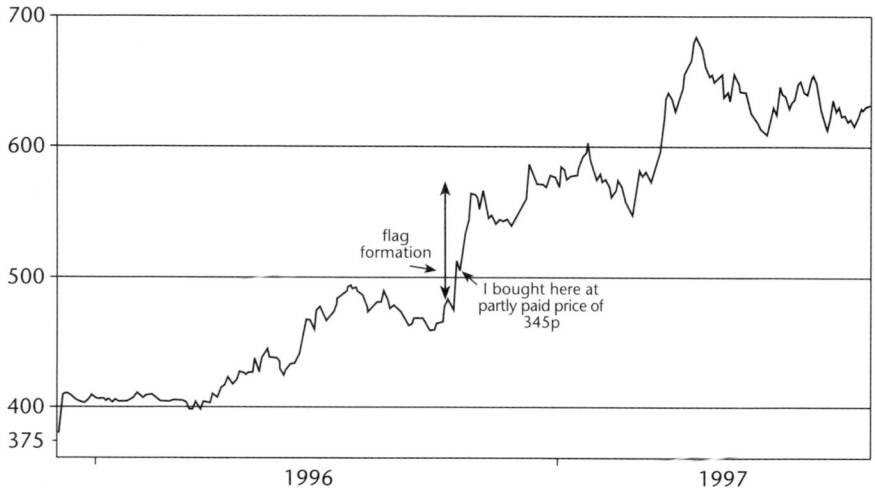

**E: Efficient Management.** Sir Bob Horton was chief executive of BP before moving to Railtrack to become its chairman on privatisation. His stay at BP was turbulent and he was firmly committed to making a success of rail privatisation. However, as he approached retirement at age 60, a successor was being sought early in 1999.

**R: Rich in Cash.** Railtrack negotiated a very profitable contract to build the track links for Eurotunnel and that operation has increased borrowings. However, the company secured government backing to reduce construction overrun costs.

*'The P/E will tell you how many years it will take to get back your initial investment. An extremely high P/E is a handicap to a stock as it requires incredible earnings to justify the high price.'*

*Peter Lynch,* One Up on Wall Street

**G: Growth in Earnings per Share over the long term.** This measure shows Railtrack growing rapidly. EPS for 1995 were 16.7p while the corresponding figure for 1999 was 78p. Growth in EPS over those five years, therefore, was 367 per cent.

**A: Active Monitoring.** This can be just as important for a FTSE 100 company as for a smaller company, since some FTSE 100 companies experience problems that affect their ability to grow. Monitoring for Railtrack is necessary because the share price could quickly suffer if the regulatory climate became adverse. The appointment of a new regulator in autumn 1999, Tom Winsor, and the anticipated costs of improving rail safety after the Paddington rail crash adversely affected investor sentiment.

**I: Institutional Support.** Such support for Railtrack in January 1999 looked weak. This could be a positive factor since if the regulatory regime proved less onerous than investors were expecting, or the new rail projects (including the Underground contract) were earnings-enhancing, more institutional investors might decide to buy a holding. However, as the year progressed, the news flow grew more negative and the share price fell to 1185p by 5 November.

**N: New Projects.** Several new projects were (at October 1999) in the pipeline for Railtrack, including improving the property portfolio, building the Channel Tunnel rail link, and contributing to the London Underground system's refurbishment. These are all unregulated projects that could enhance earnings, although they carry more risks than the regular rail revenues. However, after the Paddington rail disaster of 5 October 1999, new investment in safety systems may be required.

**S: Stock Market Direction.** In January 1999, the market was at a high, but regulatory uncertainties then held back the share price. Even so, in the autumn of 1998, several Railtrack directors bought shares, which is usually a very positive sign.

## Glaxo Wellcome For the Ultra-long Term

**F: Fundamental Facts.** Glaxo Wellcome is a tremendous UK success story. Earlier, we noted its exemplary growth during the 1980s. Analysts feared the end of patent protection for its blockbusting ulcer drug, Zantac, would substantially reduce future growth. Zantac at its peak was the world's best-selling drug. Most analysts predicted a turning point for Glaxo Wellcome in

1999, as it had a better pipeline of drugs under development than most of its peer competitors. At year-end 1996, Sir Richard Sykes, chairman, forecast two years of flat earnings followed by double-digit underlying earnings and sales growth thereafter.

**A: Annual Earnings per Share (EPS)** should show growth of about 20 per cent. EPS for Glaxo Wellcome fell 6 per cent in 1998 to 49p, down from 52.2p in 1997, due to the Zantac patent expiry and an unfavourable sterling exchange rate. In 1999, EPS was flat, at 51p; but with the excellent list of new drugs emerging in the next few years, medium term prospects look secure. In July 1999 however, the company announced it would not achieve double digit growth in sales and earnings for the year 1999.

**S: Supply/Demand** acting on the share price. As with most highly liquid FTSE 100 shares, the supply and demand factors do not make a major impact on trading in the shares; this indicator is far more important for small, volatile growth shares. Yet when an unexpected news item breaks, volumes of shares traded can rise significantly. On 2 February 1998, when Glaxo Wellcome and SmithKline Beecham announced merger plans, the share price shot up about 2000 points on the day, from 1800p to over 2000p, with around 30 million shares changing hands. These plans quickly unravelled, and over the next few months the price fell back (lower chart on page 172).

*'I realised that the whole purpose of the market is to find that particular spot where there's an equal disagreement on value and an agreement on price.'*

*Bill Williams*

**T: Technical Analysis**
Technical analysis for Glaxo Wellcome shows how long-term price patterns can reflect a company's future prospects. The shares reached an all-time high in February 1992, when a share split took them from about 1800p to 900p. The price underwent a persistent decline through 1992 to a low in mid-1993. There was a decisive double bottom, (A, in mid-1993, and B, in mid-1994, on the upper chart on page 172). The falling share price reflected investors' concerns on the ability of new products successfully to replace the Zantac patent 1997 expiry. The price took 4 years to recover from this uncertain outlook, returning to the 1992 high of around 960p in February 1996.

## Glaxo Wellcome 1988 to mid-1996

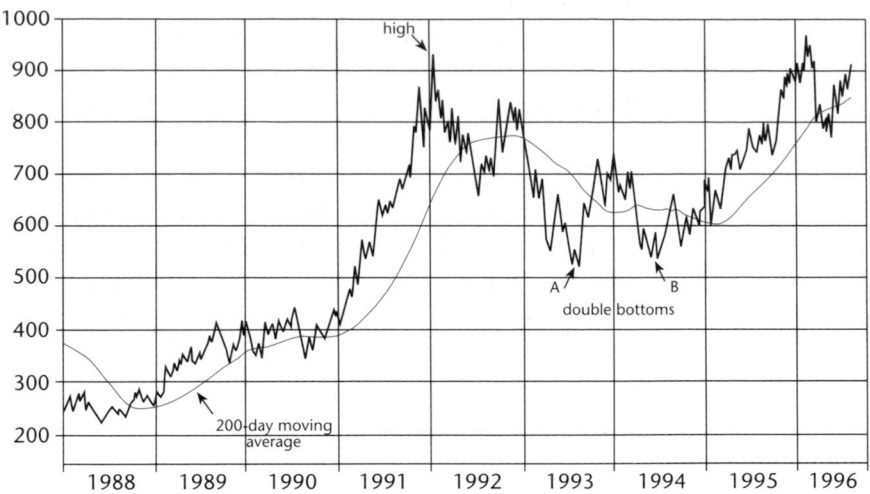

An upward breakout occurred during March 1997, with a rapid rise through 1000p and on to 1150p. Following a strong uptrend to a new high of 1400p, a clear rectangle formed, with a pronounced trading range (C on the chart below). Over a period of about 6 months, the price oscillated between 1400p and 1200p. Early in 1998, another strong upsurge occurred, briefly reaching 2200p on the profitable possibilities inherent in the SmithKline Beecham merger. In September 1998 it hit a low of 1500p, when global stock markets plunged. The long-term surge resumed during October 1998,

## Glaxo Wellcome October 1993 to November 1999

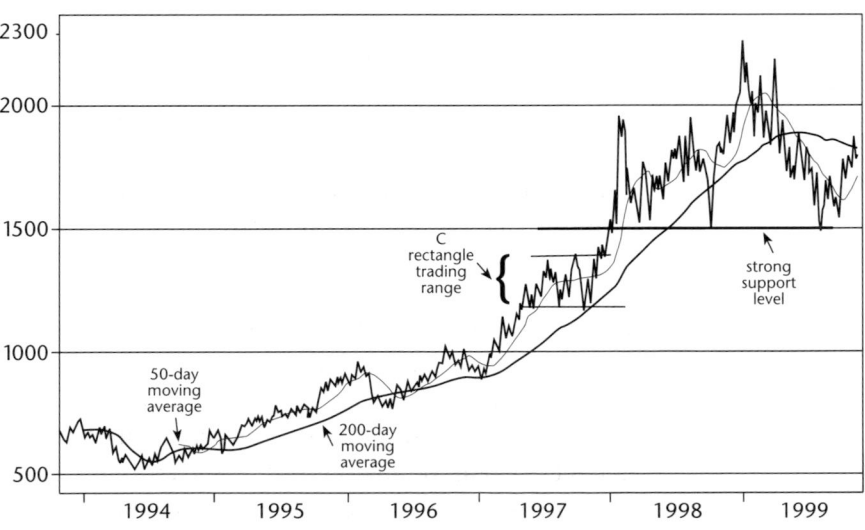

with the price back at 2000p by mid-November and reaching yet another new high in January 1999.

Is Glaxo Wellcome still a bargain at these prices? PER calculations offer guidance. At a price of 2200p, on earnings for 1999 of 51p, Glaxo Wellcome's PER was 43. Looking further out to the resumption of double-digit earnings growth as the directors predicted, earnings might reach 72.5p in 2001, and 82.7p in 2002, dropping the PER to 27. This is still rather high as a target buy price for a new holding although for a long-term investor planning to hold the shares for 20 years or so the entry price is less critical. When 1998 results were announced, brokers were divided on the strength of the drugs pipeline. This two-way pull could affect the share price during 1999. It reflects the struggle between buyers and sellers. In September 1999, with the price back at 1580p, this would have been a good opportunity to buy. All these forecasts became academic when the merger between Glaxo and Smithkline was announced in January 2000.

**E: Efficient Management.** Glaxo Wellcome's management is renowned in the drugs industry for its top-quality skills. Analysts were greatly impressed by the management of expiries for Zantac and Zovirax, the herpes treatment, both successfully absorbed during the 1998 financial year. At its peak, Zantac represented about half the company's sales, but by February 1999 it accounted for under 10 per cent and final results for 1998 revealed pre-tax profits were down only 1 per cent at £2.67 billion on flat sales of £7.98 billion, despite suffering a drop in sales of Zantac of £800 million.

## 'If we take Zantac out, 91 per cent of our business is growing at 13 per cent.'

*Sir Richard Sykes, chairman of Glaxo Wellcome, 18 February 1999*

**R: Rich in Cash.** At the time of its final 1998 results, Glaxo Wellcome still had large debts arising from the Wellcome takeover in 1995. The debts were falling consistently because selling medicines is a highly cash-generative business. Net gearing fell from 244 per cent in February 1998 to 152 per cent in January 1999.

**G: Growth in Earnings Per Share over the long-term.** This measure shows Zantac's magnificent contribution to the company's growth. In 1986, EPS were 27.1p but by September 1990 EPS were 53.1p, a rise of 96 per cent. These were the great growth years for Zantac. In 1990, Glaxo's market capitalisation was £10.9 billion at a price of 733p with cash funds of £1.16 billion. During the following years, EPS fell to around 39.9p in 1993 before recovering to 49p by 1998. These EPS movements reflect the drop and subsequent rise in the share price as noted under the Technical Analysis discussion above.

**A: Active Monitoring.** Companies such as Glaxo Wellcome are known among professional investors as **core holdings**, essential portfolio holdings because they combine a certain rising dividend with a promise of future growth. The shares do not need very active monitoring. However, before buying, check the price and the prospective PER as described above, to make your purchase at a competitive price if possible. An inflated price limits your prospects for both capital and dividend growth.

**I: Institutional Support.** Institutional support for Glaxo Wellcome is often boosted by US support. There was long-running support for the possibility of a future merger within the drugs industry involving the company, especially in late 1998, following the announcement of the merger to form AstraZeneca.

**N: New Products.** New drugs in development are, as noted earlier, a positive factor. A new drug takes at least 5 years to undergo all the research stages and reach the market. Most failures emerge at advanced testing stages. Pharmaceutical companies need enormous research and development budgets to handle potential failures while producing one major new drug. The best returns have traditionally come from those healthcare companies that concentrate research on pure pharmaceuticals, among which Glaxo Wellcome, and Pfizer of America are world-beating examples.

**S: Stock Market Direction.** This is always important for FTSE 100 shares as they dictate the overall market mood. With buoyant prices, Glaxo Wellcome inevitably participates.

## ADDITIONAL TOOLS

For up-to-the-minute share prices, the 1960s teletext system is still operational through television sets, but it has been superseded by online services where information overload is now a real possibility.

If you rarely deal in shares and price levels are not critical, the best site for intra-day prices with a 20-minute delay is offered free by Market-Eye (www.market-eye.co.uk). However, if you want real-time prices – that is, those updated as they happen – there is a monthly charge (£20 in early

1999) plus expensive exchange fees. This service carries several good features, including news items, charting options and portfolio valuations. Updated prices can be valuable because receiving company result announcements as they are made public to the exchange allows quicker decisions if you are closely following your companies. I find the charting facilities especially valuable.

While learning to spot promising candidates for your Small Company Portfolio, obtaining real-time prices direct from the stock market can be profitable because it allows rapid decisions but is expensive. I did not have this extra tool until I had been making profits for about two years. I still use the Market-Eye system, although I am far less active now than in earlier years.

Does a real-time price service earn its keep? I enjoy two important benefits. First, I use the chartist package to download a new historical chart easily and quickly when I want to examine the share price of a promising prospect before making a decision. All of the charts used in *The Wealthy Investor* were analysed while I was writing the book by using the chartist package on my Market-Eye system.

The second benefit from a real time price service is the amazing insight you gain by watching market movements as they happen. This gives superb experience for timing purchases, although that is still tricky. You watch London follow Wall Street. If the Dow Jones index falls substantially after London has closed, in the first hour of the following morning there are steep market-wide falls; if Wall Street is expected to open lower, London falls around 1.30 p.m., which is when the Dow futures market opens, indicating how the Dow will open an hour later. You can closely follow prices when you want to buy or sell, and thereby time your transactions better.

In your early days of investing, subscribing to newsletters can alert you to promising companies and broaden your knowledge about the market. Newsletters are expensive, so they must earn their keep. Some of the newsletters I used are listed in the Bibliography.

*'The first month I started trading full time, I spent over $6,000 on newsletters, figuring that the guys who were writing those newsletters knew more than I. That $6,000 ended up costing me well over $100,000.'*

Bill Williams

## PORTFOLIO PROGRESS IN LEVEL III

Stream B and C investors holding a semi-passive Top Ten Portfolio should start to follow big-capitalisation stocks to find growth stories while continuing with both the actual Top Ten and Paper Small Company Portfolios. In Level III, if market conditions look right and FASTER GAINS uncovers good growth candidates, the paper portfolio can be closed and an actual Small Company Portfolio opened. Begin by buying some of your most successful paper holdings. Use chart signals or market weakness to time purchases and spread the buying over some months when you begin this conversion. Follow the steps listed in Level II to set up the Small Company Portfolio. Stream A investors with £10,000 in savings built up in Level II should close the Paper Top Ten Portfolio and open a real portfolio.

Investors should aim to move to Level IV when the Small Company Portfolio shows consistent profits. The timing is flexible and depends both on how the market performs and on how rapidly your investment skills improve. Assess the situation using the progress analysis chart shown in the box on page 177.

*'Mainstream America delights in buying on tips, rumours, stories, and advisory service recommendations. In other words, they are willing to risk their hard-earned money on what someone else says, rather than on knowing for sure what they are doing themselves.'*

*William O'Neil, author of* How to Make Money in Stocks

**Level III Progress Report**

| Reading Schedule | Start Date | Finish Date |
|---|---|---|
| Re-read Level I<br>Re-read Level II<br>Read Level III | | |

| Net Worth Statement | Start Value (£) | Finish Value (£) |
|---|---|---|
| *ASSETS*<br>House<br>Pension funds<br>Insurance policies<br>Top Ten Portfolio<br>Savings regime<br>Other cash<br>Other assets<br><br>*Total Assets* | | |
| *DEBTS*<br>Mortgage<br>Bank loans<br>Credit card debts<br>Store card debts<br>Other debts<br><br>*Total debts* | | |
| **Net Worth in Level III** | | |

*'That confidence – which, when successful, is called daring, and, when unsuccessful, overconfidence – had always been a mark of the man.'*

*Vincent Cronin,* Napoleon

# LEVEL IV – THE SELF-CONFIDENT INVESTOR
# Your First Wealth Targets Look Achievable

*'Every single one of our Tips of the Year 1998 has gone the wrong way. You can tell IC is not subcontracting its tip choices to monkeys. Monkeys would deliver this result only once in 512 years.'*

*Investors Chronicle, 18 December 1998*
*[Investors Chronicle Tips of the Year for 1998: FKI, Dialog, Danka, Medeva, Barclays, Heal's, PowerGen, Ugland, Brooke Ind.*
*One of Investors Chronicle's Tips of the Year in 1999 was Arm Holdings, which rose by more than 2,000% over the year to 5 December.]*

In Level IV, as a self-confident investor, your first wealth targets look achievable. You learn to manage your portfolio as an active investor and follow companies with strong growth stories, whatever their size. You investigate the growth potential in recovery stories. Run the Small Company Portfolio of growth companies found by using FASTER GAINS. Continue with the semi-active Top Ten Portfolio by discarding any companies that fall below tenth position. Open a paper portfolio for FTSE 100 or 250 stocks with growth stories using FASTER GAINS if applicable. Progress to Level V when this paper portfolio shows consistent profits.

These steps together form the action plan for Level IV, as follows:

1. Learn how to manage your portfolio as an active investor.
2. Learn the important points for profitable investments in recovery stories.
3. If appropriate, close the FASTER GAINS Paper Small Company Portfolio.
4. Open your Small Growth Company Portfolio by buying companies found with FASTER GAINS in the paper portfolio.
5. Consider selling the tracker funds built up with the savings regime.
6. The proceeds of these sales can be reinvested in the new Small Growth Company Portfolio or in the semi-passive Top Ten Portfolio.
7. Continue to follow the progress of the ten companies in the partially active Top Ten Portfolio.
8. Open a paper portfolio for FTSE 100 or 250 stocks with growth stories, applying FASTER GAINS as appropriate.
9. Use extra tools: investing through the Internet.
10. Aim to move to Level V when your FTSE 100 or 250 paper portfolio shows consistent profits or when you feel ready to progress.

## BECOME SELF-CONFIDENT

Arriving at Level IV marks the watershed for the planned programme. Here, you have accepted the need to take control of your own financial future. Self-confidence flows naturally from this commitment. Self-confidence is an unshakeable belief in yourself, in your growing knowledge, in the programme you are running and in your ability to reach your set targets. It seems a heavy burden, but with the right attitude and careful preparation it is totally achievable. The essence of maintaining a high level of self-confidence springs from your decision to take control. This is one of the best ways to improve your investment skills.

A huge range of essential factors lies within your control once you focus on them. You can take control of your thoughts by pointing them in a constructive direction. Out with all those fearful negative thoughts that cramp your positive thinking. You can control your beliefs, your view of yourself, your ability to succeed and how you use your time. You can control your vision of how the future will unfold, set your own targets and manage your investments to control risk. You can learn to pay attention and gain control by increasing your skills to focus on the central issues. You can control your friendships, the people you know and work with. Finally, you can control your reaction to market movements by diligent preparation. Then, fewer events will come as a total surprise that you failed to consider in advance. Master your self-control as an investor and your self-confidence will soar.

*'What is certain is that as an administrator of an army and as a private person Marlborough hated waste, and practised the utmost thrift. Branded deep in his character was the memory of his impoverished early life, and the insecurity and ignominy that went with it.'*

*Corelli Barnett,* Marlborough

## PREPARE TO BE AN ACTIVE INVESTOR

Few investors realise how important adequate preparation is for enhanced success. Most effort is spent on stock-picking, with little attention to the finer aspects of preparation. Yet these can spell the difference between average and superb results. In the 5-Level Progression, the transition from a semi-passive to an active investment stance is a pivotal development. Level IV marks the step across a threshold – the threshold of taking control. When you follow an automatic system or hold your shares and unit trusts for years, decision-making is at an absolute minimum. When you become active, every investment decision involves the assumption of risk. This is not a problem if you are ready and properly prepared and know how to handle any unexpected events that may upset your carefully laid plans. If you approach this change in the right way, your entire attitude will be in tune with your goals, which makes attaining your targets much more manageable.

To make a success of managing your portfolio, especially when you step across the threshold from semi-passive to active investor, you must first conquer the fears you may encounter that events will not turn out as you planned. Fear is one of the most powerful emotions we have. Most fear arises from future uncertainties. Fear of the unknown can inhibit your response, rendering you unable to handle unexpected adverse events. Fear can be banished if you make careful preparation to explore all the necessary factors and strip away the ignorance that lies at the heart of fearing the unknown. Zig Ziglar, an American trader, had a memorable definition of fear: he said it stood for 'False Evidence Appearing Real'.

Overcome such fears by learning how to invest successfully with your planned programme and by knowing how to respond no matter what the market does. When you have controlled your fears, your self-confidence expands in line with your expanding knowledge. Some qualities in your investment personality will need attention so you can move more easily from a passive to an active investor stance. These are as follows:

- *You need a strategy that works and the discipline to act upon it*. Your strategy is the 5-Level Progression. After a few years of holding a passive portfolio, now is the time to harness your newly learned skills to carry the strategy forward.
- *You adopt an independent mind set*. You recognise that you alone are responsible for your investment decisions. Your willingness to accept this responsibility lies firmly with the preparation steps you follow before you finalise those decisions.
- *You understand the crucial difference between loss and losing*. Although it is impossible to avoid making some losses, as that is the nature of investment risk, when you have a proven method of controlling those losses you drastically reduce the chances of having a losing, rather than a winning, overall strategy.
- *You know the main factors that drive markets*. You can recognise the struggle between the bulls (hopeful optimists) and the bears (fearful pessimists).
- *You understand the principles of sound money management*. You never allow a single loss to get out of control and become enormous as a percentage of your total funds being managed.

## Think Like an Active Investor

It may take some time for you to hone the skills required to take control of your investment decisions so that your targets stay constantly in view. While you are in Level IV, you should focus on the attitudinal change involved in becoming an active investor responsible for your own actions. It helps if you adopt a collection of simple rules to keep you on track. Here are 12 you can consider, but you may devise your own list to fit more closely with your personal investment philosophy.

1. Have a well-defined money management programme to control the risks.
2. Focus on the most promising opportunities.
3. Be wary about adding to a losing share; add to winning shares.
4. Let the profits run to make big gains: cut the losses relatively fast to keep them really small and manageable.
5. Don't allow your ego to prevent you admitting you made a mistake.
6. Learn from your mistakes so that you don't repeat them.
7. Stay faithful to your strategies and rules.
8. Never overtrade.
9. Ignore the crowd; it is invariably wrong.
10. When in doubt, have a dry run on paper.
11. The trend is a wonderful friend: it is the secret of FASTER GAINS.
12. Have a positive attitude and avoid negative thoughts. They can become self-fulfilling.

*'Our beliefs about what we are and what we can be precisely determine what we will be. If we believe in magic, we'll live a magical life. If we believe our life is defined by narrow limits, we've suddenly made those limits real. What we believe to be true, what we believe is possible, becomes what's true, becomes what's possible.'*

*Anthony Robbins,* Unlimited Power

Pay close attention to preparing yourself to become active. Take plenty of time so that you are firmly in command of your own actions. Whenever you have doubts, run your ideas on paper. Keep a daily journal to jot down your investment ideas. If you date the entries, you can look back later and review how you were thinking six months earlier. Even if you miss a big gain, there will always be other opportunities. There is plenty to learn, and so a cautious approach might avoid a lot of unnecessary and costly mistakes.

## THE SEARCH FOR EXCITING RECOVERY SITUATIONS

Although it inevitably brings bad news, timing the onset of recession can serve as a useful indicator for investors hunting for growth because, as noted in Level III, some recovery stories become excellent growth stories. The emergence of recovery stocks is unpredictable, but many coincide with the trough of recession. Investors begin to forsake defensive sectors, like food retailers, pharmaceuticals and utility firms. The depth of the recession, therefore, is a good starting point to investigate bombed-out companies to find those with the potential for rapid recovery.

Recession can be disastrous for businesses right across the economy. A whole host of adverse factors herald its arrival. Many firms struggle to survive, while for others sales revenue and profits are decimated. As the recession deepens, more companies go bankrupt or experience serious trading difficulties. Investors sell or avoid cyclical companies, which inevitably face setbacks during recession. Cyclical companies recover as the economy recovers. They are found in sectors heavily dependent on low interest rates, a competitive exchange rate or strong economic growth – precisely the factors that disappear during a recession. The obvious cyclical stocks include construction and engineering, chemical companies, house building, textiles, air transport, leisure, media and retailing. A cyclical share can become a recovery prospect, as occurred with British Aerospace during the 1990s. Other companies, however, face such a long-lasting slump in their industries that recovery seems elusive. In the late 1990s, this fate seemed possible for Pilkington, the glass manufacturer, British Steel, and even ICI, all bastions of British manufacturing. Investor pessimism deepens as a recession develops. Investors are lured increasingly to those sectors of the economy that are sheltered from the worst effects of the slowdown because they provide goods and services widely regarded as indispensable. These sectors are safer than the rest and some – the 'defensive' sectors – are virtually recession-proof. Recession may nevertheless destroy many firms in sectors that are not recession-proof. By imposing harsh necessary measures at an early date, some companies manage to resolve their problems. Among them will be some excellent recovery situations.

Within the universe of shares, recovery situations are a unique class. When you find them, they will not be growing – indeed, they may be potential bankrupts, with monumental debts, low sales revenue, no profits, poorly performing products or managers, or collapsing markets. They are often special situations rather than cyclical stocks, that is, they have the ability to perform well as recession ends. Good timing is the key to investing in cyclical stocks. You must detect the early signs that business is falling off or picking up. The best gains in cyclical shares arise from investing as recession ends and the economic boom unfolds. As the boom peaks, the best gains will have been made for cyclical shares. Timing is less critical for recovery shares. You may miss the first surge in the share price, but if you are nimble, there will still be good profits to enjoy. Recovery shares can produce the greatest gains. In the 1990s Next, the fashion retailer, made an astonishing recovery. The share price rose from 11p in 1991 to 835p in 1998, when it again ran into problems. British Aerospace was equally amazing. The price hit 100p in 1993 but reached 2180p in 1998, before undergoing a share split.

## 'You must wait for the cycles in order for you to be able to take the profit out of the market.'

*Richard McCall, martial arts expert*

By definition, recovery situations arise in any market sector and at any time. This is a positive point for investors who are constantly searching for new candidates. They fit a whole host of possibilities. Even poorly managed cyclical stocks can become recovery stories. They usually make up lost ground quickly, once the factors for recovery are in place. Like the occurrence of young aggressively growing growth shares, the appearance of recovery shares may not be tied to the economic cycle.

Some companies will be so important to jobs or the underlying economy that the management may try to force government assistance or guarantees to avoid bankruptcy. This was a much-abused means of company rescue in the turbulent 1970s – for example with car manufacturers British Leyland and Rolls-Royce. During the 1980s, the Conservatives blocked this route, insisting companies resolve their own financial difficulties. Another type of recovery share arises almost by surprise, with investors shocked to discover a stock market favourite suddenly facing huge problems. In the late 1980s, this fate befell WPP and Saatchi & Saatchi, two of the UK's major advertising companies. Saatchi & Saatchi made an indifferent recovery, while WPP managed stronger growth and returned to the FTSE 100 élite by late 1998 after years of hard work to repay its vast debt overhang.

Another type of recovery share covers companies that insist they have met a small unanticipated problem that can soon be corrected. In such cases it is vital to predict the true extent of the company's difficulties. The adverse publicity on tobacco companies is an illustration, because years of concern over possible consumer liability held their share prices down. One further example is the group of companies where unrecognised equity is being held back by a lowly market valuation. The initial demerger of Vodafone from Racal, Zeneca from ICI and Hanson's four-way demergers were all prompted by a perceived undervaluation of profitable assets within the parent company. Finally, a major company restructure can produce exciting recovery prospects. This was a feature of many companies during the 1980s boom. BAT took over insurance companies and Argos, the catalogue retailer, precisely to exploit growth opportunities that proved elusive for pure tobacco companies in the 1980s when adverse publicity on litigation resulted in years of share price underperformance.

A summary of the types of recovery situation that can occur is given in the table below.

### TYPES OF RECOVERY SITUATION

| Recovery Type | Cause of Problems | Examples |
|---|---|---|
| 1. Important to the economy | Recession, obdurate trade union work-force | British Leyland, Rolls-Royce |
| 2. Surprise setbacks | Very high debts, over-paying for takeovers | WPP, Saatchi & Saatchi |
| 3. Unexpected problems | Various causes | Tobacco companies |
| 4. Undervalued subsidiaries | Market fails to recognise inherent value | Hanson, BT, ICI/Zeneca, Racal/Vodafone |
| 5. Major restructuring | Poor marketing, loss of markets or products | British Aerospace |

## Analysis for Recovery Shares

During a recession the list of possible recovery candidates will be extensive, and so hunting them out is fairly easy. Yet even at the height of an economic boom, some companies falter, and if you track their attempts to correct the problems they may become suitable recovery situations. Try to put each company in the right sector and decide what type of category it belongs to: growth, cyclical or undervalued. Check the price/earnings ratio to see if the share is under- or overpriced. Check on the debt levels: can the company pay off its debts or will it go bankrupt? Read all you can discover about future prospects: has it got the right products to improve future earnings? To generate high earnings some dynamic events must happen. In your reading, try to discover if there are good reasons to think the company can grow its way out of trouble. Can you find out what has to happen for the company to succeed? Are there any pitfalls to prevent this outcome? Are sales reviving? Is the level of stocks growing faster than sales? If stock levels are falling, the situation may be about to turn around. Check the percentage of earnings being paid out as dividends. If the percentage is low, there is a cushion to cover lean times; the company can earn less but still pay the dividend. Is the company likely to reduce its dividend? The market will hate this and will punish the share price, therefore you should avoid buying while the dividend payment is in doubt.

*'The difference between those who succeed and those who fail isn't what they have – it's what they choose to see and do with their resources and experiences of life.'*

Anthony Robbins, *author of* Unlimited Power

Is the company taking major steps to correct its problems? There are many varied routes to achieving this: new management, restructuring of departments, relocating factories or closing poorly performing ones, job losses on the shop floor or slimming down excess management layers. You want to know how far along its recovery route the company has progressed. Is it carrying out its stated action plan? Is there evidence that the recovery programme is working? Has the company issued new shares to raise cash for survival? This is a negative factor as excess dilution of existing shares can prevent the shares recovering, even if the company survives. There will be more shares to participate in dividends.

One of the most crucial tests for survival is the level of debt. This alone can decide which companies will ultimately fail. Pay close attention to the debt structure: is it provided by banks or secured on company assets? Examine the total debt to see whether the interest due can be paid without the company facing cash-flow problems. Small companies are more at risk from creditors than larger companies. Examine the debt structure from the balance sheet, as companies with high bank debts are the most vulnerable. Banks may suddenly call in overdrafts. Cash-flow failure will then force the company's demise, as short-term expenses such as wages cannot be met. Funded debt, secured on assets like property, with a long repayment period, is safer, but only if the company can afford the interest. When you know the total debt, calculate the debt/equity ratio. A reasonable level will be around 75 per cent of equity and 25 per cent of debt. This level can be relaxed if the company produces products or services that throw off large amounts of cash.

If recovery begins, the high PER will slowly fall as profits replace losses. Anticipate a falling PER. Eventually, if the company is not a full-blooded growth story that hit unanticipated problems, as the recovery unfolds earnings might peak. If future growth will be rather pedestrian, you might sell your holding and look for another promising situation. With the recovery complete, the company's future depends on whether it is a true growth share.

The box below gives 20 questions to ask when assessing a possible recovery stock.

---

**CHECKLIST FOR SOUND RECOVERY SITUATIONS**

........................................................................................................

1. Can the company survive a raid by its creditors, especially banks that think short-term?
2. Is there cash in the bank or enormous debts?
3. Check the debt structure: is it mainly from banks or long term, secured by assets?
4. How long can the company operate in debt without going bankrupt, while solving its problems?
5. Has the company issued new shares to raise cash?
6. Is the next dividend payment at risk due to losses or inadequate earnings?
7. Will a dividend cut destroy investor confidence in the short term?
8. If the company goes bankrupt, will there be any funds left over for ordinary shareholders?
9. How is the company going to turn itself around? Does it have a realistic plan for recovery?
10. Has it shed loss-making divisions?
11. Is business improving, stagnant or still falling?
12. Are costs being cut effectively?
13. Will these cuts be sufficient to reduce or eliminate losses?
14. If the answer to 13 is 'yes', what effect will cuts have on the company?
15. Does the company have any new products lined up?
16. Are the stocks piling up, due to reduced sales?
17. If the answer to 16 is 'yes', what is the company doing to eliminate the stock overhang?
18. Check the list of institutional shareholders. Do you know which institutions sold as the company met problems?
19. Do only a handful of institutions now own stock? This will be a positive factor as a turnaround gets underway: new investors will bid up the share price.
20. Is the PER falling?

As the recovery unfolds, investors look ahead to a full return to profitability when the earnings might peak. Once the recovery is fully over, the future for the company depends on how it moves forward from there.

---

During 1998, UK consumer spending fell dramatically and the retailing sector suffered major declines in sales and profits. Christmas trading was dismal for many. To evaluate the recovery prospects for companies in this sector in early 1999, we will look at three: Marks & Spencer, Next and Carpetright.

## Is Marks & Spencer a Sound Recovery Situation?

Shares in Marks & Spencer, Britain's top retailer, peaked at 664p in October 1997. By mid-January 1999, it had underperformed the market by 52 per cent. Priced then at 353p, it ranked 28th in the FTSE 100. An acrimonious boardroom battle was conducted in the full blast of public scrutiny by the press. When Sir Richard Greenbury was ousted as chief executive and replaced by his chosen successor, Peter Salisbury, some institutional investors observed that he was part of the management team that had created the overstocking problems in 1998. The crisis deepened with the announcement of pre-Christmas trading way below expectations, accompanied by a shock profits warning. Year-end profits were expected to almost halve, from £1.1 billion to between £625 million and £675 million. Belatedly, Marks & Spencer acknowledged it had bought too much stock, overpriced it and then been forced to slash prices to move the excess off the shelves.

*'It appeared he (Peter Salisbury – new chief executive of Marks & Spencer) did not know what the problem was – and if he doesn't know what the problem is, how is he going to fix it?'*

Comment by an unnamed institutional investor after a meeting with Peter Salisbury, 28 January 1999 (quoted in the Financial Times)

The dreadful Christmas trading figures damaged the powerful brand name. The supply chain was evidently in a mess and it could take up to eighteen months, to mid-2000, to resolve the problems. The stark reality of this abysmal performance exposed some fundamental flaws in the company's retailing culture, although confronting the issues could trigger a sense of urgency to address the problems. One of the earliest announced changes was a new emphasis on marketing to ensure the company was more in tune with the shopping tastes of its customers. Before long, a management reconstruction was also put in train.

Declining prospects for Marks & Spencer forewarned investors on the dangers in committing money to cyclical stocks at a time of economic uncertainty. In January 1999, it was unclear whether a recession would be mild, severe or avoided altogether. Early in 1999, some prices were rising but the economy was not in a deflationary spiral, although several areas of retailing were. Christmas trading statements showed many retailers were unable to raise prices to protect margins. This deflationary impact was mainly affecting retailers with mediocre management or no decisive selling formula. This was clearly the dilemma facing Marks & Spencer but Kingfisher and Dixons, among others, were trading more successfully.

Could M&S recover its premier status? The brand name had a long-standing powerful international appeal and the company was still a giant concern in the high street, valued at £10,049 million, although this was almost 50 per cent below its market capitalisation in October 1997. By 1999 it was clear major changes would be needed to correct the principal retailing errors. The company needed to be more price-competitive, restoring its market share by winning back customers from rivals, which, incidentally, include Next. It would have to be tougher with its suppliers, perhaps through greater use of foreign producers for the clothing ranges. The percentage of British goods – such a hallmark of the company's buy-British approach – was falling, from 70 per cent to 60 per cent, with the possibility of further falls, so that half of all goods would be bought or manufactured overseas in the near future.

In its foreign territories, M&S trades as a premium retailer with higher prices, attracting a different consumer than its basic quality-for-the-mass-market philosophy in the domestic market. However, this difference is based on the inflexibility of the supply chain that arises from the strong commitment to a UK supply base. Global expansion for a retail department store carrying 20,000 different lines is clearly more complex than it is for premier brands like McDonald's and Coca-Cola. Major adjustments to the overseas policy would ultimately be imperative, although the costly expansion planned in 1998 was rapidly frozen as the domestic problems began emerging later that year.

The potential for recovery in one of Britain's stalwart growth companies offers prospect for super gains, but can we assess how elusive or substantial that gain will be? Interestingly, Marks & Spencer suffered a similar down-turn in its fortunes during 1988. Profits growth then was held back by heavy development and start-up costs on its foreign expansion. Vigorous correc-tion of that profits decline saw the company's shares outperform the market by 90 per cent in the late 1980s. Several major plus factors support the company's revival. In January 1999, it had 14 per cent of the UK clothing market and a reputation as Britain's premier retailer stretching back decades. In the 1980s it entered the financial services sector, years ahead of other competitors. This early start allowed it to build a profitable business worth £100 million annually from its credit card and unit trust products.

The size of the expected profits decline in 1999 was substantial, at over 43 per cent, leaving a big question mark hanging over the safety of the final 1999 dividend as an interim 3.7p was paid in January 1999. If earnings for the year were 15.9p and the dividend remained unchanged at 14.3p, the **dividend cover** would be a lowly 1.11 (15.9p ÷ 14.3p = 1.11). The dividend cover is the number of times the dividend is covered by earnings, and a safe cover would be a minimum of 1.5 times. If earnings are 15.9p, a maximum cautious dividend for the year would be around 10.6p (15.9p ÷ 1.5 = 10.6p). After deducting 3.7p for the interim dividend already paid, the final dividend ought to be no greater than 6.9p (10.6p − 3.7p = 6.9p) instead of the 12.2p that investors would be expecting (15.9p − 3.7p = 12.2p).

By comparison with foreign companies, UK investors receive fairly large dividends and build income estimates around them. In consequence, they are greatly shocked and displeased when dividend cuts occur. The share price can suffer a dramatic slump in response to such an announcement. For Marks & Spencer, the shock of a reduced final dividend, if it occurred, might sharply reduce the share price as the final dividend cut could be a drastic 43 per cent [(12.2p − 6.9p = 5.3p)/12.2p × 100 = 43 per cent]. With this caution, it would be safer to watch developments unfold to see whether sales revenues had improved enough by the announcement of annual results in July 1999 to provide more cover for the estimated payment. During the summer and autumn, Marks & Spencer continued to issue flat trading statements and although the dividend was not in jeopardy, it was clear that recovery to its former status would take years, not months.

*'Apart from the fact that the whole world needs to save and invest more to pay for pensions, it seems daft to worry at investment's dangerous implications.'*

*Fund Manager,* Investors Chronicle

## Recovery Prospects at Next?

The fashion retailing chain of Next suffered a serious collapse in confidence when it admitted in 1998 that its autumn/winter 1997 collection had performed poorly. This resulted in a larger than usual end-of-season sale to clear surplus stock. Eliminating high stock levels adversely affected forecast profits for 1999. Next was no stranger to shock profits warnings, as noted earlier, but by January 1999 Next was further on in dealing with its merchandising problems than Marks & Spencer. It reported that, from 2 November to 24 December 1998, sales in Next Retailing were 17 per cent higher than in the previous year. Compared with Marks & Spencer, Next is a retailing minnow with a market capitalisation of merely £2,386 million, almost one-fifth of the size of Marks & Spencer. Next is a member of the FTSE 250 index, ranked 112th in January 1999. There are only 374 million

10p ordinary shares in circulation, compared with 2,863 million 25p ordinary shares for Marks & Spencer. To compare the two companies on a more equal line of inquiry, we can check their fundamentals, etc. using FASTER GAINS.

## Marks & Spencer and Next Compared

**F: Fundamental Facts.** Comparisons between some of the figures that indicate the fundamental position in both companies revealed interesting contrasts, such as dividend cover and **shareholder funds**. A positive figure at the bottom line of the balance sheet shows shareholder funds. These are the company's assets minus its debts or liabilities. These funds accumulate over the years by transferring profits from the profit and loss accounts into reserves for future expansion or unexpected problems. Early in a company's recovery, the assets might be lower than the debts, creating a negative shareholder funds balance. A negative figure for shareholder funds usually implies high debt levels that may ultimately result in bankruptcy.

The dividend at Marks & Spencer was covered 1.11 times in 1999 but the corresponding figure for Next was a healthier 1.62. Shareholder funds for Next had almost doubled, from £243 million in 1994 to £490 million in 1998, indicating its high growth rate. Shareholder funds for Marks & Spencer grew a more sluggish 52%, from £3,324 million in 1994 to £5,066 million by 1998.

**A: Annual Earnings per Share (EPS).** Although this measure should be growing at about 20 per cent for a growth company, this does not apply for recovery shares. A negative figure for 1999 was forecast for both companies. The expected 1999 downturn in EPS at Next was –11.7 per cent, with –43 per cent for Marks & Spencer. The greater reduction was an indication that Marks & Spencer faced much more profound problems than Next had faced.

**S: Supply/Demand** acting on the share price. As with most highly liquid FTSE 100 shares, supply/demand issues are not a key factor on trading in Marks & Spencer shares. However, the announcement of adverse news items did affect the volumes of shares traded. Enormous numbers of shares were dealt in Marks & Spencer on the expected profits downturn announcement before Christmas 1998 and again with the profits warning in January 1999. Volumes of shares traded are much lower for Next, often below 1 million a day.

**T: Technical Analysis.** Signals for Marks & Spencer showed some interesting features in February 1999. The price had entered a strong uptrend in March 1995, when it first rose above the medium-term 50-day moving average. Shortly after, the price rose through the declining long-term 200-day moving average. In May 1995, a golden cross appeared (A on the chart) as the 50-day moving average shot up through the 200-day moving average which had stopped falling, flattened out and begun to rise very slightly. The uptrend lasted for nearly three years, finally faltering in January 1998. At this point, the price fell below the 200-day moving average. After a brief recovery above it in March 1998, the price continued falling at a steeper gradient. The 50-day moving average also began falling and made a dead cross with the still-rising 200-day moving average in March 1998 (point B on the chart). This was a very negative chart signal, suggesting more selling than buying of shares. In February 1999 there was no buying signal at all on the chart.

**Marks & Spencer 1994 to January 1999**

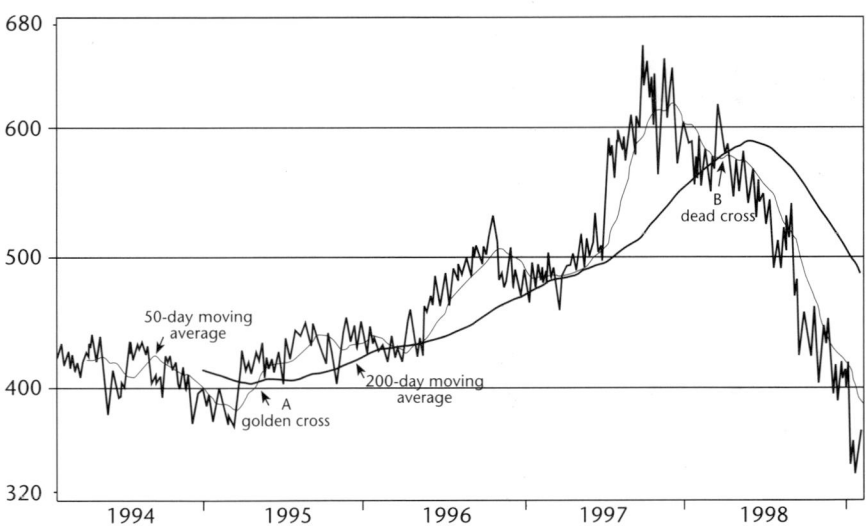

By comparison, the chart of Next's share price showed a completely different story. The price was in a base-building range from October 1994 to March 1995 (A & B on the chart on page 194). After this, a steep uptrend developed. March 1995 was, as noted in Level I, the start of a new bull market. The share price spent almost a year in a rectangle trading range with a resistance level of 600p, which was hit about eight times in the second half of 1996 before a decisive breakout occurred, taking the price up to 835p within 6 months. The shock that Next investors suffered with the profits warning announcement in March 1998 is clearly seen with the collapse of its share price (point C on the chart below).

By a pure coincidence, I printed out this chart to show the closing price on 5 February 1999. The falling 200-day moving average was just making a golden cross with the rising 50-day moving average (point D). This is a very bullish sign. Depending on other factors it might suggest a buying opportunity. The fundamentals looked encouraging, by comparison with those for Marks & Spencer. However, I thought the stock market might fall during February, so the better response was to watch the price movement for a few weeks, to see how it behaved if the market did fall.

**Next 1994 to January 1999**

*'If they are going to make informed decisions about the future, they have to have informed decisions about the past.'*

David Clarke, The Museum of Scotland

**E: Efficient Management**. Public boardroom arguments accompanying management changes at Marks & Spencer early in 1999 revealed the top managers as far too complacent about the company's performance. Without major changes, deep-rooted problems might not be adequately addressed. Some institutional investors were unhappy with the outcome of the management reshuffle that left Peter Salisbury in charge, because he was in the team that had initially created the merchandising errors. At Next, the extent of the poor stock selection errors seemed more localised and amenable to correction.

**R: Rich in Cash**. At the time of its final 1998 results, Next had lower debts and a better cash position than Marks & Spencer. Gross gearing, in *Company REFS*, was 21.7 per cent in February 1999 for Marks & Spencer; the corresponding debt figure for Next was 1 per cent. No figure for net cash per share appeared for Marks & Spencer, but Next had 38p net cash per share.

**G: Growth in Earnings per Share Over the Long Term**. Comparisons revealed another key contrast. Checking the 5-year EPS growth record, Next had almost doubled, from 18.1p in 1994 to 35p in 1998, a rise of 93 per cent. For Marks & Spencer, EPS grew from 21.5p in 1994 to 28.1p in 1998, a rise of just under 31 per cent. The figures illustrate the more pedestrian growth rate of Marks & Spencer.

**A: Active Monitoring**. When you buy a recovery share, you should be prepared to follow its fortunes more closely than you would with a true growth share, in case sudden setbacks delay the recovery story. This close monitoring is needed to apply for both Marks & Spencer and Next.

**I: Institutional Support**. Marks & Spencer's reputation had been severely damaged by January 1999. Many analysts and brokers were advising investors to sell because they considered turning the company around would be a long-drawn-out process. If you keep back copies of *Company REFS* or *The Estimate Directory*, as I do, they are a valuable databank of information when you are researching suitable candidates. By looking back to earlier issues, I discovered only the Prudential Corporation owned a declarable interest, that is over 3 per cent, in Marks & Spencer. In January 1999, Prudential held 4.98 per cent in Marks & Spencer, down from 6.25% in mid-January 1994. In such a huge enterprise, this lack of institutional holdings above 3 per cent is an interesting reflection on investors' attitudes to the company. For Next, the holdings of institutional investors were equally informative. In mid-January 1994 and again in January 1998, there were no investors holding a declarable 3 per cent interest. However, by November 1998 Tiger Management Corporation held 11 per cent, and this was unchanged at February 1999.

**N: New Products**. Renewed and more vigorous attention to addressing their problems would be the top priority for both companies. As noted, new management changes were afoot at Marks & Spencer, with new attitudes to merchandising at Next.

**S: Stock Market Direction**. This is always an important aspect for recovery shares. In February 1999 it was unclear whether the expected recession would be mild or serious. A severe or prolonged downturn might delay the anticipated recovery for retailers in the clothing and fashion industry, as consumer spending would stay low. A negative factor for both companies was that they compete for the same fashion-conscious customers.

*'I knew about money and the injustices associated with it long before I was big enough to earn any of my own.'*

*Nuruddin Farah,* False Accounting

## Recovery Prospects at Carpetright?

When we examine recovery prospects at Carpetright, the carpeting retailer run by Lord Harris, the picture is again startlingly different from the previous two companies. The household sector of retailing, including carpeting and furniture suppliers, sustained a brutal collapse in consumer spending during 1997, but it deteriorated even further in the second half of 1998. The share price of Carpetright fell steadily from an all-time high of 651p in late 1996 to hit a low of 171p in late 1998. Prior to this dreadful setback, Carpetright was a classic FASTER GAINS candidate. I held it for over three years, but sold during 1997, as the price continued falling from its earlier high.

Compared with Marks & Spencer or Next it is a retailing tiddler, although at the price peak in late 1996 the market capitalisation was £518.2 million. This fell to £189 million by 1 February 1999, indicating its savage fall from grace. Carpetright is a member of the **FTSE SmallCap** index, ranked 474th on 1 February 1999. In January 1998, there were only 79.6 million 1p ordinary shares, but in 1998 the company asked its shareholders for permission to buy back up to 10 per cent of the company's issued share capital. As noted, this is very positive because earnings per share improve after buy-backs. By February 1999, the numbers of shares in issue were down to 77.3 million.

In June 1998, Carpetright reported that 'in the last four months of our financial year, trading conditions have been the most difficult we have ever experienced.' However, the company later announced that November, always the strongest trading month, had returned like-for-like sales 7.2 per cent ahead on 1997. Early in 1999, it acquired 27 stores from Allied Carpets, a competitor that was experiencing even worse trading difficulties. Having eliminated Marks & Spencer from our immediate buy list, we now compare Carpetright with Next on a similar line of inquiry by checking its fundamentals with FASTER GAINS.

## Carpetright and Next Compared

**F: Fundamental Facts.** Carpetright is totally focused on carpet retailing, with no other distractions. It is a highly cash-generative retailer. The dividend has always been generous but by 1999, at a forecast 22p, in line with the payment made in 1997, like Marks & Spencer the dividend was only covered 1.08 times. The forecast figure for 2000 was a little better at 1.15 times. Shareholder funds for Carpetright are even more impressive than for Next. They had risen from £16.4 million in 1994 to £41.4 million in 1998, a growth of 152 per cent over 5 years. This rate of growth indicates how well the company could do once the retailing slowdown ends.

**A: Annual Earnings per Share.** As for Next and Marks & Spencer, the latest annual earnings per share growth would be negative for Carpetright for 1999, at an estimated −8.05 per cent. This is smaller than the expected 1999 downturn in EPS at the other two companies. The smaller reduction in EPS for Carpetright suggests its difficulties could be milder than theirs.

**S: Supply/Demand.** Supply and demand pressures acting on the share price are much more important for a small company like Carpetright. Volumes of daily shares traded are usually even lower than for Next – often below 500,000 a day.

**T: Technical Analysis.** Signals for Carpetright reveal the huge share price decline, from the late-1996 peak. However, by late 1998 there were signs of a revival, beginning with a clear 'double bottom' pattern (A on the chart on page 198). The share price then embarked upon a decisive uptrend, and in December 1998 it quickly rose above the golden cross that formed when the rising short-term 20-day moving average shot up through the rising medium-term 50-day moving average (B). Shortly after, the share price shot through the 200-day moving average that was still declining (C). If the price continues to recover, the 200-day moving average will stop falling and begin to rise. Early in February 1999, the rapidly rising 50-day moving average was on the point of cutting up through the falling 200-day moving average. If this happened, it would create another golden cross. These were all positive signs. However, the primary cause for the rapid share price rise was open support for the company by two brokers in January, neither of them being brokers to Carpetright. Support from two outside observers is another positive sign.

Looking back, the price pattern that developed in October 1994 can be compared with the price action developing in late 1998. With the price around 230p, several golden crosses occurred within a short period as the share price cut up through all three moving averages. This move was followed by both the 20-day and 50-day moving averages cutting up through the flat 200-day moving average in February 1995, just prior to the start of a major market rise. Carpetright's strongly rising share price coincided with the arrival of that market rise, showing the powerful impact a young bull market can have on the performance of a favourite small growth share. The 1994 action also produced a small double bottom in October at a price of about 225p, with a strong surge to over 640p in little more than a year.

In early 1999, with strong signals emanating from the technical analysis and broker interest, were other fundamental factors positive for Carpetright?

**Carpetright January 1994 to February 1999**

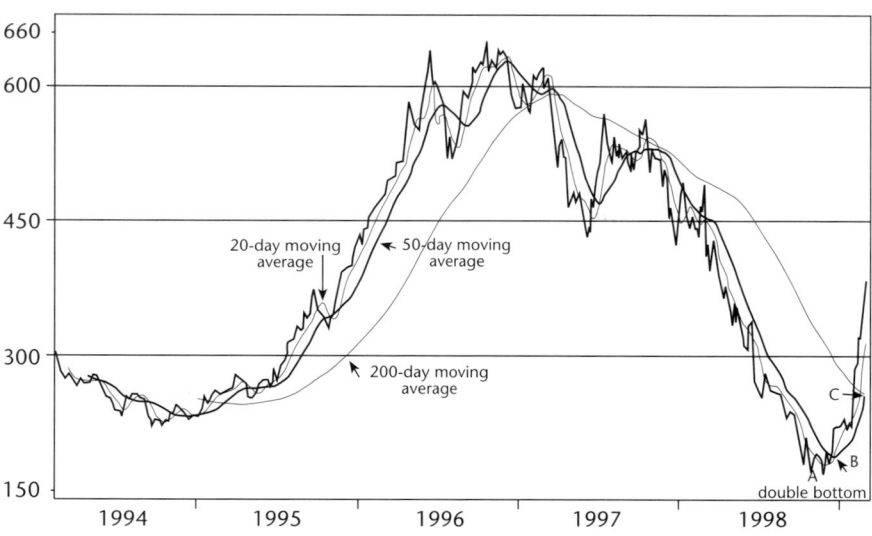

**E: Efficient Management.** Among Britain's great entrepreneurs, Lord Harris is an exemplary champion. Under his stewardship, when consumer confidence recovers, Carpetright could regain its growth path. In contrast to both Marks & Spencer and Next, Lord Harris was steadily buying more shares as the price fell, indicating his own vote of confidence in recovery. In January 1998, he held 15.5 per cent of the shares. By February 1999, this had risen to 17.7 per cent. It is another very positive signal when directors (he is chairman and chief executive) buy large holdings in their company. The holding signifies a personal commitment to the company and confidence in its future. Lord Harris will be as concerned as all shareholders to safeguard future dividends, as his own income will fall if a cut in the dividend is proposed.

**R: Rich in Cash.** Cash reserves are another strong feature for Carpetright. At the time of its final 1998 results, there were no debts, but net cash per share was 5.73p. This was a better financial situation than existed for both Next and Marks & Spencer.

**G: Growth in Earnings per Share Over the Long Term.** This measure revealed another strong feature for Carpetright. The five-year EPS growth record showed Carpetright had enjoyed a rise of 114 per cent, while for Next the 5-year growth was 93 per cent. The higher growth rate suggests that good momentum could return with recovery. If this occurs, Carpetright is not just a recovery situation; it might become a true growth story again, once its trading difficulties are resolved.

**A: Active Monitoring.** Close monitoring will continue to be important for Carpetright. Following its fortunes will be necessary – as with any small growth share – in case it hits more unforeseen setbacks that delay the recovery.

**I: Institutional Support.** Institutional support for Carpetright was damaged by the sharp decline in its future prospects. In mid-January 1994, National Westminster Bank plc held 4.96 per cent of the shares and Provident Mutual Life Assurance held 3.26 per cent. In February 1998, three growth institutional investors, including Fidelity and Legal & General, held collectively 14.9 per cent of the issued share capital. By February 1999, the major shareholdings had fallen to 10 per cent and Fidelity no longer had a declarable 3 per cent interest. If the company shows good recovery prospects, more institutional investors should buy a holding.

**N: New Stores.** Stores bought from a competitor offer an opportunity for Carpetright to improve margins and profitability on its acquisitions. This is another positive factor.

**S: Stock Market Direction.** The same caution applies to Carpetright in February 1999 as to the other retailers discussed. However, on a longer-term view, signs that it is recovering suggest taking a small holding soon would not be too risky, if the intention was to ride out the rough patches, expecting a recovery soon to emerge.

## Summary on the 3 Companies Under Review

Although we have only examined one sector where recovery appeared possible from mid-1999, the three companies cover the wide range of size that we want to explore within a paper New Millennium Portfolio. Marks & Spencer may have the potential to recover its ranking within the top ten on the FTSE 100, although I am very sceptical. Nonetheless, its prospects are sound, although, judging by the high PER on its February 1999 price, the turnaround may take longer than the market expected. Next is a middle-ranking company, although it did manage to join the FTSE 100 élite during 1997, but lost its place in 1998 after the profits warning. Yet with a dedicated approach to recovery, it might regain that ranking. Although Carpetright is tiny compared with Next and Marks & Spencer, it has greater potentials for superior gains and a reinstatement of its role as a small growth-company favourite. A robust recovery could return the company to its former status, with a large following of discerning private investors hunting for 'ten-baggers'.

## RUNNING YOUR PORTFOLIOS

You should now be running the Small Company Portfolio to hold growth companies with big potentials that you found by following FASTER GAINS. Allocate 15–20 per cent of your total equity capital to building up this portfolio. Sell some of your tracker fund units or cash that you have saved to top up either the new Small Company Portfolio or the Top Ten Portfolio. At least once every year, add these savings, reinvesting dividends and interest earned into one of these portfolios. Try to keep a list of between three and five small companies in reserve as possible future purchases. Follow their progress in case you have to replace one of your current small companies because the growth story has hit difficulties. Continue to monitor the Top Ten Portfolio by replacing companies that fall below rank 10 by new entrants to the top-ten, perhaps once a year.

You can now open a new paper portfolio to follow the progress of growth and recovery shares listed in the FTSE 100 or 250 indices. This is the next stage of converting the semi-active Top Ten Portfolio into the New Millennium Portfolio, so we will now discuss the sequence of steps involved.

## CREATE YOUR PAPER NEW MILLENNIUM PORTFOLIO

The steps to be taken to create your New Millennium Portfolio on paper are as follows:

1. Prepare a new worksheet in your personal organiser or PC to record paper selections for the active New Millennium Portfolio.
2. Keep the portfolio records entirely separate from your other paper and Top Ten Portfolio records.
3. Allocate between £15,000 and £25,000 to this paper portfolio.
4. Search for the genuine growth candidates whatever size they are and include possible recovery candidates.
5. Select at least 5 of these companies, using FASTER GAINS if applicable.
6. Spend £3,000–£5,000 on each purchase.
7. Record each transaction on your portfolio worksheet, so that you can easily calculate the portfolio value.
8. Keep a separate record of your reasons for every purchase and sale made.
9. Create a file of press cuttings for all the companies you 'buy' or follow, for later reference.
10. Enter all the dividend details for the due date and amounts 'paid', in order to 'reinvest' them at least once a year.
11. Follow the progress of your 5 chosen companies, plus those on your stock watch-list.
12. Keep changes of sales and repurchases to a minimum.
13. Monitor the portfolio's progress regularly, at least once a month.

As noted in Level III, try to avoid buying a portfolio that is heavily focused on too few sectors, to minimise risk. If I had bought 3 bank shares in mid-July 1998, the paper portfolio would have shown a bigger loss than it did during the September global financial crisis, when share prices of banks around the world slumped. This example illustrates the importance of reducing risks to the lowest possible level. It may seem difficult to do in practice, since the FTSE 100 index has become more concentrated. The largest UK companies where British management excel are in oils, banks, pharmaceuticals and telecommunications. This limitation should constantly be borne in mind when composing your Top Ten Portfolio. Take suitable measures, similar to those I used when I bought the Paper Top Ten Portfolio in Level I.

Before acting, examine the latest top 10 companies and compare them with your existing portfolio. Always review the composition of your portfolio each time you make a change. To see this work in practice, we will look at a paper version of a New Millennium Portfolio, conforming to the asset allocation and sector analysis we discussed in Level III. When you establish your Paper New Millennium Portfolio, you will be running your own semi-active Top Ten Portfolio. The additional holdings you buy on paper will be from companies ranked below the top ten FTSE 100 firms. They should be run on paper quite separately from your Top Ten Portfolio, to avoid confusion. The paper portfolio shown in the table below covers the remaining Top Ten plus the new additions, as an illustration only.

*'As a rule, there is nothing that offends us more than a new type of money.'*

*Robert Lynd (1879–1949), journalist and essayist: wrote for* New Statesman *1913–45*

### General Guide to Portfolio Progression

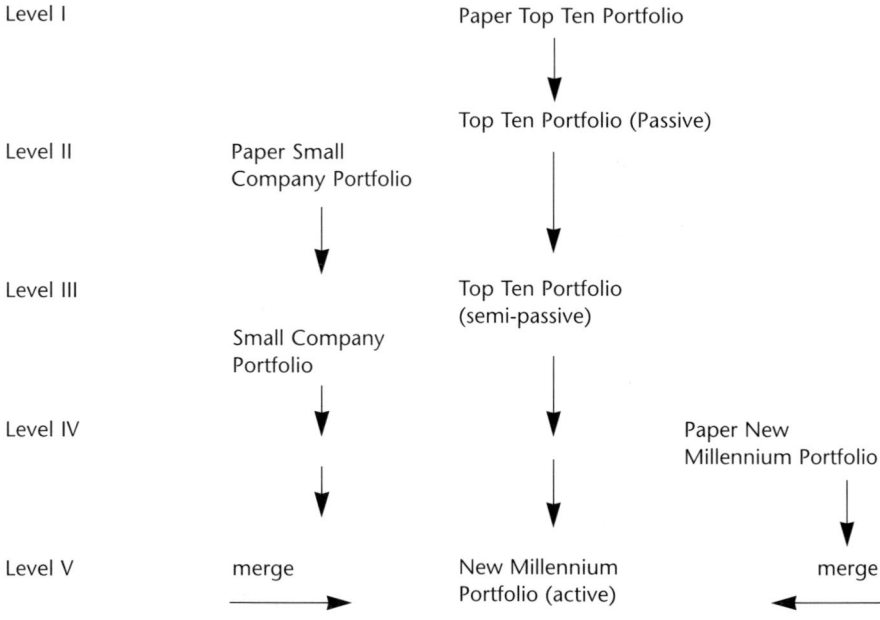

**THE PAPER NEW MILLENNIUM PORTFOLIO STARTED 4 JANUARY 1999 (INCORPORATING PART OF THE ORIGINAL JULY 1998 TOP TEN PORTFOLIO)**

| Share no. | Rank on 4 Jan 99 | Company | Number of Shares | Price (p) | Cost of Holding (£) | Sector |
|---|---|---|---|---|---|---|
| *Initial Holdings from July 1998* | | | | | | |
| 1. | 1 | Glaxo Wellcome | 51 | 1884 | 986 | Pharmaceuticals |
| 2. | 2 | British Telecom | 118 | 820 | 993 | Telecoms |
| 3. | 5 | Lloyds TSB | 103 | 940 | 993 | Banks |
| 4. | 3 | BP Amoco | 113 | 862 | 999 | Oils |
| 5. | 4 | SmithKline Beecham | 124 | 786 | 1,000 | Pharmaceuticals |
| 6. | 8 | Vodafone AirTouch | 111 | 875 | 996 | Telecoms |
| 7. | 9 | AstraZeneca | 39 | 2240 | 899 | Pharmaceuticals |
| 8. | 20 | Allied Zurich | 67 | 876 | 587 | Insurance |
| Sub-Total | | | | | 7,453 | |
| *Additional Holdings added 4 January 1999* | | | | | | |
| 9. | 128 | Airtours | 253 | 384 | 997 | Leisure |
| 10. | 924 | BWD Securities | 386 | 252.5 | 1,000 | Other Financials |
| 11. | 478 | Carpetright | 430 | 227 | 1,001 | General Retailers |
| 12. | 19 | GEC[a] | 179 | 542.5 | 996 | Electronics |
| 13. | 120 | Logica | 274 | 522.5 | 1,457 | Support Services |
| 14. | 176 | Perpetual | 35 | 3062.5 | 1,097 | Other Financials |
| 15. | 38 | Railtrack | 62 | 1571 | 999 | Transport |
| Sub-Total | | | | | 7,547 | |
| **Total Cost (spread over 11 sectors)** | | | | | **15,000** | |
| Cash including dividends (spent on LOG & PER) | | | | | (£83) | |
| **(Initial Capital** | | | | | **15,000)** | |

[a] GEC subsequently became Marconi

Seven additions to the portfolio doubled the sector number from 5 to 11. Compared with the original Top Ten Portfolio, I omitted two companies that I personally do not favour: Diageo and Shell, as explained in Level V. The Paper New Millennium Portfolio contained only one bank, Lloyds TSB. If I were to start the Top Ten Portfolio again, I would only include one bank however many were listed among the top ten. The banking industry consistently confronts its shareholders with unpleasant surprises. Lloyds TSB is the notable exception. In February 1999, it amazed its fans in the City with final results well above most analysts' forecasts, increasing the 1999 dividend by a huge 29 per cent. One point to note is that the final dividend for Lloyds TSB was the same, at 15.5p, as for Glaxo Wellcome. Yet because £1,000 initially only bought 51 Glaxo shares compared with 103 of Lloyds shares, the dividend payment for Lloyds TSB was over double the Glaxo payment. This difference illustrates how important it can be for future profits to buy your shares at low prices.

All the new additions to the paper portfolio are companies I think have strong growth potential, although some will doubtlessly perform better than others. You will note that of the 7 additional shares bought on 4 January 1999, I made a larger investment in Logica than in any other new holding, spending £1,457 to buy 274 shares, while for the other 6 companies I only spent approximately £1,000 on each. The reason was that right through 1998 I watched my personal holding of Logica perform extremely well. As a paper holding after watching for 1 year I was so confident about its future prospects I was happy to buy a larger holding in January 1999. If the holding performs well, it would galvanise the portfolio's value. The date for adding these companies to the portfolio was not my preferred choice, because I had felt for some months that the markets were due for a large fall. Yet the fall, when it came in September 1998, comprised just a swift plunge and equally rapid recovery. I thought another drop would come in 1999. When I assembled the Paper New Millennium Portfolio in January 1999, I considered that the prices I paid on paper were probably too high. By following the movements of the markets and the stories of the companies during the first 3 months of 1999, I hoped to buy the actual holdings of those companies I was not invested in. This is a sound approach when you buy shares for your paper portfolio. If prices fall back and you still like the growth story in the companies you are following, the share price weakness becomes a buying opportunity.

When you build a Paper New Millennium Portfolio, you will be holding your own semi-active Top Ten Portfolio, in which the laggards that drop below the top ten positions will repeatedly be sold. I do not advocate holding more than one paper portfolio at any time, so now, if you have not done so earlier, you should close your Paper Small Company Portfolio. Buy shares in the best-performing small companies you have been following to create a real Small Company Portfolio as outlined in Level III. You will then be ready to open a Paper New Millennium Portfolio, separate from the semi-active Top Ten Portfolio you own.

My portfolio is a mixture, including some companies from the original July 1998 portfolio, plus the 11 September 1998 adjustments, and is for illustration purposes only. It begins with a handicap because 6 of the FTSE top ten shares were bought at the 20 July 1998 market peak when prices were relatively high. Using the 11 September purchase prices would show larger gains, but we will use the July 1998 data to see if the total portfolio can recoup the early handicap over the course of 1999. Several of the companies in the January 1999 Paper New Millennium Portfolio I was already holding in my own portfolio. The only ones I was watching, with a plan to buy in due course, were Carpetright and Airtours, a FTSE 250 company. Airtours is a front-runner in the holiday industry whose share price had fallen on the possibility of a recession during 1999. Railtrack was chosen on the promising potential of the transport sector over the next few years. BWD Securities is a small fund management and brokerage company with an excellent FASTER GAINS profile, and it runs one of the highest-performing income unit trusts. In early February 1999, BWD produced brilliant final results that did not get a mention in either the *Financial Times* or *The Times*. One reason smaller companies do not perform well is that even the financial press often ignore them. This did not stop the share price, however, and it rose steadily right through January and February. At that time, BWD was relatively undervalued, so the final dividend at 8.5p (12p for the whole year) produced a yield of 3.4% for the portfolio.

BWD and Perpetual, as members of the Specialty and Other Finance sector, should do well if the long bull market of the 1990s continues. The profits of fund management companies are geared to the share indices. Most of their costs are fixed, but their annual income rises in tandem with the portfolios they manage. They make a turn on the sale of new units, which increase in buoyant markets. This gearing works in reverse when the bull market ends: clients sell units as share prices fall. Fund management companies are therefore attractive growth stocks during bull markets, which means active monitoring is essential when holding these companies, so you are ready to act if market conditions deteriorate.

However, the record shows that owning fund management companies is more lucrative than buying units in their funds. In March 1999 M&G agreed a takeover price with Prudential, the insurance giant, at £25 a share. If you had bought shares in M&G in spring 1984, you could have grown your money 30 times over by March 1999 when the take-over was announced. Your money would have only grown fivefold if you had invested it in the highly successful M&G Recovery Fund instead. The takeover of M&G left Perpetual as the largest quoted independent fund manager, and so the possibility of further takeovers is another plus point if there is further consolidation in the financial services sector. On the day that the M&G takeover was announced, Perpetual's share price shot up from 3600p to 4042.5p. An investor who held the shares from the spring of 1987, when they were floated at 100p, would have seen his investment multiply fortyfold in twelve years.

*'It is said that Victor Kiam, the memorable razor sales-man, liked the product so much, he bought the company.'*

Logica is my preferred choice for the support services sector, as I believe it has a strong long-term future. In January 1999, its market capitalisation was

£1,929 million. It might become a candidate for the FTSE 100 list if it continues to grow by increasing the numbers of new contracts it signs over the next few years. Early in 1999 GEC announced the sale of its defence arm, Marconi, to British Aerospace at the high valuation of over £8 billion. The rump GEC was intending to become a growth telecommunications company. Carpetright was chosen for its recovery potential. Despite the gloom of the collapse in consumer spending during the second half of 1998, by February 1999 it seemed to be on the mend again. We examined earlier the case for Carpetright as a recovery situation.

## USING FINANCIAL WEB SITES

Electronic investing, while still in its infancy, is a new departure that investors need to become familiar with. By early 1999, about 7 million people in Britain were able to access the World Wide Web, and this number is increasing every month. From familiarity with the Web, it is just a small step to consider the advantages of online investing. It is an attractive option for private investors as it can be used as easily at work as at home. Several online brokers offer facilities to allow investors a greater level of control over their investments – for example, by daily updates of the entire portfolio, which is viewed on screen.

In 1994, practically no one bought or sold shares online. By early 1999, in America, an estimated 5 million people had opened online accounts and many were highly active dealers. UK investors lagged far behind, with only about 6,000 open accounts, but this was primarily due to the lack of services offered. Online investing is expanding so rapidly in America that industry commentators forecast that numbers of accounts will climb to 14 million by 2002. In Britain, as new local services are introduced, the numbers of accounts could reach 150,000 by the year 2000.

Even if you decide that online investing is not for you, there are numerous other ways in which you can utilise the Web to expand your available information. Professional investors have all the advantages of readily available in-depth analysis and information and there is now an excellent range of free resources that independent-minded private investors can tap into. You can research companies online before making a final investment decision. Prices are readily available, either free or at modest cost; many newspaper archives can be accessed; and hundreds of listed UK companies make information available on their Web sites, although the type and quality of data provided varies greatly. By January 2000 there were 1,000 sites devoted to money and investments.

## Handling the Information on the Web

So much new material is being added to the World Wide Web on a daily basis that, were it not for the numerous free tools available, the problem of information overload might become more serious than having access to too little information ever was. While you are finding your way around the confusion of information on the Internet, one short-cut to accessing helpful sites is by using existing directories or established 'search engines'. Some of the searchable directories are enormous and contain investment and financial information that will probably provide most of the basic information you want to find. The Yahoo! directory (www.yahoo.com) contains massive quantities of financial-related material. In the UK, Find (www.find.co.uk) is a classified directory with links to finance more specifically related to non-American users, and of course www.ft.com is the Financial Times Web site.

Another avenue to explore is the use of 'jumping-off points', which are large collections of finance-related topics split into different categories. They can save time by avoiding the need to identify Internet addresses of special types. Useful jumping-off points for UK users are Interactive Investor (www.iii.co.uk) and Moneyworld (www.moneyworld.co.uk). Qualisteam (www.qualisteam.com) has links to a great many banks' broking and stock-exchange Web sites around the world. All these established sites can be useful starting points for novice Internet users.

However, when you have become more accustomed to using the Web, one useful technique is to create your own set of web browser 'bookmarks' by finding the sites that contain what you require and then using them as necessary. The most popular sites will include a site for price information, a site for market news, and a comprehensive newspaper archive. When you have found sites covering these issues, which you think you will return to repeatedly, if you establish a bookmark for them you can greatly speed up the process of information retrieval.

In November 1999 my own website (www.mrscohen.com) had a complete makeover. It now provides extensive information on investment and personal finance themes. I write a diary every day, giving details about my own share portfolio and a commentary of any news items that are of special interest to small investors. The associated site www.citywire.co.uk gives up-to-date financial news as it happens.

There is an opportunity for you to e-mail me any questions you may have on investment issues and the answers will appear on the site.

*'Buy a share of stock as though you were buying a whole company.'*

*Warren Buffet*

## PORTFOLIO PROGRESS IN LEVEL IV

At this stage, all investors will be holding a semi-active Top Ten Portfolio plus a separate Small Company Portfolio. The Paper New Millennium Portfolio will be running and you will be on red alert to find exciting companies to follow, regardless of size. You are preparing to make the biggest jump yet, the move to Level V when you will convert the paper into a real portfolio and finally merge all three portfolios together.

Apart from the first pivotal leap when starting your programme, bounding from Level IV to Level V is the most crucial test. Stay as long as you feel is necessary in Level IV, honing your investment skills to become knowledgeable and fully confident before moving on. Complete Level IV Progress Report and make this last megamove when the Paper New Millennium Portfolio is showing consistent profits.

## Level IV Progress Report

| Reading Schedule | Start Date | Finish Date |
|---|---|---|
| Re-read Level I<br>Re-read Level II<br>Re-read Level III<br>Read Level IV | | |

| Net Worth Statement | Start Value (£) | Finish Value (£) |
|---|---|---|
| *ASSETS*<br>House<br>Pension funds<br>Insurance policies<br>Top Ten Portfolio<br>Savings regime<br>Other cash<br>Other assets<br><br>*Total Assets* | | |
| *DEBTS*<br>Mortgage<br>Bank loans<br>Credit card debts<br>Store card debts<br>Other debts<br><br>*Total debts* | | |
| **Net Worth in Level IV** | | |

*'It's impossible to take an unnecessary risk. Because you only find out whether a risk was unnecessary after you've taken it.'*

Giovanni Agnelli, President of Fiat

## LEVEL V – THE WEALTHY INVESTOR

## Initial Targets Are in Sight

*'When we started this company in 1977, the market was at 1000. In 1982, it was still at 1000. During that period we compounded assets at 38 per cent per year.'*

*Mario Gabelli, Chief executive of Gabelli Funds*

In Level V, your initial targets are within sight. You continue to run the portfolio of small growth companies with big potentials based on timing market cycles and FASTER GAINS. The two portfolios that have been running separately during Level IV, the Top Ten Portfolio and the Small Company, are now merged. You close the paper portfolio for large-capitalisation growth companies while continuing to follow suitable candidates to find reliable growth stories. Buy the successful growth companies being followed in the paper portfolio to replace some of those in the Top Ten Portfolio. This now becomes your actively managed New Millennium Portfolio, a self-chosen portfolio where each company held shows the best possible chance of creating real wealth over 10–20 years.

We look at how to choose companies to hold in this portfolio; and how to decide if or when to sell. Continue with the savings regime, directing all savings into the combined portfolio. You look at new industries with high growth potentials and exciting futures. Allocate 5–8 per cent of the portfolio for special situations or alternative investments. These could include warrants, derivatives, futures, traded options, highly speculative small growth companies, special tax-free schemes or additional properties to rent out. This portfolio section can enhance overall growth, but needs careful monitoring and is an optional addition.

You aim to own a balanced portfolio of 12–15 companies, to provide a rising income plus capital growth. Aim to build around £500,000 within 12–15 years of beginning your programme. These steps are the action plan for Level V, which is as follows:

1. Continue to run the portfolio of small growth companies with big potentials based on timing market cycles and FASTER GAINS.
2. Merge this portfolio into the Top Ten Portfolio.
3. Close the paper portfolio for large-capitalisation growth companies.
4. Continue to follow suitable candidates to find reliable growth stories.
5. Buy the successful growth companies you are following in the paper portfolio to replace some in the Top Ten Portfolio (now the New Millennium Portfolio).
6. Learn how to choose companies to hold in the New Millennium Portfolio.
7. Continue the savings regime, periodically directing all savings into the combined portfolio.
8. Learn how to decide if or when to sell.
9. Examine new industries with high growth potential.
10. Look for special situations to enhance the portfolio's growth.

In my opinion, putting your money to work to become wealthy has never been easier than it is today. When I began investing in 1990 to escape from huge debts, I had no idea where to find investment books for beginners.

When I finally discovered a bookshop chain specialising in financial topics, I bought books written by American gurus, including Peter Lynch, William O'Neil and Stan Weinstein, because I couldn't find easy books written by UK authors that focused on investment skills applicable to the UK stock market scene. If there were tracker funds, I was ignorant about them and certainly do not recall seeing them advertised in the financial press as they are today. Helpful newsletters were being produced but I had not heard of them and never noticed any relevant advertisements. I had no idea how to obtain real-time stock market prices, nor could I find low-cost software packages designed to allow private investors to monitor their portfolios and follow the charts. Fortunately, all this has now changed dramatically for the better. For investors who want to be seriously rich, the opportunities are now there for everyone to grasp.

## INVESTING IN LEVEL V

When you reach Level V, the value of your portfolio should have grown considerably from the initial £10,000 with which you set out several years before. You should feel comfortable with the self-selected portfolio you have chosen, perhaps through trial and error on your paper holdings. Your investment skills will have been honed through years of activity and experience. The ultimate goal, to achieve £500,000 within 15 years of effort should look eminently feasible, although a 20-year period is more likely for novices with no starting capital.

Continue to run your Small Growth Company Portfolio, relying on FASTER GAINS and timing the market cycles. The two portfolios, the Top Ten and Small Company Portfolios that were running separately through Level IV, can now be merged. The paper portfolio for large-capitalisation growth companies is closed while you continue to search for suitable candidates with good growth stories. You should now buy the successful growth companies that you are following in that paper portfolio to replace some of the laggards in your Top Ten Portfolio. By doing this, you have created your own actively managed New Millennium Portfolio. It is a self-selected portfolio of companies where each one shows the greatest potential of creating real wealth over the next 10–20 years. Shortly, we will look at how to choose companies for this portfolio: how to decide which shares, if any, to sell and when. You continue with your savings regime, directing all savings into the new combined portfolio.

## The Portfolio Balance

By the time you arrive at Level V, there is a strong possibility that your portfolio will have become unbalanced since it will have been running for a few years. Over time, what started out as an equal distribution of money among your top 10 companies grows increasingly unbalanced as the winners romp away from the rest and the laggards dawdle frustratingly behind the crowd. The changing fortunes of your chosen companies can create amazingly wide variations in values. We saw this operating for the *Investors Chronicle* portfolio, but it is almost inevitable that some of your 10 will seriously lag, while others become outstanding performers. The whole purpose of becoming active is to improve the performance of your growing portfolio, and so regular monitoring and pruning is the best route to enhance that growth.

*'For investors who want to be seriously rich, the opportunities are there for everyone to grasp.'*

To discover the range in valuations, calculate the total value of your fund, work out the percentage of each holding within that total, and then judge the degree of balance that has been lost. To illustrate the process we calculate the percentages of the total for each holding in the *Investors Chronicle* portfolio when it closed in mid-1998 (see table below). Again, the figures ignore the demergers of ICI, BG, Hanson and BAT.

**PERCENTAGE OF HOLDINGS IN THE ORIGINAL *INVESTORS CHRONICLE* PORTFOLIO AS AT MID-1998**

| Company | Value of Holding (mid-1998) (£) | Percentage of Each Holding (% by value) |
|---|---|---|
| BAT | 5,600 | 11.6 |
| BG (British Gas) | 5,400 | 11.2 |
| BP | 5,700 | 11.8 |
| BT | 5,300 | 11.0 |
| BTR | 1,600 | 3.3 |
| Glaxo | 10,100 | 21.0 |
| Hanson | 2,100 | 4.4 |
| ICI | 2,700 | 5.6 |
| Marks & Spencer | 3,900 | 8.1 |
| Shell | 5,800 | 12.0 |
| **Total** | **48,200** | **100.0** |

(Initial 1988 Capital £10,000)

As we would expect, since 5 of the shares were valued at around £5,500, these 5 were each on average about 11.5 per cent of the total. One share (Marks & Spencer) was about 8 per cent, while three (BTR, Hanson and ICI) were in low single figures. Glaxo Wellcome, the star performer, commanded 21 per cent of the portfolio. If you have been following the progress of your companies, as members of your investment family, you might be quite comfortable holding over one-fifth of your assets in a company like Glaxo Wellcome, which has proved to be an outstanding British success story.

You will now be thinking like a part-owner of the companies you hold, rejoicing when their fortunes flourish and anxious when events look uncertain. Many directors in your companies will themselves own large shareholdings in addition, perhaps, to share options relating to the company's future performance. You can check in either the annual reports, *Company REFS* or *The Estimate Directory* to see what percentage of Glaxo Wellcome, BP Amoco, BT or any of your companies is held by the directors. Some will be holding hundreds of thousands of shares, worth many millions. You may think that, as insiders, they have better access to information on when the shares are vulnerable to heavy falls, perhaps if profits have declined substantially. However, company directors are forbidden to buy or sell their own shares in the two months ahead of results announcements as this is when more detailed accounting information on the company's progress will be revealed. You, as an independent part-owner, are in a better position. You are not constrained by any selling timetable and can make impartial decisions.

Although the gurus warn that it is dangerous to fall in love with your company shareholdings, when you see an unbalanced result, as in *Investors Chronicle* portfolio, you may think it is appropriate to make some adjustments.

## THE SELLING DECISION – OFTEN THE HARDEST TEST

If your portfolio looks unbalanced, does it matter if it has developed a major tilt in favour of one or two companies? If Glaxo Wellcome had been sold, perhaps in 1994 or 1995, the *Investors Chronicle* portfolio would have lost its only ten-bagger and its 1998 value is very likely to have been lower. We already know that because the demerger effects of BAT, ICI, BG and Hanson were excluded, the end result was greatly understated.

By March 1999 Glaxo Wellcome stood at a price of 2050p. With forecast earnings of 63.2p for 2000, it was trading on a prospective price/earnings ratio of 32 (2050p ÷ 63.2p = 32). Was this a reason to sell or should you just hold, regardless, for the ultra-long term? The estimated dividend for 2000 was 44p or £440 on a holding of 1,000 shares. Looking ahead over another 5 years to 2005, people will still need the medicines that Glaxo Wellcome produces. With one of the best drug development pipelines in the industry, earnings could reach 110.3p by 2005 and the dividend could be 77.2p. If the share price is split in two, your position will be unaffected because you would own twice the number of shares, say 2000. Then, the earnings per share would be halved (110.3 ÷ 2 = 55.15p), as would the dividend (77.2 ÷ 2 = 38.6p), but you would still receive a dividend payout of £772 (2000 × 38.6 = £772). By 2005, on your share price of 2050p (1025p after a two-way split), the price/earnings ratio would be 18.6, which is reasonable for a long-term growth company. And who can say what Glaxo Wellcome will be earning on its products *another* 5 years on, in 2010?

*'The decision to sell the company's holding in McDonald's was a very big mistake . . . Overall, you would have been better off last year if I had regularly snuck off to the movies during market hours.'*

*Warren Buffett, annual report 1999 revealing details of the company's failure to match the gain in the broader stock market, a very rare event*

Within the unbalanced portfolio, if selling Glaxo Wellcome would not be a sensible idea, how *should* you decide which shareholdings, if any, to sell? Among seasoned investors, a popular catch phrase is 'run the winners and sell the losers' as a certain way to boost your results. Yet this behaviour seems contrary to common sense. Small investors tend to rationalise their investment decisions in the opposite direction. Anxious to protect a gain, they are tempted to sell winning shares and bank the profit. Gains are obviously at risk if a high-performing share, at a peak, suddenly declines. The poorly performing share, by contrast, is only showing a loss on paper. It might recover and ultimately register a gain. Selling before that turnaround will crystallise the loss; the paper loss will become real.

This logic looks impeccable, but it is flawed because it ignores the long-term promise that is inherent in well-run, successful companies. Selling the winning situations eliminates potential ten-bagger growth companies: holding the losing positions exposes you to the risk of greater loss if adverse news is subsequently announced. Hoping for a revival in the fortunes of a share that is showing a loss in the portfolio could prove a long wait. Adopting the reverse strategy, namely selling losers and running winners, can transform your portfolio results.

Another way to transform your portfolio results is to buy a larger than average holding in companies you think have excellent prospects because you have been following these companies on paper for some time. We will see how this works in practice on page 223 when we update the 4 January 1999 New Millennium Portfolio.

## *'Risk comes from not knowing what you are doing.'*

*Warren Buffett*

In Level IV, the Paper New Millennium Portfolio, begun on 4 January 1999, held shares in 7 extra companies below the top 10 FTSE 100 rankings: Airtours, BWD Securities, Carpetright, GEC, Logica, Perpetual and Railtrack. Of the original 10 in the July 1998 portfolio, only 6 remained; Glaxo Wellcome, BT, BP, Lloyds TSB, SmithKline Beecham, and Vodafone (now Vodafone AirTouch). Allied Zurich was retained, after the BAT demerger but AstraZeneca had replaced Barclays. Shell and Diageo were both excluded.

In 1999, Diageo was an unknown quantity. Formed in 1997 by the merger of Guinness and Grand Metropolitan, it had only a short history following the merger. However, the drinks and spirits sector was badly affected by the international global downturn of 1998. Sales of wines and spirits to emerging and Asian economies were adversely affected, as Diageo's interim results in early March 1999 revealed. These results knocked Diageo out of the top 10 rankings but I had decided to eliminate it back in January. The share price slide coincided with a surge in NatWest and Barclays shares, responding to merger activity in the French banking sector. NatWest and Barclays rose up into 9th and 10th places. Diageo was therefore a recovery situation, awaiting a global economic upturn.

The situation with Shell and BP Amoco looked similar. They became recovery stocks when oil demand slumped during 1998. If you find yourself holding these or similar stocks, you might decide to stay with them, trusting that the long-awaited recovery will materialise. In January 1999, BP Amoco looked in better shape than Shell, and so a comparison between the two, using FASTER GAINS, may explain why I decided to retain BP Amoco but not Shell in my paper portfolio.

## The Future For Shell Transport and Trading Co.

**F: Fundamental Facts.** Shell is a multinational oil company, part of the Royal Dutch Shell Group. It has a long track record but faced severe problems in 1999 due to the oil price collapse of 1998. Press comments on the outlook expressed frustration at Shell's seeming inability to focus on restructuring to counter the adverse impacts of the oil price. Comparisons with BP Amoco were unfavourable, as the latter had taken a more aggressive approach. BP's merger with Amoco was completed on 4 January 1999 to improve profits through cost-cutting savings. Shell was seen as poorly managed and unable to impose the vital reorganisation necessary to turn it around. Support for the company continued strongly, however, because, like Marks & Spencer, the brand is extremely powerful and the company has impressive inner resources. Investors believe an eventual turnaround seems inevitable.

Comparisons with BP Amoco revealed the latter to be more in control than Shell. Although the two companies face similar problems, they were tackling them differently. Both companies are like supertankers in terms of market capitalisation: BP Amoco, ranked 1st in the FTSE 100 on 4 January 1999, was valued at £89,519 million, compared with BP alone, ranked 2nd. On 5 January 1998 BP was worth £46,297 million; at year-end 1998 immediately prior to the merger, it was 3rd with a market capitalisation of £52,808 million. The growth over one year indicates BP's greater popularity with investors. On 5 January 1998, Shell was ranked 3rd with a market capitalisation of £44,547 million. A measure of its difficulties is gleaned from its position on 4 January 1999, when it was ranked 8th with a market capitalisation of £36,642 million. After announcing annual results in February 1999, Shell fell to 9th position; if its relative decline continues, it might fall below the top ten.

As both companies are potential recovery situations, we will look at dividend cover and shareholders funds. The 1998 dividend at Shell was forecast to be covered only once, down from 1.34 times in 1997. The corresponding figure for BP was a more robust 2.00 for 1997, falling to a forecast 1.51 times in 1998. Shareholder funds for BP had risen from £9,748 million in 1993 to £14,112 million, almost 48 per cent, by year-end 1997. Corresponding growth for shareholder funds at Shell were from £13,944 million in 1993 to £14,581 million by 1998, a paltry rise of 4.5 per cent. Over that 5-year period, BP's shareholder funds grew so strongly that they had almost caught up with Shell, being just £469 million behind (£14,581 − £14,112 = £469).

**A: Annual Earnings per Share.** Although the EPS should be growing at about 20 per cent, this will not apply for Shell or BP in January 1999 as they are prospective recovery stories. The forecast 1998 EPS figure for Shell was 13.6p, down 22.7 per cent from 17.6p in 1997. The 1999 EPS for BP was forecast at 36.1p, down 17.9 per cent from 44p in 1997. The forecast 1999 EPS for the merged BP Amoco was down 27.8 per cent at 31.8p, reflecting merger costs.

*'It is better to be certain of a good result than hopeful of a great one.'*

*Warren Buffet*

**S: Supply/Demand.** Supply and demand pressures acting on the share price face the same considerations as we noted with all highly liquid FTSE 100 shares. Supply/demand issues are usually not a major factor on trading in these shares.

**T: Technical Analysis.** Analysis of the Shell share price shows the collapse that had occurred since mid-1998, coincidentally with the fall in the oil price. In June 1998, both the 50-day and 200-day moving averages turned down and a dead cross formed in July 1998 as the 50-day moving average cut down through the 200-day moving average, both following the falling share price. The lines marking the downtrend (A and B on the chart) created a steadily falling channel from mid-1997 to mid-1998. Then, after a major drop during the summer of 1998, the price continued falling, but closer to

**Shell Transport & Trading Co. August 1994 to January 1999**

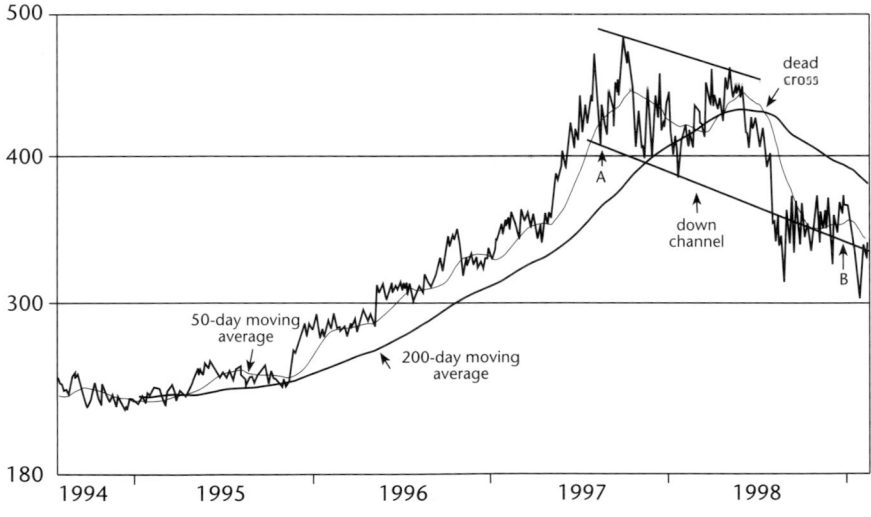

the lower line (A), leaving the upper line far above the price action. There was no sign of recovery by February 1999 as the price was still below both moving averages.

Fortunately, the chart of BP Amoco (shown below) was still relevant after the merger, because Amoco was treated as a take-over and incorporated into BP, leaving the long-term chart picture intact. The contrast between the charts for BP and Shell was instructive. It revealed a divergent investor attitude towards each company. The share price for BP Amoco lay squarely within a rectangle, begun in mid-1997 and still in place in February 1999. Support for the shares emerged on two occasions when the price fell to around 750p, while on four separate occasions, 960p marked a resistance level at which sellers emerged to pull it down again. One interesting feature on the chart is the behaviour of the 50-day and 200-day moving averages. Throughout the period when the share price was in the trading range from 960p to 750p, the two averages switched place several times, as the shorter-term 50-day moving average kept crossing up and down through the slower-moving 200-day average. This behaviour is typical of moving average patterns in a prolonged trading range.

**BP Amoco January 1994 to February 1999**

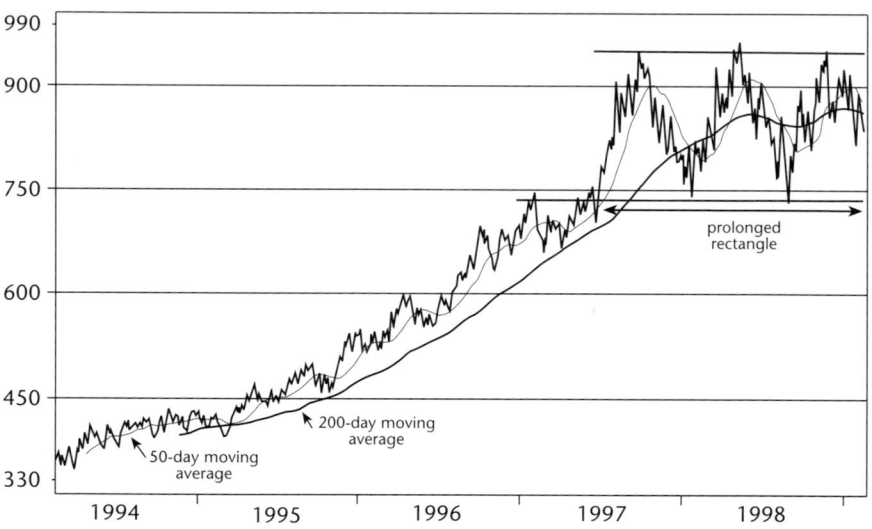

**E: Efficient Management.** Sir John Browne, chief executive of BP Amoco has a high reputation in the City for management skills. He has proved himself an able negotiator in bringing the Amoco merger to a successful conclusion within a very short period of announcing it publicly. In contrast, in February 1999, on announcing the poor preliminary results, Moody Stuart, managing director at Shell admitted his position would be untenable if a turnaround in the company's fortunes did not materialise soon.

**R: Rich in Cash.** At the time of its final 1998 results, BP Amoco's debt situation was fairly low, while at Shell debts were even lower.

## 'It only takes a handful of big winners to make a lifetime of investing worthwhile.'

*Peter Lynch*

**G: Growth in Earnings per Share for the Long Term.** Comparison here shows another contrast, with 5-year EPS growth more than doubled for BP, up from 16.8p to 44p, a rise of 162 per cent. For Shell, EPS grew from 9.68p in 1993 to 17.6p in 1997, a rise of about 82 per cent, illustrating again, a lower growth rate for Shell.

**A: Active Monitoring.** In January 1999, when the price of Shell fell to 304p, the dividend yield of 5.7% was higher than 10-year gilts were paying. Institutional investors began aggressively buying the shares for the high income on offer at that price. With recovery shares, active monitoring is necessary, in case there are unexpected setbacks. Analysts at a meeting with BP Amoco management in mid-February 1999 raised questions on the figures for return on capital, which were apparently falling due to the merger. Some analysts thought the share price was too high, and it duly fell, down to 820p within a few days.

**I: Institutional Support.** Institutional support for BP Amoco was very high in February 1999, at 41.9 per cent compared with only 3.5 per cent at Shell, a declarable interest held by Prudential Corporation.

**N: New Products.** As we noted in Level III, the dramatic fall in the price of oil during 1998 prompted a spate of megamergers among the oil industry giants. These can be interpreted as a new approach to restructuring. Shell, however, had made no moves in this direction: although it reported that restructuring was firmly on the agenda, it had not by then produced concrete improvements.

**S: Stock Market Direction.** In the context of a recovery for the oil majors, the price of crude oil dominates their prospects even when efficiency savings and cost reductions remain high priorities. By February 1999 there was no firm evidence that an end to the globally low oil price was in sight. However, during March 1999, the prospect of the OPEC countries reducing their quotas to bring about a better supply/demand situation in the marketplace set both share prices alight: Shell recovered to 405p while BP Amoco shot up above 1000p. By November 1999, the price of oil had recovered to hit a 3-year high of $25 a barrel creating a recovery scenario for both companies.

### Summary of the Comparison Between Shell and BP Amoco

This analysis between two comparable companies is a useful exercise for investors who are trying to decide in favour of one company rather than another. As funds are always limited, choosing between two close options becomes a disciplined exercise when using the FASTER GAINS criteria. As you research each possible growth or recovery situation, always try to compare the share you favour with another close competitor in its sector, as illustrated in Level IV with Next and Carpetright. With a comparable analysis for BP Amoco and Shell, a more reasoned assessment is possible. I see the pedestrian growth at Shell and its apparent inability to grapple with the complexities of reorganisation as discouraging signs for future prospects. However, if very slow progress continues, a management reshuffle could be a positive outcome. Investors who prefer the value approach will favour Shell for the relatively high dividend.

By the time *The Wealthy Investor* is published, Shell will either have made a decisive impact on its difficulties or, on current form, it might be out of the top 10 rankings so that you will not need to buy it even for your passive portfolio. However, you may still find you are holding companies with a similar profile of declining investor support. If so, use this exercise to decide whether to eliminate them from your portfolio and buy companies with better growth prospects or stay with the recovery stories.

*'If a stock is down but the fundamentals still look good, hold on or, better still, buy more.'*

*Peter Lynch*

On 12 March 1999, the value of the Paper New Millennium Portfolio was £18,035. If it had started with £10,000 instead of £15,000, it would have grown to £12,023. Therefore, the New Millennium Portfolio was over 20 per cent up within about 9 weeks of launch.

Although these figures looked promising, 9 weeks is too short a test for the portfolio. By 5 November 1999 the Paper New Millennium Portfolio had been running for 10 months and the breakdown of its value on that date is shown on the table below.

### THE PAPER NEW MILLENNIUM PORTFOLIO STARTED 4 JANUARY 1999 AS AT 5 NOVEMBER 1999
### (INCORPORATING PART OF THE ORIGINAL JULY 1998 TOP TEN PORTFOLIO)

| Share no. | Rank | Company | Number of *Shares* | Cost (£) | Price (p) | Value on 5.11.99 (£) |
|---|---|---|---|---|---|---|
| 1. | 4 | Glaxo Wellcome | 51 | 986 | 1856 | 947 |
| 2. | 3 | British Telecom | 118 | 993 | 1102 | 1,300 |
| 3. | 8 | Lloyds TSB | 103 | 993 | 852 | 878 |
| 4. | 1 | BP Amoco | 226 | 999 | 541 | 1,223 |
| 5. | 7 | SmithKline Beecham | 124 | 1,000 | 880 | 1,091 |
| 6. | 2 | Vodafone AirTouch | 555 | 996 | 317 | 1,759 |
| 7. | 6 | AstraZeneca | 39 | 899 | 2818 | 1,099 |
| 8. | 25 | Allied Zurich | 67 | 587 | 777.5 | 521 |
| Sub-Total | | | | | | 8,818 |
| *Additional Holdings added 4 January 1999* | | | | | | |
| 9. | 137 | Airtours | 253 | 997 | 343 | 868 |
| 10. | | BWD Securities | 386 | 1,000 | 411 | 1,586 |
| 11. | | Carpetright | 430 | 1,001 | 475 | 2,043 |
| 12. | | GEC | 179 | 996 | 736.5 | 1,318 |
| 13. | 74 | Logica | 274 | 1,457 | 1062 | 2,910 |
| 14. | 181 | Perpetual | 35 | 1,097 | 3410 | 1,194 |
| 15. | 53 | Railtrack | 62 | 999 | 1185 | 735 |
| Sub-Total | | | | | | 10,654 |

| | |
|---|---|
| **Portfolio Value on 5 November 1999** | **£19,472** |
| Cash including dividends | 407 |
| **Total Value of Holding** | **£19,879** |
| **Initial Capital** | **(£15,000)** |
| **Portfolio GAIN** | **£4,879, 32.5%** |

| | | |
|---|---|---|
| FTSE All-Share index | 30.12.98: 2673.92 | |
| | 5.11.99: 2894.74 | |
| FTSE All-Share index  GAIN | | + 220.82, 8.3% |
| FTSE 100 index | 30.12.98: 5882.6 | |
| | 5.11.99: 6356.6 | |
| FTSE 100  GAIN | | + 474, 8.06% |

The New Millennium Paper Portfolio's impressive showing was partly due to the strong performance of 3 of the additional stocks chosen but also because the market rose strongly during 1999.

The excellent gain of 32.5 per cent for the 10 months that the 7 additional shares were held, relied primarily on an outstanding performance by Logica and Carpetright. They both grew by 100 per cent or more, a money-doubling of the initial stake in just 10 months. In addition, BWD Securities rose by almost 60 per cent. The results for these 3 together far outweighed the laggard performances by Airtours and Railtrack, illustrating how important it is to spend time learning the skills to pick good quality companies to hold for the long term. Active investors who are good at building wealth-creating portfolios should easily improve on the performances shown by the passive Top Ten Portfolio.

The performance of Logica was most impressive. On 4 January 1999, it was ranked 120th with a market capitalisation of £1,929 million. By 5 November it was ranked 74th with a market value of £4,224. But it was still on the FTSE 100 reserve list because at the September 1999 review, although it was ranked 95th and worth £3,353 million, there were other candidates ahead of it who entered the FTSE 100 at that date. This situation was rectified on 11 November when Logica entered the FTSE 100 list. Unlike many fast-growing shares for 1999 in the technology sector, Logica has all the hallmarks of a soundly-based, well managed company as revealed by a FASTER GAINS analysis.

*'Only enthusiasts close to the game [investing in Internet stocks] have benefited. However you try to value the stocks, they look expensive, so maybe they are. Otherwise what is the point of modern analytical techniques?'*

*Fund Manager,* Investors Chronicle, *January 1999*

## NEW INDUSTRIES WITH HIGH GROWTH PROSPECTS

During the last few years, news items on emerging industries have begun to hit the headlines. Although the impact was initially slow, as the nineties ended the momentum was gathering at quite a hectic pace and a cluster of 30-something-year-old founder-entrepreneurs were making stunning fortunes.

Most of the new industries come under the broad umbrella of 'high technology', but this now covers a wide and varied range of exciting new ventures. Spotting winners is clearly not easy, but if you adopt a highly disciplined approach, having arrived at Level V, your ability to take advantage of these outstanding opportunities will have risen substantially. Now you have acquired the necessary investment skills to increase your wealth by taking your own investment decisions, you are as well equipped as the professionals to benefit from this upsurge of new opportunities, because winners and losers here are equally difficult for everyone to spot.

The spread of new ventures offers plenty of exciting options (see box below). They include biotechnology companies, mobile telecommunications, niche information technology, companies producing state-of-the-art software, the merger potential of computing and mobile telephony, termed convergence, and, of course the Internet, within which are a whole host of amazing adventures, like stock market investing on the net and e-commerce. Investing in any or all of these avenues could produce opportunity gains for those who are early investors. Fledgling companies continually emerge with new technologies for many of these areas, especially in software and Internet products, and so it is worthwhile watching for new appearances. New issues are reported weekly in *Investors Chronicle* and in the financial press. Obviously, there are high risks, the technology may be too obscure for mainstream investors to understand, and you might choose to invest in one of the many new entrants that fail spectacularly without ever making profits. Choosing between the numerous prospects on offer seems like a game of chance, but there are a few general rules to follow to reduce the chances of picking too many losers. We will consider some useful rules when we have examined a few of the emerging industries more closely.

---

**EMERGING INDUSTRIES WITH HIGH GROWTH POTENTIAL**

1. Biotechnology companies
2. Mobile telephony
3. Mobile computing
4. Niche information technology companies
5. Computer applications such as direct sales to consumers
6. Software niche products
7. Internet providers
8. E-commerce
9. E-trading

## High-Tech Pharmaceuticals Risks – British Biotechnology

Biotechnology companies were among the first group to make headline-grabbing news. They were frequently featured, but often for the wrong reasons, reporting failed tests, the abandonment of a promising line of research, boardroom disputes, or endless calls on shareholders for more cash. Some companies will certainly make exciting breakthroughs, but a long string of UK failures has damaged the sector's credibility with investors.

The fall from grace of British Biotechnology, at one time so highly valued that it was briefly poised to join the FTSE 100 index, reveals the inherent investment dangers. In 1997, it was the established standard-bearer for the flourishing UK biotechnology scene. It had captured the imagination of investors with its pioneering science and its upside-down business model, which used 'burn rates' rather than profits because, like most research companies, profits were non-existent. The ultimate emergence of profits depended heavily on the research outcome. The tempting promise that British Biotechnology dangled before investors was its decision to retain full ownership of value in its novel cancer drug marimastat, then under development. The huge promise inherent in this drug was its potential to arrest the spread of many different types of tumour, making it highly valuable in the fight against cancer. By shunning alliances with pharmaceuticals companies and recruiting its own marketing salesforce, the company would retain all the profit from the new drug. This bold decision underscored British Biotechnology's confidence in this product. On the strength of this promise and the potentially wide application of the drug, the company's market value soared to nearly £2 billion in 1996.

Unfortunately, biotechnology companies do not research scores of drugs as pharmaceutical companies do: all their effort is directed into only one or two major projects. If marimastat proved unsuccessful in the long trial process, the overhyped share price would quickly crash – which, sadly, was the ultimate outcome.

In 1998, controversy was sparked when the clinical research director expressed concerns that the company was sending too optimistic a message to investors. He was sacked for this outspoken disloyalty, but earlier doubts had been planted in investors' minds and the share price had already begun a precipitous slide. The final fall from grace was the announcement in early 1999 that marimastat appeared to be no more effective than existing treatments. From its high of 326p in May 1996, the share price underwent a prolonged decline, falling another 4.5p to 20.5p on this dismal announcement. The company was then worth little more than its cash value. Like a temperature chart of a patient in terminal decline, the chart for British Biotechnology reveals its miserable fate.

**British Biotechnology 1995 to May 1999**

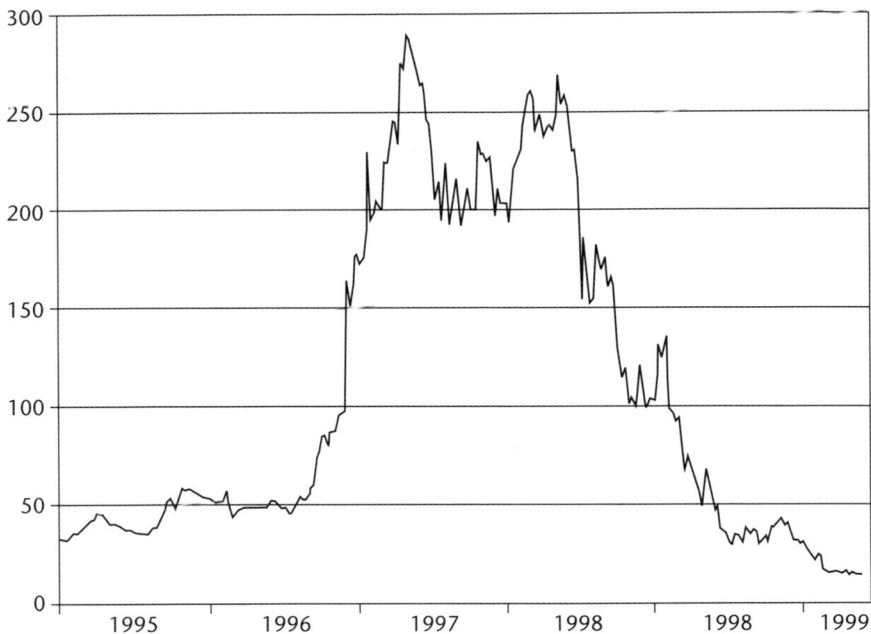

British Biotechnology then joined the growing band of biotechnology start-ups whose early promise had foundered. Most drugs take 10 years to develop and the vast majority of drugs fail during tests, never to reach the market. The technology is obscure, there are no profits or price/earnings ratios, and few investors have any idea how to value the companies since one of two dramatic fates awaits them: the science involved fails and they become worthless; or it succeeds, turning them into billion-pound ventures. Yet there is a middle way. Some companies seek alliances with an industry giant, usually a long-established pharmaceutical company, to share the research or participate financially in some aspect of drug development. Although this route inevitably means sharing future profits, it is obviously a more cautious way for start-up companies to proceed.

*'But these companies are not going to evaporate overnight. And a couple of them are going to make absolute fortunes. The difficulty is spotting them.'*

*Erling Refsum, analyst at Nomura International*

## The Internet Explosion

The explosion of interest and company value in everything relating to the Internet took investors and commentators completely by surprise during 1998. Its rise and growth was a phenomenon of unparalleled speed. According to the US Securities and Exchange Commission, a quarter of US retail share trading was on the Internet by early 1999. The number of online accounts had doubled to 7.8 million in one year. Many of these investors were not traditional clients of US retail brokerages such as Merrill Lynch and Paine-Webber; the profile of the day-trader is younger and poorer. They buy shares in the small US Internet stocks on a daily basis, taking quick profits and losses on the day. Their activity grew so rapidly that the illiquid Internet stocks they were trading became hugely overvalued.

*'It is still too early to pick individual firms, but the winner's business model is clear: an asset accumulator that provides advice and can leverage technology, the Internet in particular, to build deeper relationships with customers.'*

*Henry McVey, analyst with Morgan Stanley*

Trends that start in the United States often cross the Atlantic following a delay. After two years of Internet fever in America, the craze reached Britain in early 1999. Any UK company with even a remote Internet connection was suddenly a red-hot favourite for investors. Shares in the computer retailing giant, Dixons, doubled in value in a matter of weeks when it announced it had attracted over 1 million members to the Freeserve site it set up as an Internet Service Provider in September 1998. On-line, a tiny concern, soared from 12p in early January to 275p within 3 weeks, before rapidly plunging down below 100p again. Some companies with proven records of considerable revenue growth will undoubtedly be immensely profitable. But, clearly, care is needed when sorting through potential candidates since few of the current crop, either in Britain or the United States, have made profits or are likely to do so for many years to come.

However, the possibility that huge profits *will* ultimately emerge made every US Internet flotation an immediate success. Astronomical valuations on the new issues from the first day of trading created an Internet bubble of monumental proportions. In November 1998, Theglobe.com, a Net community site, made overnight millionaires of its two co-founders, Stephan Paternot, aged 24, and Todd Krizelman, 25. Floated at $9, it hit $97 and ended its first day at $63.5 for a 600 per cent rise, but was down at $41.81 by late January 1999. Market Watch, a business-news provider, was floated in January 1999 at $17 and soared to $97.5 by the close of trading on its first day as a public company.

One reason for the phenomenal rise in net stock values is the limited float size and the limited number of shares in issue. As we know, demand and supply operate to favour share price rises for small-capitalisation stocks. Another reason was the incredible feedback loop of novice investors buying and selling Internet stocks over the Internet on an hourly or daily basis, operating as day traders. Like any new computer game, people can become proficient at beating the computer by spending hours on a game, measuring their progress against their previous scores. With the right competitive approach, this can work for trading Internet stocks as if they were a computer game but instead generating hard cash profits or losses. However, all this Internet trading carries immense risks not seen with most computer games. A dramatic fall on the shares might wipe out many of these day traders in a colossal meltdown. Some of the largest discount brokers, including Charles Schwab, banned trading in new net stocks to protect their most naïve customers from possible losses, because they were not using limit prices on orders for volatile new issues. Nor were they setting stop-losses to reduce the risks of a sudden price collapse.

In 1999, a survey showed that 70 per cent of American day traders made losses, not profits from their daily efforts. High prices were not restricted to new issues, however. Well-established companies, such as Amazon.com, the online bookseller, and Yahoo!, the popular US search engine, were trading at levels about 10 times higher than a year earlier. Amazon did not expect to make a profit until 2003, and Yahoo! not before 2004. Soaring optimism on future net profits fuelled a rash of spectacular merger deals. One of the largest at the time occurred in October 1998, when America OnLine (AOL), the largest online service, bought Netscape, the Web browser and net software maker, for $4 billion.

Analysts thought that the price/earnings multiples applied to net companies resembled the seventeenth-century Dutch tulipomania bubble. However, like all stock market bubbles, the enthusiasm has some basis in reality. US retail sales made over the net were 3–4 times greater in the last quarter of 1998, at $3.5 billion, than the corresponding quarter of 1997. Forecast sales were predicted by Forrester Research to reach £108 billion by 2003. Interestingly, many people seemed to be fully aware of the net's revolutionary impact. Stephan Paternot, co-founder of the net community site, Theglobe.com, saw the Internet as one of the biggest social changes in world history. Not only is it here to stay, but it is also improving rapidly.

Steve Case, AOL's boss, was the first to recognise the enormous potential and the need for a specific approach to develop his business by pursuing an advertising model. He spent several years of revenue bombarding the public with millions of free AOL computer disks. His business model was to spend 100 per cent or more of revenue on advertising and marketing in order to build brand awareness and a place in the market. Lack of profits was unimportant as long as the stock price continued rising. No other online service was prepared to allocate advertising spend of that magnitude but his strategy eventually paid enormous returns. AOL shares rose almost 7 times during 1998 and he was able to absorb or crush almost all his rivals. This advertising strategy proved equally successful for Amazon.com. It could probably make profits by reducing the advertising budget, but it continued advertising in order to ensure that all of the new people coming on line knew about it and used it. However, if the bull market founders, investors may worry about those missing profits.

*'There is no way a company such as On-line can be at the valuation it was. The rise in the share price was, I think, due to a combination of massive investor ignorance, profit-taking and people jumping on the band wagon.'*

Nick Gibson of Durlacher, the brokers

## Mobile Computing?

By the end of the twentieth century, the hottest technologies were those promising new convergences such as mobile phones with the Internet. The cellular phone market was growing by 40 per cent a year in Europe and almost 30 per cent in America. Forecasts for 2004 suggest that more than half the developed world's population will then own a mobile phone. In Scandinavia, numbers of mobile phones are likely to exceed numbers of people.

Analysts have predicted that combining hand-held cellular devices and the World Wide Web would create 'killer applications' producing the biggest-selling consumer electronic devices of the next decade. In 1999, hot on the heels of the proposed merger of Vodafone and AirTouch, a new buzzword entered the high tech lexicon: mobile computing. This new market will be carved out for cellular data devices made and sold by alliances between computer and telephone companies. The technology for these gadgets is still being developed, but analysts estimate sales of hand-held computers and 'smart' phones will reach 600 million a year by 2003. Such sales will be over three times greater than for personal computers, and more people will be using wireless or portable phones than the wired version.

Several alliances of companies were announced in 1998 and 1999, to win a dominant place in this emerging market. Microsoft formed a joint venture with Qualcomm to develop wireless data and teamed up with BT on a range of new Internet and corporate data-communications services for customers worldwide, with tests due to begin within a year of making the tie-up. AT&T, the American long-distance carrier, reported that it was discussing ways to expand its international wireless business with BT, sparking rumours of a full merger between the two groups. At that stage (1998), it was unclear which competing format would survive. For instance, in 1998, Psion, a pioneer in the hand-held computer market, faced the prospect of being eclipsed by competitors like 3Com, Sharp and Hewlett-Packard. Its shares collapsed on a profits warning, but surged later in the year when Psion announced an alliance with Motorola, Ericsson and Nokia followed by link-ups with Japan's telecommunications giant, NTT.

## An Investment Strategy For Emerging Industries

Running a portfolio of emerging industries may look like choosing winning lottery numbers. However, there are a few rules you can follow to reduce the risks of heavy losses. The Fund Manager's Diary in *Investors Chronicle* has highlighted the approach of James Dines, an influential American commentator who has written an investment newsletter since 1960. (I have his book, *The Invisible Crash*, which describes the collapse of the market in the 1970s, using extracts from his newsletters.) He has suggested that the only way to work with Internet stocks is to select one or two possible leaders in each subgroup as it gets defined, and then buy a basket of such stocks. As an example, he had American Online, Amazon.com and Yahoo! in his first basket – and, holding just *one* of these treasures in the period since their flotation would have made you a fortune. This idea has a wider use: it can be applied to all emerging industries.

*'Everyone has the brain power to make money in stocks. Not everyone has the stomach.'*

Peter Lynch

Yet this is not a foolproof system, as we saw with the disastrous history of British Biotechnology, a leading-edge company in its field. Clearly, it is essential to spread the risks in as many ways as is prudently possible (see box below).

If you spot a promising biotechnology stock – or, indeed, any emerging industry company – only invest a modest sum so as to avoid the nasty shock of discovering its projects are ultimately all failures. Use a stop-loss system, with a price decided in advance on which you will sell if the share price moves against you. This may be after a 20 per cent fall, when the chart shows the price diving below the trendline or a dead cross appears. If the growth story falters, as it did with British Biotechnology, be firm and sell.

It is better to have a cluster of small holdings rather than only one or two, although if you have the winning talents of James Dines, stay with the leaders in each field. Do not be too greedy if you are fortunate to discover one of these little gems early in its rise. Either sell half while the good growth story is intact, or sell out completely if you have made a good gain and you think the price is greatly overvalued. Finally, only allocate 5–8 per cent of your total portfolio value to any high-risk areas you diversify into.

---

**WAYS TO REDUCE RISKS WITH HIGH-RISK COMPANIES**

1. Choose a group of companies, rather than only one.
2. Stay with one or two leading-edge companies in the field.
3. Set stop-loss prices at which you will definitely sell.
4. Follow sell signals on the charts, such as the price dropping below the lower trendline, or the appearance of a dead cross.
5. Don't be greedy if the price rises way beyond what you consider 'reasonable'.
6. Consider selling perhaps half, if not all, of a holding if the growth story hits problems.
7. Invest only a small percentage of your total wealth in highly speculative areas.

---

*'It [the Internet frenzy] consists of a bunch of venture capitalists who don't have a long-term commitment to their investments, employees who don't have a long-term commitment to their company, and companies that don't have a long-term commitment to their customers.'*

*Michael Saylor, founder of MicroStrategy, a Net sales and marketing company*

# ADOPTING A HIGH-GROWTH STRATEGY

There is a wide range of high-risk areas you might consider to boost your portfolio performance. They include derivative trading, such as options or futures or emerging markets in underdeveloped areas that fell heavily in the global crisis of 1998. Then there are tax-free schemes, such as venture-capitalist trusts, becoming an 'angel' for new theatrical productions, or buying property to let long term.

You might explore the whole spectrum of alternative investments. A list of these ideas is given in the box below.

---

**POSSIBLE ALTERNATIVE INVESTMENTS**

Antique silver
Antique furniture
Antique porcelain (Japanese, Chinese, European, English)
Paintings (oil or watercolours)
Clocks
Coins, Medals, Stamps
Antique books (first editions, signed copies)
Dolls and dolls' houses
Teddy bears, toys
Mechanical toys and antique mechanical gadgets
Old comics, rare maps, letters by famous people
Military uniforms, guns and memorabilia

---

It can add spice, excitement and hard cash to your efforts if you specialise in one of these areas and turn it into a stimulating hobby to improve the growth trend in your wealth-creating skills. But it must be treated seriously because heavy losses in this sideline could undermine some of your previous efforts. If you decide to stay with UK equities, you might make a speciality of following the fortunes of obscure small growth companies or 'blue sky' shares. A 'blue sky' company is very young, with huge start-up debts, low sales revenues and no profits. Companies like British Biotechnology epitomise this breed. Indeed, examples include the majority of new issues in biotechnology and technology companies, especially those linked to the Internet.

## The Sky may be the Limit

In 1998, the three best-performing companies on the London Stock Exchange were Colt Telecom, Orange and Telewest, all in the fever-hot telecommunications sector. Apart from being in the much sought-after telecoms sector, they share several other features in common. Strong institutional support enabled all three to join the élite FTSE 100 group, although between them they had forecast losses for the year of about £450 million. Astonishingly, Colt, the best-performing share, was almost a five-bagger in one year, rising by 482 per cent during 1998 even though it had never made a profit. The same nebulous story supported another blue-sky share, Orange, the mobile telecommunications company, with nothing but huge debts and promises of future earnings to support that price. In October 1999, Orange agreed a takeover by the German conglomerate Mannesmann, valued at £19.8 billion and it had still not made a profit.

The best- and worst-performing FTSE 100 companies during 1998 are set out in the table below. The emphasis on telecommunications among the 'winners' is clearly shown.

### 1988 WINNERS AND LOSERS

| FTSE 100 WINNERS for 1998<br>% Change on the Year | | FTSE 100 LOSERS for 1998 | |
| --- | --- | --- | --- |
| Colt Telecom | + 481.7% | ICI | − 45.2% |
| Orange | + 164.6% | BTR | − 34.6% |
| Telewest Communications | + 147.9% | Marks & Spencer | − 31.2% |
| Vodafone | + 122.3% | British Airways | − 27.6% |
| British Telecom | + 89.2% | | |
| FTSE 100 | + 14.5% | | |

You cannot, of course, calculate a price/earnings ratio for a company with no earnings, but this does not deter some optimistic investors. You can make amazing gains by investing in these companies, especially when their popularity is soaring and before a serious setback emerges. But it would be foolish to underestimate the risks. Never be greedy. Take the profits long before the company announces bad news that shocks the market out of its euphoria. This frequently means leaving the scene while the price is still rising. I did this with my holding of Unipalm, which I thought was grossly overvalued at 500p when it announced it was in talks with a bidder. Unipalm was one of the first UK Internet Service Providers and the price soared above 700p with the bid story in full swing, but I was happy to sell at 425p on 21 August 1995, doubling my money in three months. My investment in Unipalm is described in *The Armchair Investor*.

If you stay on board too long, one of many disasters could strike. There may be further or unexpected delays for profits, the need to raise more cash from shareholders might arise, or products that do not live up to early expectations may suddenly be withdrawn.

Set out below is a table of the technology mini-portfolio I was running and writing about in the *Financial Mail on Sunday*, in 1995, long before the flaming high-tech fever really hit Wall Street and London. A sixth company, Coda, a software producer, announced a profits warning about two weeks after I sold it for a sizeable gain. Later, it became a take-over prize at a far lower price, but I had stopped following the story and so it is not included here. None of the shares listed stayed for the long term in my portfolio because, in 1995, I was still a greenhorn and was certainly not thinking like a long-term investor; chopping and changing was the order of the day. But the table shows that only 3 of the 5 selections turned out to be sound long-term investments: Filtronic, Real Time Control and Unipalm. I lost 20 per cent in two days on my Calluna holding, but the price on 12 March 1999 was down to 15.5p. A long-term hold of this small company, developing a revolutionary mini-disc drive that has been beset by problems, would then have been worth £775 for a loss of 72 per cent.

*'But the market phenomenon of 1999 so far is the Internet. Web stocks, and particularly those linked particularly to "e-commerce", are going through the roof.'*

John Authers, Financial Times, *10 January 1999, reporting on Wall Street*

## MY TECHNOLOGY MINI-PORTFOLIO OF 1995

| Share | Date Bought | Number Bought | Price (p) on Purchase | Total Cost (£) | Price (p) at 5.11.99 | Value (£) at 5.11.99 |
|-------|------|--------|-----------|------|-------|-------|
| Filtonic | 15.2.95 | 3,000 | 215 | 6,450 | 1257.5 | 37,725 |
| Telspec | 4.5.95 | 853 | 459 | 3,985 | 60.5 | 516 |
| Real Time | 22.6.95 | 1,250 | 165 | 2,098 | 880 | 11,000 |
| Control | 29.6.95 | 1,250 | 182 | 2,306 | | 11,000 |
| Unipalm | 29.6.95 | 1,429 | 203 | 2,966 | Sold on 21.8.95 at 425p | 6,073 at time of sale |
| Calluna | 10.7.95 | 5,000 | 55 | 2,799 | Sold on 12.7.95 at 45p | 2,235 at time of sale (£564 loss, or 20% in 2 days) |

**Total Cost of Mini-Portfolio: £20,604**
**Total Value on 5.11.99: £68,549**

*'When the facts change, I change my mind.'*

John Maynard Keynes (1883–1946), one of the greatest economists of the 20th Century

## CONTINUING PROGRESS IN LEVEL V

You can stay for ever in Level V, enjoying the benefits of years of effort and application. Once you have achieved your own level of financial security, which will be special to you and your particular circumstances, you can motor along at whatever pace you feel comfortable with. Keep track of how you are faring by using the progress box below. Try alternative investments, or just relax and enjoy the gains you are making on your New Millennium Portfolio. You decide. If you feel lucky or uncertain when making financial decisions, why not send me an e-mail via my web site (www.mrscohen. com)? Or join me there online for an update on financial and investment matters.

We should not be ashamed of making money. When we have it, there are so many wonderful things we can do with it to help others less fortunate than ourselves. As your wealth increases, pay off all your debts, give money to members of your family or your favourite charities, or spend it on luxuries that you always thought were totally out of reach. You might like to give talks as I now do, on how to spread this gospel of self-help to other people in your community or neighbourhood. Teach your children and grandchildren the value of money to make their lives easier as the twenty-first century unfolds.

In my opinion, the prospects for becoming superbly wealthy have never been better. When I was miserable and in debt, I always cheered myself up by the thought that the money was sitting there in the market. I could see it there every time a company announced a special event: a new merger, new product, big contract, a positive trading statement. I knew the money was there waiting for me to take my share of it. All that was needed was a method by which I could learn how to capture some of that cash for myself. Naturally, it takes some effort, application and a willingness to learn. I hope it doesn't sound too trite, but as my expertise grows, so I believe does my knowledge about myself and the world. I see this knowledge as one of the greatest benefits I am gaining by trying to become wealthy through stock market investing.

You can participate in this truly exciting adventure. Get wise to get wealthy and discover how to be magnanimous with your own money. If you haven't already done so, are you now keen to get started? Today is the perfect day to begin.

**Level V Progress Report**

| Reading Schedule | Start Date | Finish Date |
|---|---|---|
| Level I<br>Level II<br>Level III<br>Level IV | | |

| Net Worth Statement | Start Value (£) | Finish Value (£) |
|---|---|---|
| *ASSETS*<br>House<br>Pension funds<br>Insurance policies<br>Top Ten Portfolio<br>Savings regime<br>Other cash<br>Other assets<br><br>*Total Assets* | | |
| *DEBTS*<br>Mortgage<br>Bank loans<br>Credit card debts<br>Store card debts<br>Other debts<br><br>*Total debts* | | |
| **Net Worth in Level V** | | |

*'Wealth isn't something to admire. It is something you create.'*

# REFERENCE INFORMATION

## SUGGESTED READING

### Introductory Works

Here is a short list of introductory books on general investment topics. They cover a wide range of different investment approaches. They are listed in alphabetical order as there is no preferred reading order.

Bryan, Mark and Cameron, Julia, *The Money Drunk*, Ballantine Books, 1992.

Cohen, Bernice, *Treasury of Investment Wisdom*, Orion, 1999.

Drury, Tony, *Investment Clubs: the Low-Risk Way to Stockmarket Profits*, Rushmere Wynne, 1995.

Lefevre, Edwin, *Reminiscences of a Stock Operator*, John Wiley, 1993.

Linton, David, *Profit From Your PC: How to Use a Personal Computer to Buy and Sell Shares*, Rushmere Wynne, 1995; and an updated version, *More Profit from your PC*, 1996.

Lynch, Peter, *One Up On Wall Street*, Simon and Schuster, 1989.

Schwager, Jack D., *Market Wizards*, Harper & Row, 1990.

The Beardstown Ladies, *The Beardstown Ladies Common-Sense Investment Guide*, Hyperion, 1994.

Vintcent, Charles, *The Investor's Guide: Be Your Own Stockbroker: The Secrets of Managing Your Own Investments*, Pitman Publishing, 1995.

### Starting Out

It is helpful to have a beginner's investment guide as it covers the main essentials and explains investment jargon in simple terms. Any one of the following four would be a good starting point. I have included my own book on investments for beginners because it deals extensively with how I learnt to handle the skills of investing for myself.

Chase, Lorraine and Shaw, Adam, *Money and How to Make More of It*, Orion, 1997.
Cohen, Bernice, *The Armchair Investor*, Orion, 1997.
Gray, Bernard, *Investors Chronicle Beginners Guide to Investment*, Business Books Ltd, London 1991.
Slater, Jim, *Investment made Easy*, Orion, 1994.

## Making Progress

Finally, here is a list of books for investors who want to progress to higher levels.

Cohen, Bernice, *The Edge of Chaos*, John Wiley & Sons, Inc., 1997.
Dines, James, *The Invisible Crash*, Random House, 1975.
Glassman, James K. and Hassett, Kevin, A., *Dow 36,000*, Random House, 1999.
Hagstrom, Robert G., *The Warren Buffet Portfolio*, John Wiley & Sons, Inc., 1999.
Hagstrom, Robert G., *The Warren Buffet Way*, John Wiley & Sons, Inc., 1994.
Kirzner, E. and Berryessa, N., *Global Investing*, Dow-Jones Irwin, 1988.
Schwager, Jack D., *The New Market Wizards*, Harper Business, 1992.
Train, John, *The New Money Masters*, HarperCollins, 1989.

## USEFUL TELEPHONE NUMBERS AND ADDRESSES

National Debtline: 0645 500511.
Consumer Credit Counselling Service (CCCS): 0800 1381111. Nine around the country for face-to-face interviews.
National Association of Citizen's Advice Bureaux (Nacab). There are 17,000 bureaux around the country with general and specialist advisers.
Institute of Financial Planning: 0117 930 4434.
BEST Investment provides a guide to PEP and ISA Best Buys: 0990 112255.
PIA (Personal Investment Authority) Helpline for pensions mis-selling victims: 020 7417 7001.

# NEWSLETTERS AND JOURNALS

*Financial Times*, Number One Southwark Bridge, London SE1 9HL.

*Investors Chronicle*, Greystoke Place, Fetter Lane, London EC4 1ND.

*Moneywise*, RD Publications Ltd, 10 Old Bailey, London EC4M 7NB.

*Money Observer*, Garrard House, 2/6 Homesdale Road, Bromley BR2 9WL or *Money Observer*, FREEPOST NB 2019, Bromley BR2 9BR.

*Company REFS* (Company Really Essential Financial Statistics), Hemmington Scott Publishing Ltd, City Innovation Centre, 26–31 Whiskin Street, London EC1R 0BP.

*The Estimate Directory*, Barra Global Estimates, Barra International, Sovereign House, 12–13 Young Street, Edinburgh, EH2 4JB.

# SOFTWARE PACKAGES

## Budgeting by PC

There are a number of software packages for budgeting, among the most useful are:

MICROSOFT MONEY

QUICKEN

## Share Information by PC

There are several software packages and systems that provide a variety of share price information, portfolio management or technical analysis. The ones I have experience of using are provided by:

*Market Eye*, ICV Ltd, 23 College Hill, Cannon Street, London EC4R 2RA.

*Synergy Software*, Britannic House, 20 Dunstable Road, Luton LU1 1ED.

*Updata Software*, Updata House, Old York Road, London SW18 1TG.

Also

Teleshare, by phone. tel no: 0906 4711 077

# WEB SITES

The following are useful Web sites:

*AAA Investment Guide*: www.wisebuy.co.uk (facts on 93 different types of investments and savings)

Bernice Cohen's website: www.mrscohen.com

*Financial Times*: www.ft.com

Hemmington Scott (the publishers of *Company REFS*): www.hemscott.com

*Mrs Cohen's Money* on www.Channel4.com

Updata: www.updata.co.uk

www.fund.co.uk

National Savings ISA on www.nationalsavings.co.uk

# GLOSSARY OF TERMS

**Active fund manager:** one who runs an actively **managed fund** (q.v.), aiming to outperform the market.

**Advisory broker:** one who offers advice on which shares to buy/sell.

**Analysts:** professionals who work for the big brokerage and merchant banking houses. They analyse and report on national economies, companies and various sectors of a stock market.

**Annuity:** a form of income, guaranteed and fixed for life, that is bought through insurance companies with an accumulated pension fund.

**Annual General Meeting (AGM):** an obligatory yearly meeting at which the company announces its results for the year.

**Annual Results:** a company's yearly statement on its trading activities.

**Assets:** physical and intangible goods (such as goodwill) that a person or a company owns.

**Auditor:** an outside accountant employed to make routine checks on a business to ensure the company's accounts are being kept properly.

**Balance sheet:** the statement of the capital position of a company at any one time. It shows what it owns (assets) and what it owes (its liabilities).

**Bear** and **bull markets:** a bear market is one where prices are falling over a period of weeks, months or years. A bull market is one with rising prices. Investors who think the market is about to fall are bearish; those who think the market will rise are bullish.

**Bid price:** the price at which the professionals will buy shares back from investors.

**Blue chip:** shares in a sound, highly regarded company.

**Bonds:** a bond is a certificate of debt issued by companies and governments to raise cash. It usually pays interest and can be traded in a market.

**Brokers:** professionals who buy and sell on behalf of their clients. They are sometimes called intermediaries.

**Bull Market:** a market in which prices are rising in general.

**Capital:** a lump sum of money that can be invested in assets or is available to invest.

**Capital gains (or growth):** the increase in the capital value of investments.

**Capital Gains Tax:** this is a form of government taxation, payable on profits above a set level, from the sale of stock market investments (particularly shares).

**Capital-secure:** a description for Capital that is not exposed to price volatility.

**Collective funds:** any scheme where investors pool their resources to spread their investment risks. The term covers UK unit and investment trusts and US mutual funds.

**Compound growth:** a method of growth in which the interest is added back to the capital at each stage to increase the total all the time.

**Conglomerate:** a group of diverse subsidiaries brought together under one holding company.

**Core holdings:** shares held as ultra-long-term investments within a portfolio.

**Corporate bond:** a fixed-interest loan raised by a company that guarantees to repay the capital on an agreed future date.

**Credit:** credit is given by banks when they advance loans to their customers, and businesses when they allow their customers to take goods and defer payment for them.

**Creditors:** companies or individuals to whom money is owed.

**Cyclical companies:** are companies whose activities closely follow the phases of the business cycle.

**Dax:** the benchmark index for the German stock market.

**Default:** fail to pay a debt.

**Defensive sector:** includes companies whose profits are not too adversely affected by recession.

**Deflation:** the opposite of inflation: general prices in the economy are falling

**Demutualise:** when companies cease to be owned by their members.

**Depreciation:** the loss in value of an asset with time or through usage.

**Deterministic chaos:** is defined as unpredictable behaviour that is governed by rules. These rules may or may not be known, but they still apply, regardless.

**Diversify risk:** spreading the risk.

**Dividend:** the proportion of a company's profits paid out twice yearly (as an interim and final payment) to its shareholders.

**Dividend cover:** the number of times the dividend is covered by earnings. A safe cover would be 1.5 times.

**Dividend yield:** the ratio between the dividend and what was actually paid for the share.

**Dow Jones Industrial Average:** this is a list of thirty US major blue chip companies. It is unweighted with each of the thirty shares having an equal weighting in the index. Despite this defect the DJIA is the benchmark American index.

**Earnings yield:** this measure is the inverse of the price/earnings ratio. It is the amount an investor would receive if a company paid out all its attributable earnings each year.

**Economic cycle:** this is a round of economic events that proceed in an irregular succession.

**Equity (ies):** another term for **ordinary shares** (q.v.) of a company. They are freely traded stocks and shares in publicly quoted companies that do not carry a fixed rate of interest but entitle holders to a share in the growth of the company through annual dividend payments.

**Equity premium:** a measure of the difference between the annual returns on equities and gilts. The long-term difference is 6 per cent (8 per cent for equities minus 2 per cent for gilts).

**Execution-only broker services:** all shares must be bought or sold through a broker, but dealing is cheaper with execution-only brokers because they just make a transaction and do not give advice.

**Fixed-interest investment:** an investment that pays a certain amount of interest until maturity.

**Flag formation:** a chart pattern that unfolds in two stages with a pause in between. It may involve a price rise or a price fall.

**Flotation:** a flotation is a new issue of shares available to the public which occurs when a private company sells a percentage of its shares to whoever among the public wants to buy them.

**Fractal:** a graphic representation of chaos, (q.v. **deterministic chaos**).

**FT 30 index:** the oldest London index commenced on 1 July 1935. The thirty constituent companies were chosen on the basis of being actively traded, leaders in their sector and domestically focused.

**FTSE 100 index:** monitors the performance of the top 100 publicly quoted companies by market capitalisation (market value) on the London stock market. It is weighted to take account of the largest- and smallest-sized companies on the list and is updated throughout the day. The initials stand for Financial Times Stock Exchange; completing the range of indices is a joint venture between the *Financial Times* newspaper and the London Stock Exchange.

**FTSE 250:** this index works like the FTSE 100 and monitors the performance of 250 medium-sized companies that together comprise this index.

**FTSE 350:** this index covers the companies in the FTSE 100 and FTSE 250 shares. All three indices are updated continuously throughout the working day.

**FTSE SmallCap:** this index covers some of the small companies on the UK stock market

**FTSE All-Share index:** covers about 850 shares on the UK market. It is updated at the start of every working day.

**Gearing:** the relationship between the size of the borrower's initial debt and the lender's initial share of an asset on which a loan is made. High gearing means high borrowing relative to a borrower's contribution to the value of the asset. Gearing is used by homebuyers and companies.

**Gilts** or **Gilt-edged bonds:** British government loans that carry a fixed level of interest.

**Gilt-edged investment funds:** a managed fund that only invests in gilt-edged stocks.

**Gross:** interest or dividends for investors, before deduction of income tax.

**Gross Domestic Product (GDP):** the amount of goods and services produced by a country in one year.

**Historic prospective:** this relates to actual (generally latest) figures rather than to future figures.

**Illiquid assets:** assets or securities, such as houses or commercial property, which are not easily transferable into cash.

**Income:** money earned or received from a regular and reliable source.

**Income fund:** a unit trust that focuses on companies that pay out dividends large enough to provide an income to the investors.

**Independent financial adviser (IFA):** an adviser who offers 'best advice' on a wide range of investments and financial products and is not tied to any particular company.

**Index:** a selected list of publicly quoted shares that represent all others of that type.

**Indexation:** a system by which the value of securities and/or interest payments are linked to inflation, particularly for index-linked gilts, annuities or National Savings products.

**Individual Savings Account (ISA):** a new tax-exempt savings scheme introduced in April 1999.

**Inflation:** a percentage measure of the amount by which the prices of goods and services rise in the economy over a period of time, usually one year.

**Interest:** a regular payment, usually made twice yearly, to savers who keep their money in deposit accounts with building societies or banks.

**Interim report:** half yearly results issued by a publicly quoted company.

**Investing:** putting money into real financial assets, with the hope of increasing the size of the original investment through future growth at the same time as receiving a regular and rising income.

**Investment bond:** an equity-based investment issued by an insurance company.

**Investment trust:** a company that is quoted on the stock exchange and exists to invest in the equity of other companies. It is used by large institutions and also small investors to gain a wide spread of investments.

**ISA:** *see* **Individual Savings Account.**

**Leading indicator:** occurs before changes in the business cycle occur.

**Liability:** an amount of money owed to other people; a debt.

**Liquidity:** a market for a financial commodity is liquid where there are many buyers and sellers, so that it is easy to deal. Cash is the most liquid asset as it is free to buy any other asset.

**Managed fund:** a broadly based investment fund run by a professional manager in a pension or insurance company.

**Market capitalisation:** a company's total value. The number of shares in issue multiplied by the share price at any time.

**Market makers:** professionals who set the prices at which shares trade.

**Mid-price:** the price that is set between the bid (sell) and offer (buy) prices.

**Money supply:** the amount of money circulating in the economy. There are several different ways to measure it.

**Mutual:** a company structure where the members (borrowers, savers or policy-holders) own all the assets of the company, which may be a building society or insurance company.

**Mutual funds:** the US version of UK unit trusts.

**National Savings:** low-risk savings schemes run by the UK government.

**Negative equity:** the difference between the initial price paid for a property and its current value if the latter is lower.

**Net:** after tax (not to be confused with the Internet).

**Net worth:** the value of a set of assets after deducting all debts (liabilities).

**Nikkei 300 index:** Benchmark index for the Japanese stock market.

**Nominal value:** the numerical value of an item, ignoring the impact of inflation.

**Nominee account:** is held by an intermediary on behalf of the investor.

**Non-redeemable gilts:** gilts without a maturity date.

**Offer:** the price at which the professionals will sell shares to investors.

**Ordinary shares:** the commonest form of shares in a company; *see* also **equities.**

**Partly-paid:** a public offering of shares where the payment is made in instalments.

**Pension:** a savings scheme whereby the contributions create a fund which from a specified date will return an income to the saver.

**Portfolio:** a group of company shares held by an investor at one time, or by a group of investors.

**Premium:** the amount that an asset (such as an investment trust) is selling above its intrinsic value.

**Privatisations:** state-owned organisations sold to the public by an issue of ordinary shares.

**Profits:** the cash left in a business after deducting all expenses from the revenues earned.

**Publicly quoted companies:** companies that are listed on a national stock market.

**Purchasing power:** the amount of goods and services your money will buy.

**Pyramiding:** adding more shares to your holding on a new buy signal.

**Real (real-terms) . . . :** after taking account of inflation.

**Real assets:** assets that hold or increase their value over time, in spite of inflation.

**Real financial assets:** assets in financial investments that tend to hold or even increase their value over time, in spite of inflation.

**Real growth:** growth after deducting for inflation.

**Real rate of return:** capital growth plus income earned on an asset after deducting inflation.

**Recession:** a downturn in activity across the economy that lasts more than six months.

**Reserves:** money put aside out of the profits of a company to build up the internal resources that the company holds for future use, including expansion.

**Retail Prices Index (RPI):** the measure of inflation in the economy. It is calculated by weighting the cost of goods and services to approximate to a typical family's spending patterns.

**Retained earnings:** company profits that are retained in the business and not distributed to the shareholders as dividends.

**Rights issue:** an issue of shares made when a company asks its shareholders to subscribe for new shares, often at a discount to the current market price, to fund expansion or pay off debts.

**Risk:** a measure of the possibility that an investor will sustain a financial loss from an investment.

**S&P 500 Index:** a benchmark index for the New York Stock Exchange covering 500 shares.

**Saving:** Putting aside a sum of money for future use.

**Securities:** tradable financial products, such as shares or bonds.

**Shareholder funds:** the money belonging to the ordinary shareholders in a publicly quoted company.

**Solvency:** a company is able to meet all its legal financial obligations including paying wages and repaying debts.

**Stockbrokers:** *see also* **Brokers**; professionals who buy and sell shares for their clients.

**Stock market:** the market for equities, or shares, in public companies. In London, it is called the **Stock Exchange**. A buyer is actually purchasing a share in the ownership of a company.

**Take-home pay:** pay after all deductions have been made, including tax and national insurance contributions.

**Take-over:** arrangement whereby a company offers to buy out the shareholders of another company.

**Tied agent:** a financial adviser who works for a single company and is legally bound to offer advice regarding only that company's products. He cannot therefore offer impartial advice over the whole field of financial investments.

**Time series:** a series of data covering a specified time period of days, weeks or years.

**Total return:** the addition of the capital growth plus the dividend income received on an investment in real financial assets.

**Tracker fund:** a fund designed to follow some stock market index by investing in a range of shares that behave similarly to that index.

**UK growth and income trusts:** Unit trusts that invest in publicly quoted companies aimed to give investors either a high rate of growth or a high annual dividend payment.

**Unearned income:** income derived from assets rather than work.

**Unit trusts:** A form of investment where investors' money is pooled in order to purchase a spread of shares to spread the risk. This enables an investor to have exposure to a larger range of companies than individual resources alone might allow.

**Value investing:** seeking out potentially profitable stocks that are selling at cheap or reasonable prices.

**Volatility:** a measure of the frequency with which share prices move up or down.

**Variable interest rates:** Interest rates that vary as general levels of interest in the economy change.

**Yield:** The annual rate of return on a share or bond that the investor would earn from that security at the current market price.

# INDEX